Praise for Kiyah Wright

"Kiyah is one of the most talented hair stylists in the industry, and beyond her talent she is an amazing person. There is nothing better than to go to work with someone you want to be around. She is always so much fun! I am so proud of her accomplishments; she is the definition of hard work and determination. The ultimate hustler! I know whatever she puts her mind to she will get it done and it will be a success."

—**Ciara**

Praise for *From Beauty to Business*

"I could not be more proud of Kiyah and the business that she has built. Her story is a beautiful example of how hard work and immense talent can transform your dreams into reality. I know her journey, her determination, and her success will provide inspiration to many aspiring and established hair artists and entrepreneurs alike."

—**Jennifer Hudson**

"Kiyah is not only talented, but also a true role model and a great inspiration to other stylists. I love that she is sharing her learnings with others as we can all learn from her positive energy, hustle, and honesty."

—**Frederic Fekkai,** founder and CEO of FEKKAI

"The hair industry is full of opportunities, but without proper guidance, business strategies, and a long-term plan, many stylists can find themselves stuck and discouraged. Kiyah Wright, one of our most innovative and powerful leaders, holds nothing back in her guide to building a successful beauty business. Kiyah is authentic and transparent about her journey, using her life experiences as a blueprint for success. This is an industry defined by the relationships you nurture, the art you can create or redefine, and the impact we have on the way people see themselves. This book shows exactly why Kiyah Wright is one of the best."

—**Dr. Kari Williams,** celebrity stylist, trichologist, and creator of the Goddess Locs

"Kiyah's book will LITERALLY set you up for next-level success. It's filled with priceless information that will save you tons of time and costly mistakes. If you want to set your business up to win, I suggest grabbing this book and keeping it within arm's length at all times."

—**Larry Sims,** celebrity hairstylist

"This is the book the beauty business has been waiting for! Few have shared the wealth of priceless information that Kiyah has provided in *From Beauty to Business*. It's through her hard work, consistency, and trial and error that allowed this alignment with a game-changing purpose! Bravo, Kiyah, I'm so proud of you!"

—**AJ Crimson,** founder and CEO of AJ CRIMSON Beauty

"I met Kiyah when she first landed in LA, and I knew right away that I needed to introduce her to my agent because she was the right combination of talent and ambition. The rest is hair history. She went on to be everything that a celebrity beauty expert dreams about being. She fulfilled all of her wishes to the point where she is now writing this amazing, resource-filled book for all future and aspiring beauty entrepreneurs."

—**Rea Ann Silva,** founder and CEO of Rea.Deeming Beauty Inc. "Home of the Original Beautyblender"

"Dream big, work hard, and learn the 'Wright' way to succeed in the beauty industry."

—**Sam Fine,** CEO of Fine Beauty Inc.

"Every service provider needs to focus on managing their careers as much as they focus on their craft in order to be successful. Kiyah has proven to be an innovator in her work. She has a unique ability to brand, market, and grow her beauty career. *From Beauty to Business* is full of practical and aspirational advice to elevate your beauty profession.

From Beauty to Business gives you the power to transform your beauty career by providing you the tools to stay inspired, while you grow and bulletproof your business. As a leading beauty agent working globally, I have learned from Kiyah. Her depth of knowledge, vision, and tenacity is a testament that needs to be shared. This book is a must-have for the majority of beauty service providers who must agent themselves."

—**Madeline Leonard,** founder and director of Cloutier Remix, more than 30 years representing beauty artists and experts globally

"My mind is completely blown after reading *From Beauty to Business*. Kiyah explains everything from applying for a Tax ID to joining the union in a way that's easy to understand, and she even includes QR codes, making everything she references easily accessible to the reader. As an agent in the beauty biz, I had the pleasure of managing Kiyah for many years and, ironically, I learned a great deal from her about the art of negotiation, which she also covers in the book. If you are a beauty pro or interested in becoming one, I promise you'll need this textbook in your collection! Class is in session!"

—**Erodney Davis,** CEO and agency director of Basic White Shirt LTD

"As a talent and brand manager that has worked with Kiyah over the years, I know she understands how helpful this book will be to stylists and aspiring stylists. Check it out and enjoy all the knowledge gems!"

—**E. J. Jamele,** CEO of crowdMGMT

From BEAUTY to BUSINESS

From *From* BEAUTY *to* BUSINESS

The Guaranteed Strategy to Building, Running, and Growing a Successful Beauty Business

A practical guide for hair and fashion stylists, estheticians, and makeup artists—from an expert who's been there

Kiyah Wright

2x Emmy Award–winning celebrity stylist

with SHIRLEY NEAL

BenBella Books, Inc.
Dallas, TX

BenBella

BenBella Books, Inc.
10440 N. Central Expressway
Suite 800
Dallas, TX 75231
benbellabooks.com
Send feedback to feedback@benbellabooks.com.

BenBella is a federally registered trademark.

Printed in the United States of America
10 9 8 7 6 5 4 3 2 1

Library of Congress Control Number: 2021050583
ISBN 9781637740910 (paper over board)
ISBN 9781637740927 (electronic)

Editing by Rachel Phares
Copyediting by Lyric Dodson
Proofreading by Denise Pangia and Cape Cod Compositors, Inc.
Indexing by Debra Bowman
Text design and composition by PerfecType, Nashville, TN
Cover design by Oceana Garceau
Cover and interior author photo by Cheryl Fox
Additional cover images © iStock / mouu007 (foil texture), didecs (hair tools), Fototocam (makeup brushes), HomePixel (blush), koosen (compact mirror), AndreaAstes (lipstick), imagehub88 (eyeshadow), Luda311 (lip gloss)
Printed by Lake Book Manufacturing

Special discounts for bulk sales are available. Please contact bulkorders@benbellabooks.com.

I wish someone had given me a road map when I started my business. That inspired me to write this book for all the beauty pros out there who had no guidance and didn't know where to start to get their businesses in order, or even where to start to make their brands a real business on paper. I dedicate this book to you.

CONTENTS

Introduction   1

PRINCIPLE 1
DEVELOP A SUCCESS MINDSET

1: Full Dream Ahead   9

2: Entrepreneurial DNA—Do You Have the *Wright* Stuff?   21

3: Have the Courage, Live Out Your Dreams   25

PRINCIPLE 2
UNDERSTAND THE BUSINESS OF OUR BUSINESS

4: Business Basics 101: Get Started   47

5: Marketing, Part 1: The Basics   61

6: The Bigger the Dream, the Bigger Your Team   77

7: Taxes, Tips, and Tough Lessons   89

8: The *Wright* Ways to Manage Your Money   115

PRINCIPLE 3
FIND YOUR NICHE

9: Find Your Niche and Build Your Brand   129

10: Marketing, Part 2: Define Your Niche   137

PRINCIPLE 4
DIVERSIFY WITH MULTIPLE STREAMS OF INCOME

11: Secrets of Upselling   147

12: Getting Freelance Work   153

13: How to Break into TV and Film   165

14: Product Lines: From Selling to Launching Your Own   177

15: Weaves to Wigs to Wealth—Taking Your Product Line to
the Next Level   187

PRINCIPLE 5
GROW YOUR PLATFORM TO GROW YOUR PROFITS

16: Marketing, Part 3: Platforms and Strategies to Boost Your Brand   199

17: Attracting Sponsors, Securing Sponsorships   223

PRINCIPLE 6
PREPARE FOR THE UNEXPECTED

18: Preparing for and Surviving Natural Disasters and Other Crises   235

PRINCIPLE 7
PREPARE YOUR FUTURE, TODAY

19: Growth and Start-up Funding   251

20: Planning for Retirement   259

21: A Positive Mindset Breeds Opportunity   271

Acknowledgments   273
Appendix: Additional Resources   275
Notes   283
Index   285

INTRODUCTION

From as early as age fourteen, I've had a passion for doing hair. I guess you could say it was in my blood.

When I was growing up, my paternal grandmother owned a beauty salon in Southeast Washington, DC, called The Wright Salon, where she did hair for a loyal customer base—everything from press and curls to roller sets. To keep me busy on weekends, my mom would send me over to my grandmother's shop to help out. For a few bucks, I'd run errands for my grandma, sweep the floors, and do whatever else she needed done.

I began to love the beauty industry itself. I loved being in the salon, seeing my grandmother whip up those styles and making her customers smile, but I was also impressed with her independence and the fact that she was able to make money doing what she loved. At twelve years old, seeing my grandmother own her own successful beauty business inspired me to aim for success of my own. So, while my mom was at work in the evenings, I'd sneak girls in our basement to do their hair. One night, my mom came home early.

"Kiyah! Who the hell are you sneakin' in this house?!"

Busted!

"That's it," she said. "Your butt is going to hair school!" If I was going to be running this makeshift business out of our basement, she wanted me to really know what I was doing.

With my mother's $150 investment, I started going to a trade school that offered regular courses like science and biology and also taught trades like carpentry and cosmetology. This is where I officially began my journey toward becoming a hairstylist.

Most of the kids in my class were white, which was only a problem when we had to work on each other's hair, and at that time, I only knew textured hair. But the experience of working with all hair textures eased me out of my comfort zone and made me realize how good I was.

The more hands-on training I received at school, the higher I raised my small fees doing hair in our basement. I was hustling left and right—ten dollars here, twenty dollars there. I was so into the whole salon experience, I even had my grandmother buy me a pedicure set so I could start doing nails, too. I started out as an entrepreneur.

I remember watching the GRAMMY Awards on TV around this time and hearing huge stars like Anita Baker and Madonna thank their hairstylists as they accepted their awards. Seeing the fashion and hairstylists get that kind of recognition made me realize what was possible for me in the beauty industry. I was like, *Wow! You mean this could actually be a career? And I could get to work with celebrities? That's what I want!*

After that, I decided I didn't want to just do hair. I wanted to do "Hollywood hair," and I wanted to be so good at it that I would one day be recognized on a big stage as the best, just like I'd seen on TV. Little did I know, almost twenty years to the day that I first daydreamed about doing celebrity hair in Hollywood, I was living it, walking up on stage as the first Black female hairstylist to *ever* win an Emmy Award for Outstanding Achievement in Hairstyling for my work on *The Tyra Banks Show*. The following year, I won a second Emmy and became the first and only hairstylist to win back-to-back Emmy Awards in that category. Thanks to my unfaltering passion, determination, hustling abilities, prayers, manifestations, and hard work, my life's dream came true, and then some. I've traveled the globe, worked with some of the world's biggest celebrities, and had my work featured in *Vogue, Essence, Vanity Fair,* and more.

I know it might sound like a magical fairy tale, but my journey from the hood to Hollywood was pretty rough. Sadly, my mother died of an aneurysm right before my eyes, shortly after she'd given me the $150 to buy my beauty kit for hair school. Unfortunately, she never got to witness my success and the fruits of her investment. The trauma of losing her at such a young age

PHOTOGRAPHY BY TYREN REDD

led me down a destructive path for a few years. Without adult guidance, I started acting up in school—missing days, smoking weed, and getting in trouble with the popular girls and my drug dealer boyfriend. I even tried selling drugs for a while until they got stolen—$20,000 worth. I was done after that!

I managed to graduate at seventeen—but without my cosmetology license. Unfortunately, I'd missed way too many school days to complete the coursework at that time. But rather than let the tragedies, pain, and distractions in my young life keep me down, I used that adversity to strengthen my backbone. I was determined to stay the course and make my mom proud, and I ultimately surpassed my own expectations, becoming something I never knew I would become. Oh yeah, and of course, I eventually got my cosmetology license.

Maybe you've had a rough upbringing or experienced other challenges along your journey. Life continually has pitfalls, but it's how we choose to look at them and learn from them that determines our destiny. Many of the early lessons I learned were painful and costly. But as the saying goes, you never know how strong you are until being strong is the only choice you have.

For over twenty-five years, I've dreamed big, worked hard, and learned a lot. I have managed to stay focused and relevant over the course of my career, working with many of the best in the entertainment industry. I've observed and studied the top minds in business, self-motivation, finance, entrepreneurship, and spiritual leadership roles. I perfected my craft early on and have earned a reputation as a *go-to* stylist, both in the entertainment industry and among my personal clients. More importantly, I've taken the time to pay closer attention to my finances and am excited to share with you my resources for succeeding in the *business* side of the beauty industry.

So, with this book, I want to pay forward all the knowledge I've gained along the way. I want to inspire you to follow your dreams and find success, no matter where you are in your life or career. Think of it as a master class in surviving and thriving in the beauty business. Like Bill Gates, Ralph Lauren, and Steve Jobs, I'm living proof that you don't need a business degree to be a successful entrepreneur, but you do need to know how the business works. In our industry, you need passion, experience, and proper guidance from someone who has been where you want to go.

I'm a "tell-it-like-it-is" type, so in *From Beauty to Business*, I share my triumphs, tribulations, philosophies, advice, and resources as well as essential information I've learned about our business's business—from the consequences of not doing your taxes to starting your own business to marketing yourself and beyond—all in one place. It's the practical guide I wish I would have had when I was starting out, and I've designed it to be both comprehensive and easy to apply to your own life.

Scan the QR code to learn more on why I wanted to write this book and what I hope you'll get out of it.

I've divided the advice in this book into seven sections, which I'm calling the **Seven Principles for Success**. In these seven principles, I offer proven business strategies not taught in *beauty* schools, along with resources on how to grow and survive in the beauty industry that are not taught in *business* schools. In **Principle 1**, I'll teach you how to develop a success mindset, including how to visualize your dreams and determine if you're ready to dive into the business side of beauty. In **Principle 2**, I'll teach you all the basics you need to know to run a successful business, including marketing yourself and harnessing the power of social media, hiring employees, handling your taxes, and managing your hard-earned money. In **Principle 3**, you'll learn about finding your niche and building your brand. **Principle 4** will help you take your business to the next level by adding multiple streams of income—whether that's through upselling; freelancing in TV, film, or elsewhere; or launching and growing your own product line. In **Principle 5**, I'll help you grow your platform even further to increase your profits, including attracting sponsors. In **Principle 6**, you'll learn how to prepare for—and survive—the unexpected, whether that's a natural or human-made disaster, an inability to work, or something else. And in **Principle 7**, I'll share strategies on preparing for your future, including advice on start-up funding, planning for your retirement, and staying positive through it all. Finally, I've included an appendix in the back of the book with additional links and resources you can reference any time.

Through helpful exercises, case studies from my experiences, checklists galore, and information I gleaned from experts in business, finance, and motivation, I also aim to inspire you to *grow*—not just in business, but as a person—and be successful in the process!

From Beauty to Business is a passion project for me and my gift to you.

Let's face it—we creatives have short attention spans and like to cut to the chase. I wanted to make sure this book not only inspires you but also gives you the resources you need to help you realize your professional success and provides you with the armor necessary to achieve your personal goals!

KIYAH *Wright*

Principle 1

Develop a
Success Mindset

CHAPTER 1

Full Dream Ahead

The biggest *adventure* you can take is to
live the life of your **DREAMS**.

—Oprah Winfrey

I love being a celebrity hairstylist, but it's the everyday woman who really inspires me—the woman who wants that new image or Hollywood look. "When you change your hair, you change your life" is my trademark and the inspiration behind what I do every day.

You see, I'm an *image maker*, so when I give my client a new look, I get excited because I can shift her mood, change her whole energy, and literally transform her life just like that. That moment when I spin her around to look in the mirror and she starts to cry or smile because she loves what she sees—*wow*! That really motivates me to keep striving to be a better hairstylist.

What is it that inspires *you*?

Better yet, can you remember what inspired you to make a career out of your passion for doing hair, nails, brows, makeup, lashes, facials, waxing, fashion, or whatever else you might do in the beauty service industry?

My first gig doing Hollywood Hair—in West Hollywood!—was at a spot called Millennium on Third and Fairfax. At 2,500 square feet, Millennium was large as salons go, and it attracted a lot of celebrities and several of the top barbers and hairstylists in town. By the time I came along, the owner was in desperate need of a new hairstylist, so he hired me on the spot. God was definitely in the details!

I got the prized chair—but not the clients. I sat there every single day waiting for customers. I'd inherited only a few and picked up maybe two or three new people, but I didn't fret about it. I understood that I had to earn everyone's trust as the new girl in a new location. Everybody was sitting around waiting to see how good I was. Me? I already knew I was really good. I had rebuilt a clientele two times over in two different states and had over four hundred clients in each location when I was just twenty-three years old. By the time I arrived in LA nearly eight years later, I was more experienced, faster, and my work and reputation had grown quite a bit. I knew I could make it in LA! It was just a matter of time.

Thankfully, by my third month at Millennium, things started to pick up. I enjoyed staying busy, and even though I knew my stuff, I learned so much from the other stylists by just working there.

In my down time, I freelanced on a video shoot for singer Faith Evans with celebrity makeup artist Rea Ann Silva (who later invented the Beautyblender). She mentioned that she was about to work on Angela Bassett for a *What's Love Got to Do with It* promo shoot.

I thought, *Damn! I wish I could do Angela Bassett. She's one of the biggest in the business!* I didn't come out and ask point-blank, but I let Rea Ann know matter-of-factly that I would love to be on a shoot where I could do hair for Hollywood celebrities.

The next day, when I went into the salon, the owner said, "Hey, Kiyah, Angela Bassett came by here looking for you."

"No way!"

I'm still not sure how it happened, but God bless Rea Ann for throwing my name out there!

In addition to doing Angela's hair for the promo shoot, I also got to do a few days of grooming for Laurence Fishburne, who co-starred in the film, which grossed almost $40 million domestically.

Working that gig with Angela Bassett set off all kinds of opportunities for me to work with more A-list celebrities, including Patti LaBelle, Chaka Khan, Kerry Washington, Tyra, Zendaya, Venus and Serena Williams, Ciara, and Jennifer Hudson.

All the success I achieved started with my dream of knowing what I wanted to do in life and believing I could do it. So, however you define *success* for yourself—whether it's having millionaire wealth, being able to live well and pay your bills, or just doing what you love to do—there are three tried and true steps that successful entrepreneurs take to maintain their status: believe in yourself, define your goals, and place your goals front and center.

BELIEVE IN YOURSELF

I started my career as a hairstylist, then expanded to create a product line, a wig line, a virtual retail store, and ultimately a global beauty conglomerate. Getting here didn't require a huge financial investment, but it did require a serious time investment and belief in myself. Confidence is key; you have to believe you have what it takes to succeed and refuse to let the fear of failure keep you from pursuing your dreams. Before asking myself, "How can I do it?" I convince myself, "I *can* do it!"

The bigger the dream, the stronger your faith needs to be. Try to resist second-guessing yourself or giving in to naysayers.

I'll never forget the day I told my family I was moving from DC to New York to pursue my dream of becoming a celebrity hairstylist. My old-school Southern naysayer grandmother, my mother's mom, didn't hesitate to tell me how skeptical she was. She said, "New York? You'll never make it up there. New York is a hard place."

Now, get this: she'd never been to New York—or outside of her hometown, for that matter. She'd never been on a plane and never even traveled on a bus. She had no idea what New York would be like for me. She was just scared and worried for me and parroted what she had heard. My aunt was just as cynical, saying things like, "Your mom just passed less than ten years ago. You're doing well here. Why go now? It's a mistake!"

I know they meant well. But they had never been outside of their comfort zones, and they were projecting their fears onto me unfairly. So I ignored them.

Kicking fear to the curb, I took a leap of faith, and I haven't regretted it. Moving to New York helped me grow my personal brand, improve my craft, and ultimately gave me the courage to diversify and expand my businesses.

Remember this: no one can build your dreams for you. If you want to succeed, you have to believe you can. So dream big, arm yourself with knowledge and confidence, set your goals, and watch what happens!

DEFINE YOUR GOALS

When I first decided I was ready to make my leap from basement side hustle to working at a real salon, I intuitively knew I had to do more than keep saying, "I wanna get rich doing Hollywood Hair!"

Not long after I graduated from hair school, I was flipping through TV channels and caught one of those thirty-minute infomercials from the iconic self-help motivational speaker and bestselling author Tony Robbins. He talked about the value of setting goals and seeing yourself as the person you want to be, moving with action and intention in life. I was so totally pulled into what he said that I begged my grandmother to help me order his CDs (that was back in the mid-nineties before digital downloads). At that point in my life, I was about seventeen years old. My mom had died three years prior, and I was searching for answers for my life.

I listened to those CDs night and day. On one of them, Tony asked, "What do you love the most? What is most important to you? And what is the order of priority they fall in?" I had already believed in myself and my ability to achieve my dreams, but his questions got me thinking more seriously about *how* I would achieve them.

In one exercise, he prompted listeners to list the five most important things in their lives and the order they'd like for them to come true. Here were mine:

1. Success
2. Money
3. Power
4. Career
5. Family

Every five years or so, my priorities shift a little, but success has always remained at the top of my list, even to this day.

No matter how defined you think your goals already are, I urge all new and even seasoned beauty professionals to do this exercise periodically. It really helps to put some intention behind your goals, reassess your priorities, and ensure you aren't living on autopilot. Then, once your goals are clearly defined, take the next step to visualize them.

PLACE YOUR GOALS FRONT AND CENTER

I'm sure you've heard the adage "Seeing is believing." Well, that's certainly true for our goals and desires. Making your goals visible—that is, having a physical reminder of your goals that you'll see every day—creates a roadmap for where you're going professionally and personally. Muhammad Ali used to famously say, "If my mind can conceive it and my heart can believe it, then I can achieve it." That mentality is what helped him become the GOAT (greatest of all time) in boxing!

There are studies that support how psychological imagery is linked to success. Here are five of the most effective ways I keep my goals in front of me:

1. Vision Boards
2. Success Journals
3. Affirmations
4. Prayer and Manifestation
5. Read, Write, and Reflect

Vision Boards

Many successful entrepreneurs and celebrities like Oprah Winfrey, Steve Harvey, and Ellen DeGeneres swear by vision boards—I do, too!

I once read that Oprah Winfrey had a picture of then-senator Barack Obama on her very first vision board, as well as a picture of the dress she would wear to his presidential inauguration. Of course, we all know how that dream manifested.[1]

Dr. Stacia Pierce—a success coach and client of mine—inspired me to start creating vision boards as an adult. She told me she built several successful companies by using the boards, manifested her dream homes and cars, and continued to grow her business and empower her clients.

Vision boards are easy and fun to make. All you need to get started is:

- Foam core, cork, or poster board
- Scissors
- Tape or glue
- A focused mind

Start by imagining your future and how you want it to look. Think about the places you want to go, your dreams, your goals, and where you see your life going. Maybe you want to be a personal stylist for celebrities, own a brow bar, increase your sales, or get a corporate sponsor. Maybe you want to lose ten or twenty pounds, travel to Africa, or have a lavish wedding. Start with small things you can achieve in the next year and maybe just a few that will take longer. If you do this exercise right, you can usually see your dreams begin to manifest within one year.

Next, think about your vision board title to help you hone in on what you want out of life. I love the title "If You Can Dream It, You Can Do It" based on the famous quote by Walt Disney. Then, grab all the magazines you might have lying around your house, your friend's house, your mama's house, and those out-of-date magazines you used to keep around in your salon pre-COVID. You can also find pictures online and print them out. Cut out images that represent your goals and lay them all on a flat surface. Use tape or glue to affix each cutout onto your foam, cork, or poster board. You can arrange the images randomly or prioritize them based on what you want to happen first. You can cut out words and phrases related to your goals and add them to the board, too.

Here's a picture of me creating one of my vision boards:

PHOTO BY MARS WHITE

After you finish creating your vision board, put it in your kitchen, bedroom, bathroom, or any other place you'll see it every day and remember that your dreams are closer than you think.

Try to review it every night so it's one of the last things on your mind before you go to sleep.

Feel free to add to your vision board as often as you want to, when you think of new goals. By continuing to add images, you'll expand your belief to make things happen through visualization and manifestation.

I travel a lot and can't have my vision board with me all the time, so I also carry around a more portable tool for visualizing my dreams: a success journal.

Success Journals

A success journal is different from a typical diary or planner; it's an interactive manifestation tool that uses prompts to help you target specific areas of your future success. My friend and client, Dr. Stacia, who reintroduced me to vision boards, created the success journal I use the most, which is available on her website at Staciapierceshop.com.

Even though I like recording my thoughts and wildest dreams on my phone, there's something freeing about actually putting pen to paper and writing out my goals, desires, to-dos, and wildest dreams. It helps me maintain focus. Plus, most success journals are pretty easy to navigate because they provide prompts to help you organize and crystalize your thoughts.

You don't have to journal every day, but it's a good idea to create a routine like writing at night before you go to bed, particularly if you make a "Things to Do" list for the following day. Or if your mind is clearer in the morning with a cup of coffee, that is a good time to spend journaling before your day gets full.

Success journals are a great way to maintain a clear head and positive outlook. The ones I use by my good friend Dr. Stacia include an area for me to write my favorite affirmations or create my own, which include where I'm headed professionally.

Affirmations

Affirmations are another powerful and valuable tool to get us closer to realizing our professional goals and personal dreams while overcoming self-sabotaging, negative thoughts.

My introduction to affirmations came when I was about seventeen years old, still trying to cope with my mother's death. A friend gave me the book *The Wisdom of Florence Scovel Shinn*,[2] a classic, four-part collection of inspirational volumes about the power of affirmations. In them, the author teaches that you can create anything you want simply by aligning your thoughts and words with the perfect good that resides divinely within you. In other words, if you think it, believe it, and say it with intention, it will happen. The book also includes exercises for turning defeat into victory, lack into prosperity, fear into faith, and resentment into love. To this day, it's still my go-to book whenever I feel a bit off track.

For affirmations to be most effective, you should recite them a minimum of once a day and believe in what you are speaking. When I do it, I can't help but feel empowered!

You can also find tons of positive quotes on the internet that are created to uplift your day. I've posted many of these positive quotes on my Instagram and website. They focus on self-esteem, love, forgiveness, happiness, prosperity, and more.

Add positive affirmations to your vision board, in your journal, or scribble them on paper that you keep in your purse, pocket, phone, or anywhere you can easily see them. Develop a routine of reciting them every day. Once you start, stay the course! You'll begin to see how empowering these simple words can be. I'm a walking, breathing testimony that if you have *faith* in what you ask for, your dreams will come true—in God's time, of course!

Prayer and Manifestation

You will see throughout my journey that God has been very prominent in my life. I know He's always with me because some things that have happened to me just don't make sense otherwise. I'll say, "God, I want to work at the hottest salon in New York. Dear God, I wish I could win an Emmy. God, I want to do Hollywood Hair! God, bless me to be a successful millionaire hairstylist."

I've gotten mostly everything I asked God for! In my early years, when I wanted to work at those hard-to-get-into salons, something unexpected would happen just before I showed up, and I would get the job. I'd be standing there wondering, *Uh, what just happened?* Sometimes the situations were so unreal, I knew that only God could've opened the doors.

I talk and pray to God throughout each day, and He lets me know when I'm on the right path, even when I feel discouraged or believe it's taking too long.

Whatever kind of higher power you believe in or can connect to—including nature, your community, meditation, or anything else—this form of manifestation is powerful. So, if you believe in the power of prayer, *pray!*

Read, Write, and Reflect

The last thing I do to manifest my dreams and success is follow the five-hour rule practiced by many self-made millionaires, billionaires, and other famous people you may know. The five-hour rule[3] says that no matter how busy you get, you should always set aside at least one hour a day—or five hours a week—that can be considered deliberate practice, learning, reading, or reflection. This is even hard for me at times, but it's really helpful.

When I first heard about this rule, I was like, "Who has time to read books?" Then I learned that while he was running the free world, President Barack Obama read every day, and he credits books to surviving his presidency. Oprah Winfrey said the same thing; it's why she ultimately started her book club. And they are not alone: Warren Buffett reads five newspapers a day, Mark Zuckerberg reads a book every two weeks, and Mark Cuban reads more than three hours a day.

I've never been big on reading, but once I found a rhythm, I realized it's not as hard as it seems to make a habit of it.

Try devoting just twenty minutes a day to reading, learning, or reflecting, then slowly work your way up to an hour. Read about your competition, latest products, or new ways to color, braid, or give facials. Watch DIYs to learn new techniques for waxing or layering lash extensions. You can also dedicate part of that hour or all of the time to reflection. Whether it's staring at a brick wall, writing in your journal, or praying, take time to think and clear your head. Sometimes I just pull out my phone and record videos of myself. It's a calming release for me, where I can talk through my thoughts and feelings. It gives me clarity and helps me shape my vision.

You might not think that simply *believing* in yourself or, say, creating a vision board will actually result in tangible changes in your life. But trust me when I say these things really work (and if you need even more convincing, check out the sources I've cited throughout this section). When you follow even one or two of these proven steps for success, you'll not only begin to *think* and *dream big* but also manifest your goals—*if* you believe!

RECAP

THREE PROVEN STEPS FOR SUCCESS

* Believe in yourself.
* Define your goals.
* Place your goals front and center.
    - Build a vision board
    - Write in a success journal
    - Practice positive affirmations
    - Harness the power of prayer and/or manifestation
    - Read, write, and reflect

CHECK OUT THESE VIDEOS

Creating My Vision Board:

Keep Your Mind Right with a Success Journal:

Staying Motivated:

CHAPTER 2

Entrepreneurial DNA—Do You Have the *Wright* Stuff?

Don't *talk* about it.

BE about it.

—Sean "Diddy" Combs

In 2017, *Forbes* magazine called the hair and beauty industry a "gold mine for self-made entrepreneurs."[4] I wasn't at all surprised. If you were to observe the success stories of people like John Paul DeJoria (Paul Mitchell), Lisa Price (Carol's Daughter), Mary Kay Ash (Mary Kay), Rihanna (Fenty Beauty), Pat McGrath (Pat McGrath Labs), and hey, even me, you'd find that we've all made millions of dollars in this field. Now, let's be clear, I can't say that I stand shoulder to shoulder with some of these visionaries, but we do all share one thing in common. Take a guess!

It's not family money because John Paul DeJoria once lived in his car (it was a Rolls-Royce, but still, it was a car). We didn't all inherit the success gene because no one in my family could even tell me how to balance a checkbook.

Give up? The one characteristic we all have in common is *entrepreneurial DNA*,[5] and no, not the DNA used to pinpoint your ancestors or place you at the scene of a crime. Not even close! Entrepreneurial DNA consists of specific character traits you either have naturally, you have inherited from your upbringing, or you have acquired that make you successful—and it's an important part of developing a success mindset. We all know what we're most passionate about, and we work hard to get it. Sometimes a "win" can come from challenges that come our way. I have a saying: "There is no 'No' in 'Yes,'" meaning if you want something, you have to make a decision and commit. Once you decide what you want, why you want it, and how *much* you want it, you'll be ready to do the work to actually make it happen.

Of the many traits associated with determining if you have Entrepreneurial DNA, I've narrowed down my top fifteen.

DO YOU HAVE THE *WRIGHT* ENTREPRENEURIAL DNA TRAITS?		
PASSION. Do you have a passion for what you do, even if it means being on your feet for hours at a time with no break except for maybe a quick snack in the back room?	❑ Yes	❑ No
CONFIDENCE. Do you know from deep within your core that you have the talents/abilities to realize your dreams and find your niche?	❑ Yes	❑ No
RISK-TAKING. Do you have a *now* mentality that drives you to step out of your comfort zone from doing hair in the basement/room or waxing your girl's eyebrows in her bathroom, no matter how scary or impossible moving into a salon setting may feel?	❑ Yes	❑ No
BUSINESS MINDSET. Are you up to handling your finances and running a business, even if you have to hire experts to help you?	❑ Yes	❑ No

DO YOU HAVE THE *WRIGHT* ENTREPRENEURIAL DNA TRAITS?		
PREPAREDNESS TO LEARN. Are you willing to keep up with the latest trends and skills to stay current, even it means spending money to take classes or attend seminars, conventions, or beauty shows?	❑ Yes	❑ No
VISION. Are you always looking several steps ahead for growth opportunities or for ways to maximize your sales?	❑ Yes	❑ No
STRONG COMMUNICATION AND PEOPLE SKILLS. Are you able to easily relate to your clients, vendors, and anyone else you have to deal with in a professional setting?	❑ Yes	❑ No
EMPATHETIC. Are you sensitive and diplomatic enough to listen to your clients' concerns objectively?	❑ Yes	❑ No
ABILITY TO COPE WITH SETBACKS. Can you snap back from a setback, whether it's financial, personal, a pandemic, a natural disaster, or any other obstacle, without giving up?	❑ Yes	❑ No
MULTITASKER. Beyond just doing hair, facials, waxes, massages, and other beauty services in a salon setting, are you willing to diversify and try additional income streams like freelancing in editorial and TV, developing and selling products, creating DIY videos, and managing your social media?	❑ Yes	❑ No
SELLING SKILLS. Whether it's upselling services or selling products, are you comfortable and effective at creating other sources of income?	❑ Yes	❑ No
STRONG WORK ETHIC. Do you do what you say you will do and sometimes *extra*? Are you on time for your clients? Do you do your best to stick to the schedule?	❑ Yes	❑ No

DO YOU HAVE THE *WRIGHT* ENTREPRENEURIAL DNA TRAITS?		
DISCIPLINED. Are you disciplined enough to keep your website, newsletters, and social media posts up to date, whether you do it yourself or assign the task to an outside company?	❑ Yes	❑ No
FOCUSED & GOAL-ORIENTED. Are you driven and motivated enough to stay on target with your goals?	❑ Yes	❑ No
COMMITTED. Are you prepared to make personal sacrifices regarding your social life or family to build your dream?	❑ Yes	❑ No

If you're honest with yourself and believe you have all of the above-listed traits—congratulations! You definitely have the Wright Entrepreneurial DNA. If you answered no to more than a few of them, you have work to do, but it's still possible to find success; you'll just have to work a little harder. No worries! Through the exercises and information in this book, I'll help you identify your strengths and boost your confidence in your ability to achieve your career goals and live your dreams—including, most importantly, figuring out your *why*—with real advice and tangible resources to help you get there.

REMEMBER THIS

Entrepreneurial DNA is not about being born with the success gene. It's about developing a winning mindset and putting in the work to make success happen, grow, and flourish.

CHAPTER 3

Have the Courage,
Live Out Your Dreams

Choose a job that you like,
and you will **NEVER** have to
work a day in your *life.*
—Confucius, philosopher

Now that you've explored the first steps of developing a success mindset—learning to believe in yourself, defining your goals and putting them front and center, and determining that you either already have what it takes to be an entrepreneur or are willing to work hard to get there—you're ready to put those skills into action. Once you've made that decision to move forward with your dreams, whether you're coming right out of school or moving from the one-offs to the big jobs, you need to have a plan in place for reaching both your immediate and highest goals. And always remember to keep in mind your *why*.

FRESH OUTTA COSMETOLOGY SCHOOL: WHAT'S NEXT?

Don't wait until you have your license in hand to start considering where you want to work. Start thinking about it three to six months before graduation, then start applying for jobs two to three weeks before you're available to work. Generally, your first job should be in a beauty salon or beauty business retail outlet, and you should be willing to be an assistant—embrace this role! It's a great time to get your bearings and understand how every single part of this business works, from understanding hair textures to styling and treatments to scheduling and sweeping.

As you start making your plans, think about the people in your industry who you admire. Who would you like to have mentor you? Yes, mentor! Don't even think about going solo too early. By working with a mentor, you can learn the process of timing, patience, growth, and cultivating relationships. And by working at a reputable business, you'll learn firsthand how to be a good business owner before you go it alone. Plus, you'll get the opportunity to work in different settings and see how different business models work so you can make an informed decision when it comes time to take the training wheels off.

The mentorship period of my career was invaluable. I was seventeen years old, and my very first professional gig was at one of the most popular salons in Silver Spring, Maryland, on Georgia Avenue, where the DC line starts. I remember like it was yesterday, hitting the pavement and asking all my cool friends where they got their hair done. Just about all the cool girls in town went to this trendy shop called Imagine This salon. It was run by three colorful, fancy, fabulous, next-level creatives who strutted up and down the street wearing these custom-made neon spandex outfits—I'm talking body-con! At first, I labeled them as "misfits," not sure if I bought into the hype, but after seeing how people on the streets followed them to their salon like they were pied pipers, I realized they were really walking, talking marketing geniuses, attracting customers just with their images! Once people got inside their shop, the proof was in the pudding. The buzz they generated translated into a ton of clients.

After just one visit, the guys liked me enough to take a chance on me, a seventeen-year-old straight out of high school. They put me on a fifty-fifty commission (meaning I kept half of what I made, a fairly common setup for those just starting out in the beauty industry) with my own chair and their clientele. I had to respect that. It was my first real job and a big leap at being independent.

Day one at the salon was like nervously walking into school on the first day. *Am I gonna be able to fit in here? Can I keep up? Am I gonna make money? Can I hang?*

As it turned out, the guys were great! They were the perfect mentors for me, especially David Dior, the lead hairstylist. He was the real deal—fly, over the top, and one of the best in the city. Everybody wanted him to do their hair, from the drug dealer girlfriends to celebrities like Salt-N-Pepa when they came into town, and anybody else who happened to roll through DC. Back then, David was *the* go-to hairstylist. Working with him, naturally, I learned *a lot*, including how to be a good student.

BEING THE BEST MENTEE

See, I was the type of person who always wanted to be around and work with the best. I felt it was the only way I could genuinely learn. If you're serious about finding any level of success in the beauty industry, choosing the right mentor can make a big difference in your future success. After you've identified who you admire most, it's OK to contact them via email, DM, or even stop in their salon and ask, "When is a good time to chat with you?" Once your foot is solidly in the door, don't just ask for a job—sell yourself. Let them know your goals and why it would be mutually advantageous for them to mentor you or let you work with them.

Heed the following advice to make the most of your time as a mentee and what could be your defining career launchpad:

- **Soak up knowledge.** Watch what your mentor does, how they do it, and what it is about them that made you want to learn from them specifically.
- **Do what you are asked to do.** Even if you're asked to dust the product on the shelves, do it with a positive attitude, and don't be afraid to go that extra mile and take initiative.

- **Professionalism is key.** Be mindful of your environment. Image is everything. Dress the part. Act the part. Use common sense (this includes not taking personal calls or surfing your social media).
- **Ask questions.** If you don't understand something, ask. But know *when* to ask (i.e., not during a crazy-busy time at the salon) so you're not a distraction from the work that needs to get done.
- **Be flexible.** Sometimes you'll be asked to work late or come in early. Don't question it. Change your plans, if necessary, to get the work done. There will be a time in your career when you can afford to be picky about the work you take on and the hours you work, but your mentorship is not one of those times. This stage of your career is a grind, but it'll pay off if you put the work in.

Once you've soaked up all the knowledge you can as a mentee and have a little experience under your belt as an assistant, you can start considering branching out on your own.

First, you'll want to decide which business model is right for you. There is no right or wrong choice here, but each option has advantages and disadvantages. Whether you're just starting out or are looking for a change in your beauty career, use the following as a roadmap you can refer back to again and again.

SELECTING THE BEST BUSINESS MODEL

For a career in the beauty industry, you'll likely follow one of five main paths. In fact, you'll probably work under more than one of these models, and you might even work under more than one at the same time. Those five main business models are:

- Commission
- Booth Rental
- Going Mobile
- Going Solo in Your Own Space
- Salon Suite

These days, I find that most beauty pros do more than one beauty service. Like myself, I started out doing nails and hair, then I added coloring and even a little photography and creative direction. Whether your specialty is hair, nails, brows, facials, or anything else, there are pros and cons to each business model when you're working in a salon setting, so be sure you understand each one. Each model offers something different, so it's important that you know which model will work best for you at a given time in your life and career.

Commission

Working on commission means you'll operate within an existing salon environment as an employee. You'll follow their policies and procedures and will have access to their facilities and resources (including customers!). This can be a nice way to build a client base, even if it means handing over a significant portion of your earnings. And what I appreciate about this model now, looking back, is that I could leave and go on the road for months without having any salon overhead to worry about. As long as I kept up with my customer outreach, I could even keep my customers for my return (I'll cover more about taking your work on the road and retaining customers later on!). When you work on commission, you agree to give a percentage of what you earn to whoever hires you. The split can vary depending on the salon. Fifty percent is the average starting commission split these days for most independent salon owners. Don't be surprised, though, if you go to work at an upscale salon and the owner insists on a larger share of the split to cover their high-priced rent and overhead. There could be extra coins, too, through your salon product sales and tips.

Other employers offer a base hourly wage or sometimes a guaranteed salary plus tips, but with a lower commission. Aside from having to split the money you bring in, another potential downside of the commission model is that you generally won't have much say about your workdays and hours; the salon is typically in charge of scheduling. However, on the upside, you'll have fewer expenses (since the space and equipment are covered by the salon), and you can get started without already having a big client base. It can be a great model for anyone just starting out or switching between positions.

The fifty-fifty commission split I got at my first salon, Imagine This, was cool because I was just starting out and didn't have many clients yet. I was also *super slow* at doing hair at this stage while I was building up my confidence. So not having to worry as much about landing individual clients allowed me to focus on my craft. Over the next fifteen years or so, I worked on commission every time I moved to a new location (at my first salons in New York and Los Angeles, owners started me on fifty-fifty splits with my commissions growing as I excelled, though my tickets were higher as I advanced, so it all evened out), which helped me establish my reputation in a new environment each time since I could build my client base from walk-ins and salon owner referrals. Nothing says you have to stay with commissions if you start there. Trust me, you'll know when it's time to move on.

Two years into my commission at Imagine This, I was popping. I had more than two hundred clients and was making about $2,500 a week. By that point, I knew I was making way too much money to give half away, so I requested a meeting with the owners and asked for a larger commission. Unfortunately, after days of back and forth, it became clear that it wouldn't be possible. Disappointed, I left.

Thankfully, I've always been a strategic thinker, so even before I went into that meeting, I had my eye on another salon that was across the alley. It wasn't trendsetting. There was no vibe and no sexy. The salon stylists and the clients were older than I was used to, but they had an open chair, and it was nearby so my current clients wouldn't be too inconvenienced. Armed with the confidence that I could make it on my own, I made the giant leap from commission to booth rent.

Booth Rent

Unlike myself, many aspiring beauty professionals dream of having their own salon. They often say, "I'm not giving anybody half my money!" And while that's an admirable goal, it's also extremely valuable to spend some time working alongside reputable stylists in a learning environment before you go solo. The money will come! But if you're not quite ready to take that giant leap to full-on salon owner, booth rent (sometimes called the "work-share model") is the best next step, as you still get the opportunity for mentorship along with a level of independence.

When you rent a salon space (aka booth rent), you pay a weekly or monthly fee to the owner, who covers all the overhead. You will likely be responsible for more of your own day-to-day expenses under booth rent than commission (more on this below), but after these expenses, all the money you make is yours—no splitting your commission. This usually means you'll have the potential to take home much more income with the booth rent model. Plus, you don't have to worry about the logistics of running a full salon.

Although renting a booth means you aren't responsible for an entire salon, your obligations and expenses are significantly greater than they are in a commission setting. You essentially become your own small business, with many of the rewards but also responsibilities that may include:

- Hiring assistants
- Salon maintenance (product orders, washing towels and capes, cleaning, etc.)
- Paying taxes as a business owner
- Carrying your insurances
- Setting your own prices and collecting payments
- Finding and managing vendor relations
- Marketing your business

In the next section, I'll discuss the ins and outs of managing these details, but for now, let's take a closer look at the booth rent model and what you need to know to get started.

What You Need to Get Started with Booth Rent

When you commit to paying booth rent, make sure you get a **written lease or agreement** from the landlord. It will save any confusion down the line, especially with the IRS. The agreement should include the following:

- Start and end dates (common lease terms can be anywhere from six to eighteen months) as well as a clause that lays out how either party can terminate the agreement.
- The agreed-upon flat rate you'll pay for rent as well as the frequency and due date of these rent payments. Depending on your state or country, salon booth rates can range between $150 and $500 per week.

- Explanation of what you get as a renter (in addition to your booth) in exchange for your fee. This should include water, towels, lockers, parking, and in some cases, electricity. Make sure these terms are included in your lease itself rather than through a la carte arrangements.

Even though salon owners are under no obligation to give you a key, it's a good idea to ask if you can have one so you can get into the salon at any time, not just during their regular business hours.

• • •

I paid $175 a week at my first booth rent job back in the nineties, and I pocketed everything else I made. By the time I was twenty-one years old, I was grossing about $130,000 per year, about the same as I did on commission across the street at Imagine This. But after rent and other expenses, I pocketed about $90K doing booth rent versus the $65K I took home after splitting my commission in half. At eighteen years old, this wasn't so bad. Do the math!

As a booth renter, I could set my own hours, and I had the freedom to develop my brand and think about my future. Of course, none of this was a walk in the park. Going solo came with greater responsibility. I worked harder and longer hours to guarantee I made enough money every week to pay my expenses, and I got to the point that I needed help to maximize the business demand (more on hiring an assistant in chapter six).

Like I mentioned before, I have gone back to working for commission a number of times over the course of my career, but my first switch to booth rent was a better fit for me at that time because I lived on the road during tours.

WARNING: New Model for Booth Renters in Some States

The business model for salon workers has changed a lot from when I started, and even more so since January 2020. In California, for instance, commissions are practically a thing of the past, thanks to a new "gig worker" bill called AB5. It reclassified a lot of beauty professionals who worked as independent contractors into employees.

In other words, if you work under the schedule the salon owner sets, follow their rules, use their products, and they pay you any kind of wages, then you're an **employee** and not just a booth renter. The distinction is important because independent contractors are not entitled to most of the protections and benefits that employees get, including a minimum wage, overtime pay, unemployment insurance, workers' compensation insurance, and paid family leave.

Independent contractors, on the other hand, may have the potential to keep more of their earnings and write off more expenses. As long as you have the appropriate license and permits to rent a booth, come and go as you please, set your hours and prices, process your own payments, schedule your own appointments, and get paid directly by your customers, then yeah, you're a full-fledged independent contractor.

And while these guidelines are specific to California, they'll likely serve as a nationwide cosmetology industry model. So you may want to play it safe now to avoid problems with the IRS down the road.

I urge you to check out chapter seven for more specifics about your tax obligations as an **independent contractor versus an employee**, as well as tips on how to **handle your tips**.

Meanwhile, here's a snapshot of the pros and cons of the booth rent model versus the commission/employee model to help you decide which setup may work best for you:

COMMISSION VERSUS BOOTH RENT SIDE-BY-SIDE COMPARISON		
	Commission/Employee	**Booth Rent**
Pay structure	You are guaranteed a set salary or commission rate that you split and can negotiate with the salon owner.	You set your own pricing and pay rent per your written agreement, but you don't owe the salon owner any of your income beyond that.
Social security & Medicare taxes	By law, the owner covers these contributions for you.	These mandatory costs are all left up to you.

COMMISSION VERSUS BOOTH RENT SIDE-BY-SIDE COMPARISON		
	Commission/Employee	**Booth Rent**
Hours and scheduling	The salon owner sets the hours of operation.	You set your own schedule, coming and going as you please.
Cost of renting a space	The salon owner covers this.	You rent your own space and are responsible for earning enough money to cover this.
Writing off business expenses	You are an employee, and taxes are automatically deducted from your pay.	As an independent contractor, you can write off many of your expenses.
Costs for supplies, like color, shampoo, towels, tools, and more	You do not pay for products.	You are responsible for paying for the products you use.

There is no right or wrong answer as to whether you should work for commission/as an employee or pursue booth rent. As you can see, each model has its pros and cons, and there is a time and place for both, depending on your priorities and stage of life and career. But with the tightening IRS rules and classifications, more and more hairstylists, estheticians, makeup pros, and others in the beauty service industry are abandoning the commission, employee, and booth rent models altogether, opting to go it alone by opening their own brick-and-mortar shops or salon suites or by going mobile. This last option certainly has its benefits, but in my opinion, it is a risky way to get started if you haven't worked with a mentor first.

Going Mobile

With salons on forced shutdown in 2020 due to COVID-19 restrictions, many of us beauty professionals stayed afloat by doing house calls—I even added virtual consultations. This trend has continued post-COVID, with even more stylists choosing to continue offering mobile services long after restrictions were lifted. Going mobile isn't a bad option, but it's not for everyone. It takes a certain type of person to run a successful mobile beauty business, namely one who is organized and flexible.

ARE YOU ORGANIZED? Going mobile may mean having to pack and unpack different supplies every day and lug them around when you're out with clients. Otherwise, it could be a long way home if you forget something you can't do without. You need to know your schedule on a given day and plan ahead for anything you might need. Pack beforehand and review your kit several times. And stylists, *always bring extra hair.*

ARE YOU FLEXIBLE? You never know what you're walking into when you visit a client at their home or office. Can you adjust if there's not enough light in the space? Children or pets in the room? No running water? No convenient space to set up?

• • •

Like all the other business models, going mobile has its share of pros and cons:

GOING MOBILE PROS & CONS	
PROS	**CONS**
• Less overhead • Flexible hours • Minimal start-up costs • Can receive tax credits for gas, parking, car repairs, etc. (check with your accountant and insurance agent for details and savings) • Personal one-on-one service • Higher rates for at-home services	• Hard to build a client base initially, which can affect your income. • Travel time between customers, plus time spent parking, moving, and packing products, can affect the number of clients you see in a single day. • Client homes may have distractions, including pets, kids, limited workspace, etc. • Home visits lack structure. They often invite clients to negotiate lower rates. • No real haircare treatments, mainly style and go.

Another potential way to branch out on your own is to open your own salon, either at a dedicated brick-and-mortar location (recommended) or at home (approach with caution—more on this later). Either one of these paths requires a huge amount of work and commitment, and both can feel complicated and overwhelming. But the independence of working as a solo beauty artist can be incredibly rewarding and isn't as intimidating as it might seem.

Working Solo (as a Salon Owner)

Going solo is not for everybody, but for those who want a taste of true entrepreneurship, the greatest reward of working for yourself is that *you're the boss.* You get to call all the shots and keep all the profits. You can design your location with a vibe that suits you and your customers, set your own prices, market your business based on your brand and target customer, and you don't have to report to anybody other than the IRS.

But like with any small business, there are downsides. You are responsible for *everything* and *everyone,* including financial obligations that need to be met regardless of your income that month. And remember that you'll be working ten times harder than if you work as an employee, on commission, or even on booth rent.

The most crucial detail before you establish your salon is to have a Vision Plan—on paper.

Vision Plan

When you're just starting to consider going solo, all you need is a one- to two-page document that lays out your vision and goals for success. This is called a "Vision Plan." This doesn't have to be a full-blown business plan with financials, legal documents, and projections you may need after you've been operating for a while and are looking for funding (see chapter nineteen for more on how to craft an official business plan). This is just a place for you to get your goals on paper.

Creating a Vision Plan is easy. Start by writing a couple of sentences about each of the following:

- What is your business? Hair salon? Nail salon? Brow bar? Day spa?
- What makes you and your business unique?
- Who is your competition?
- How do you intend to outperform or complement your competition?
- What are your first-year goals?
- What are your ultimate goals for the business?
- Who is your client? What are the traits of the clientele you want to serve?
- Most importantly, *why* do you want to start this business?

After you complete this exercise, voilà, you will have a bona fide Vision Plan. Now it's time to start considering where you want to operate this business.

Opening Your Salon Checklist

Home-Base Location

Unless there are reasons beyond your control, I strongly recommend that you avoid operating your beauty business from your home. Why? It can be difficult to earn the respect of customers (particularly new ones) who often see home-based operations as more casual and less professional than a formal salon environment. They can also be less likely to want to pay full dollar for your services. These are obstacles you may be able to overcome but can avoid altogether if you opt for a more formal setup.

Of course, there are instances when any beauty professional *must* work from home, like for childcare reasons or other family concerns. Even if you need to work from home, it's still important to do it the right (read: professional and legally compliant) way. Consider the following for any home-based operation:

THE *Wright* CONSIDERATIONS WHEN SETTING UP SHOP AT HOME

- **Paperwork.** Along with your cosmetology license, be sure to secure your operational and retail licenses along with necessary insurances, permits, and a certificate of occupancy (see chapter four).

- **Zoning.** Are there any zoning regulations that prevent you from operating a commercial business from home?

- **Work Area.** Be sure to have a designated client service area that's separate from your living space. And be mindful of your neighbors!

- **Entrances.** If possible, do your customers have a designated entrance?

- **Dress the Part.** Are you prepared to dress for work and carry yourself like a professional as you would if you were in a salon setting?

- **Set the Mood.** Consider smell, cleanliness, sanitization, noise levels, and other distractions, and make sure your décor matches your tastes and the kind of clientele you want to attract. This is an important step. Don't disregard it.

- **Work Schedule.** Set official business hours.

- **Supplies.** Is your home-based salon equipped with all the necessary tools and products you would have in a brick-and-mortar salon setting? According to *Entrepreneur* magazine, start-up costs for home-based hair salons are under $2,000, while start-up costs for home-based nail salons can run from $2,000 to $10,000.[6]

Brick-and-Mortar Location

Opening your own brick-and-mortar salon can be an overwhelming process, but I've pulled together a list of some of the basic things you should keep in mind before you take the plunge.

THE *Wright* THINGS TO CONSIDER
BEFORE OPENING YOUR DOORS

- **Paperwork.** Along with your cosmetology license, have you secured your operational and retail licenses along with necessary insurances, permits, and a certificate of occupancy (see chapter four)?
- **Location.** Have you picked a location that's near where your target demographic shops or lives with good traffic, high visibility, adequate parking, and lots of light?
- **Competition.** Check out where your competition operates nearby.
- **Laws and Regulations.** Research all the local laws and regulations for opening a shop in that area.
- **Move-in Costs.** Determine all costs associated with moving into an existing space or purchasing a location from the ground up, which may include a security deposit that's equivalent to several months' rent.
- **Written Agreements.** Take care of all your business with the seller or lessor, which may include lease or purchase documents, and set up your utilities.
- **Supplies.** Have you purchased all the equipment and products you'll need? According to a 2020 report from SBDCNet, a full salon purchase list for a hair salon can run about $27,000, including hood dryers, shampoo, and coloring stations. The costs are less for a simple barbershop or nail salon. Used stations with chairs can range from $200 to upwards of $1,000. Supply costs for polishes, dyes, shampoos, and other products can cost up to $20,000 to start.[7]
- **Look and Feel.** Does your décor match your tastes and the kind of clientele you want to attract?

Setting Up Your Salon Space

Most brick-and-mortar salons are about one thousand to two thousand square feet and include separate areas for reception, retail, an office, storage, a changing room (the restroom can also be used for changing), and maybe a break room. Hair salons will have service areas for shampooing, styling, and cuts. Nail salons and spas may also have at least one private area for facials, waxing, and other esthetician services. This checklist is geared toward brick-and-mortar salon locations, but some of this advice can apply to a home-base salon as well, depending on your setup.

THE *Wright* CHECKLIST FOR SETTING UP YOUR BRICK & MORTAR SALON SPACE

- **Reception Area.** At a minimum, have a desk or table to check in. If space permits, include waiting chairs, plants, a TV, and speakers for music. Depending on where you're located, it may be a good idea to have a coat rack and a place for umbrellas.
- **Retail Area.** Set up your retail products near the front of the salon, close to the reception area. Make the display look as appealing as possible on glass or wood surfaces, bookcases, or metal bakers' racks. Keep products at eye level and arrange them as attractively as possible. Don't clutter the space with too many products, and absolutely keep them dust-free.
- **Shampoo Area.** Most salons keep shampoo stations in the back of the salon or as far away from the reception and waiting area as possible. These stations can be free-standing or affixed to the wall. Each station should have a cabinet or shelf for storing the products you use (ideally, they are the same products you're selling). Also, try to use this area to apply any strong chemical treatments so the fumes are as far away from the reception area as possible.

- **Treatment Rooms.** Whether you use this space for facials, waxing, or skin treatments, make it a comfortable and relaxing environment that has a door, curtain, or partition for privacy. Lighting in this space should be appropriate for the treatments you offer (i.e., brighter lights for detailed services like skin treatments and lower lights for more relaxing services like facials can be achieved with light dimmers). Ensure you have enough electric sockets, good ventilation, cabinets or drawers for storage, heating, and cooling in this area.
- **Environment.** You should give as much thought to the environment and overall feel of your salon as you do the actual décor. If you believe your clients will be offended by loud hip-hop, hard rock, or other music blaring throughout the salon or R-rated movies playing on the TV while their kids are in the waiting room, then you need to make adjustments accordingly.
- **Window Display.** Depending on whether you lease or own your space, there may be some restrictions on how much you can do for your window display. Ideally, you'll want to show your salon's name and contact info (phone number and website). The key is a clear logo, something you can see from afar. Don't list your operating hours if you're concerned about safety, but do state if you accept walk-ins. If you have a security alarm, be sure to post the security company's sticker on the door or window, where it's prominent.

I never opted to set up my own brick-and-mortar salon because I didn't think managing stylists would be good for me—it would keep me too still. But times have changed, and I've realized I can still be independent while other stylists are nearby, which is why I ultimately opted to pursue a salon suite and have the best of both worlds.

Salon Suites

What led me to eventually transition to the salon suite model after years of doing booth rent and commission had to do with circumstances beyond my control—plus, times have changed!

It was 2014, and I was renting a booth at the Warren Tricomi Salon in Los Angeles. It was in a fabulous location on Melrose Avenue near the corner of Melrose Place, surrounded by great designers like Alexander McQueen and Vivienne Westwood. If a store was high-end, you could bet it was nearby. Most of the customers were a part of the Beverly Hills salon/spa crowd. We had many celebrities come through. My celebrity clients liked it because they felt pampered by the surroundings and the customer service they got from the minute they walked through the door. It was ultimately a learning experience for me.

I had been working there for about thirteen years when the owner and my mentor, Kaz Amor, announced they were closing the salon to pursue other ventures. I was devastated.

One day, I'm a big fish in a big pond, then—*poof*—I'm without my space in one of the most highly regarded, upscale salons in town, without a plan B. I had two options:

1. Rent a booth at an equally upscale salon
2. Go it alone

Coming from Warren Tricomi, I couldn't go down. So I hit the pavement looking for an equivalent salon space where I could do booth rent. I wanted to stick with booth rent because I didn't want to worry about staffing, ordering and stocking products, profits, losses, or other stuff like that. During that time, my schedule was nuts. There was no way I was going to subject myself to that kind of pressure.

But after a week of hitting all the top Beverly Hills salons, I came up dry. *Where else can I go?*

A week before Warren Tricomi permanently closed its doors, one of the other stylists there said, "We're going to these salon suites that are opening up the street on Wilshire Boulevard. You should come with us."

Salon suites were a new trending concept across the states where, instead of paying a commission in a traditional salon, you could rent out an intimate

four-walled space in a mid-end complex with other beauty specialists who
have their own private spaces and keep 100 percent of your revenue. It's
essentially a hybrid between booth rent and working in a storefront or other
brick-and-mortar location; you get privacy for your clients in your own suite
like you would if you were in your own salon, yet you're in an environment where compatible beauty pros commune. And importantly, it can act
as your own retail space as well. Either way, you're still responsible for filling
your own back-bar with inventory and equipment, shampoo, coloring stations, scissors, clippers, products, furniture, décor, as well as setting up your
own website and online booking system. Many suites offer stylists access to
wholesale beauty supplies, parking, and a receptionist—at an added cost, of
course. Ultimately, I decided to take the plunge and take my colleagues up
on their offer to join them in the salon suite life.

• • •

The Salon Republic wasn't due to open for another two to three months,
but I committed to putting down my deposit. Like most Beverly Hills suites,
The Salon Republic touted itself as a "salon of the twenty-first century, creating a one-of-a-kind experience for professionals and their clients." The
complex had 150 transformable studios with high ceilings, free internet,
color-corrected lighting, premium equipment like shampoo stations, all-day
housekeeping services, a front desk manager and receptionist, styling chairs,
full-size mirrors, towel service, and all utilities included. Some of the suites
even had the floor-to-ceiling windows I liked.

I started with a small suite, then eventually grew into a larger one with a
street view, which, of course, came with a price increase.

After my initial skepticism, I actually liked the suite concept. I just
missed the camaraderie with other stylists.

• • •

There's no right or wrong answer when it comes to finding a model that
works for you; it all depends on what works best for you, your lifestyle, and
your budget. Nothing is permanent—you can always change things up as

you grow. As long as you've considered all your options and can make an informed decision, you'll do just fine.

KEY TAKEAWAYS

* When you're just starting out in the beauty industry or you're ready to move from the basement to the big time, find someone you trust and admire who can mentor you.
* Decide which business model works best for you (commission, booth rent, going mobile, work from home, opening your own brick-and-mortar salon, or salon suite). Do your homework by exploring all the pros and cons of each model before you make your decision.
* Write a Vision Plan as a roadmap for your short-term and ultimate goals.

Caution:

COVID-19 has changed the way our industry conducts business. Be sure you know what's required to comply with all safety protocols in your area.

Check Out This Video:

Scan the QR code to watch a video where I talk more about setting up at home versus in a traditional salon space.

Principle 2

Understand the *Business*
of Our Business

CHAPTER 4

Business Basics 101: Get Started

The secret of *getting ahead*
is getting **STARTED**.

—Mark Twain, writer

I can honestly say I never considered having a career outside of the hair and beauty industry. I love the creativity, the flexibility, and the opportunity to bring joy into other people's lives through my work. It's been an incredibly rewarding experience. But as much as I love my craft, I've had to learn that craft isn't all there is to being a successful beauty professional. It took me a minute to realize that as much as I knew about shampooing, color, and other salon 101 basics, I needed to grasp the *business* of working in the beauty service field if I wanted to make it a bona fide career. And while I've ultimately achieved a good deal of financial success, it hasn't been easy. At times, navigating the business side of beauty has been scary. I knew how to be a hairstylist early on, but I didn't always understand the other essential part of this job: how to be a business woman.

So, to spare you some of the lessons I had to learn the hard way, this chapter will break down many of the fundamentals of the *business* side of beauty—all the tools you need to get started in one place. This includes:

- Permits and Licenses
- Getting Insurance (Required)
- Applying for a Fictitious Name
- Applying for an EIN Number
- Setting Up a Business Bank Account
- Buying versus Leasing Equipment
- Setting Prices
- Paying Yourself

This is the guide I wish I'd had at the beginning of my beauty career. Use it as a roadmap to navigate the ins and outs of the business side of beauty, no matter the stage of your career or specialty.

PERMITS AND LICENSES

Regardless of where you live, you *must* have a cosmetology license to legally perform any basic hair, skin, or nail services. Requirements for licenses may vary from state to state, especially for advanced or specialized invasive services like skin care, electrology, chemical treatments, and massage therapy. The institution providing your training can guide you to the appropriate licensing boards in your area. Hairstylists can also visit the Associated Hair Professionals site (Associatedhairprofessionals.com) for state-by-state info.

Be prepared to post your cosmetology license(s) where all of your customers and the state board—who, by the way, likes to make random visits to salons—can see them.

Additional state permits and licenses needed may include:

Salon Retail Seller Permit (aka seller's permit, permit license, reseller permit, reseller number, resale certificate, state tax ID number, reseller license permit, or certificate of authority). The salon retail seller permit, which will include an account number, is really important if you plan on selling products to customers. With this permit, items from vendors like shampoo, conditioner, extensions, wigs, nail polish, skin care products, etc., are tax-free, allowing you to charge the sales tax to the customer. Most state departments of revenue will let you apply and pay for your permit and account number online.

Salon Business Operation License. All beauty professionals in the US are required to have a business license, regardless of whether you work from your house, rent a booth, or own your own brick-and-mortar salon. You can apply for your salon business operation license at the US Small Business Administration office in your state. It will likely cost between $100 and $400, depending on where you live.

Certificate of Occupancy. This certificate comes from the city you want to work in. You'll need it when you operate from any building that complies with zoning, codes, and any other local requirements—whether you're running a brick-and-mortar salon or working out of your home.

INSURANCES

Since the law requires that most US citizens have health coverage, you hopefully already have that on lock. But just as important, I highly recommend that you look into getting disability insurance. If you're like I was, you've probably put it off. *I'll get it one day. I can't afford it now.* But trust me, disability insurance is well worth the cost and can work in your favor big time if you find yourself unable to work.

The light bulb first flashed for me when I met a really successful stylist in Chicago who was in the process of building a beautiful salon from the ground up, but he wasn't working. I couldn't understand how he could afford to even start construction. As it turned out, he was suffering from a rheumatoid disease that prevented him from working as a stylist. Still, I asked, "How are you building this salon and you can't even work?"

He said, "Well, I have good disability insurance. I get about $20,000 a month."

"*What*?! How much?!"

He said, "Yeah, they base the payout on your business and personal expenses." Basically, because he was investing money into his business while being unable to work, his disability insurance payments covered a significant portion of his expenses.

It took me four years after we met to get disability insurance, mainly because it required pulling together a lot of paperwork to get the policy, but after considering all the occupational hazards in our industry, like getting scissor cuts, bruises, chemical burns, falling on set, or repetitive strain injuries, I decided it made sense to protect myself in case something happened that prevented me from working, even temporarily. So, yep, it took four years, but I got it!

Along with health and disability insurance, there are three other basic business policies I strongly recommend you consider having. These insurances are designed to protect you financially if someone files a claim against you—because you just never know!

- **Public Liability Insurance.** This covers accidental bodily injury or property damage, like if a customer or vendor happens to fall on a wet floor in your salon.
- **Products Liability/Professional Treatment Insurance.** This protects you if someone happens to suffer an allergic reaction to a product you use on them.
- **Employer's Liability aka Workman's Comp Insurance.** This is important if you're an employer; it covers claims for bodily injury or illness by an employee who, for instance, might develop carpal tunnel or back pains from standing up all day.

An insurance broker like State Farm can be a great place to start for your business, and it, or companies like Aflac or Northwestern Mutual, can help you get the best quotes for life insurance and long- and short-term disability policies. Be sure to ask the agent about bundling with your home or car insurance to get the best rates. You can also go on the web to shop around and compare rates for yourself.

As you research policies, keep in mind that the cheapest quote is not always the best way to go—the coverage you're getting matters. Also be sure to customize. Not all policies cover you for emergencies. See chapter eighteen for more information on extra coverage (aka riders) you may want to get for those unexpected crises.

CHOOSE YOUR BUSINESS NAME

Creating a fictitious name for your business or service is an option, not a requirement. But it's not a bad idea to start thinking about one when you're ready to establish your brand.

When I started at my first salon, Imagine This, straight out of hair school, I wanted to blow up fast, so I had business cards made to hand out to potential customers. I printed them with K-I-A instead of my nickname Kiyah because it's what my family called me and it was easier to pronounce.

Throwback! If you were around in the nineties, you know these were the cards at the time! Whew, have times changed ...

Years later, when I started my product line, I came up with MuzeHair as my brand name. It was the most appropriate name I could think of for my company because all of my clients—from celebrities to everyday women—have inspired me my entire career.

Before you start making business cards and signs and blasting your name all over the internet, look into filing a fictitious name statement.

Your Fictitious Name

Using a fictitious name or DBA (doing business as) strengthens your brand identity. You can incorporate your legal name in your DBA, that is, "Jane Doe Salon and Spa," or you can keep your DBA generic, that is, "Lash Boutique." The point is to choose something unique, memorable, and easy to pronounce and spell.

The process for filing for a fictitious name varies by state, but in general, you'll follow these simple steps:

1. Decide on your name.
2. Search the name online by visiting the registrar-recorder/clerk website in your county to make sure the name you want hasn't already been taken.
3. Download the fictitious name/DBA application from your county's registrar-recorder/clerk website.
4. Get the completed application notarized.
5. Mail in the notarized application to the specified address. Here's where the process may differ depending on where you live. Most states require a fee to be paid to the county clerk before you receive a certificate. These can range between ten dollars and one hundred dollars and are usually good for five years. Expect to wait about six to eight weeks for your application to be processed. When the term of your DBA expires, you renew it by paying the current fee.
6. Most states will also expect you to place a fictitious name ad in an authorized local newspaper once a week for four consecutive weeks after filing or hire a company that does all the filing for you. You can initiate the publishing yourself, or trust me, the minute you file, you'll be inundated with third-party companies offering to do the leg work for you. Typically, they'll charge a nominal fee and handle everything. Frankly, I think it's worth it to ensure this process is done correctly.
7. Celebrate your success!

. . .

If, over the course of your career, you decide to branch out from your main brand by creating sub-brands, you'll need to get DBAs for *each* entity.

For instance, after I officially launched MuzeWorld, LLC, it became a holding company for my wig business, online beauty supply store, affiliate program, and even my freelance work, which now includes Muze, LLC; MuzeWorld, LLC; Main House; Muzepreneur; and Wigs, Hair & Beauty Stuff.

Despite all my brands operating under one umbrella, I still had to separate all my companies so I would be taxed separately (see chapter seven to understand these tax rules better).

Once you've got your business name, consider using a service like LegalZoom to trademark the name as well if you want to brand the name and business and come out with your own products and merchandise (anything from t-shirts to hot tools).

EIN (EMPLOYER IDENTIFICATION NUMBER)

If you plan on having employees, filing excise tax returns, or pension plan tax returns, you'll need to apply for an Employer Identification Number, or EIN. Think of this like a social security number for your business that's supplied by the IRS for tax purposes. It's nine digits long and necessary when taxes are **not withheld** from your income—which applies to most beauty professionals. It's also mandatory if you want to open a business bank account and use it *instead* of your personal bank account. Make sure you have the necessary info ready—your business's name and address, current owners' social security number(s), the reason you're applying for an EIN, and what you expect to make in a year—and visit the IRS website (irs.gov), then search EIN for information on how to apply. Don't skip this step. The IRS will know.

This step is crucial if you plan on having assistants, receptionists, or any other employee or team member, which you should consider having because *the bigger the dream, the bigger the team*! It's a good idea to apply for an EIN sooner rather than later to start establishing an identity and credit profile for your business.

BANKING

Once you have a DBA, you can use your approved registration to open a business checking account.

Business Checking Account

Having a business checking account gives that professional appearance you need with vendors, makes credit card payments easy to process, and helps improve your credit scores. Since it is separate from your personal accounts, you are not personally liable for business account transactions or issues.

You'll want to choose a bank that meets all your needs for the long haul, so don't be afraid to ask questions like:

- Are there fees or rewards for opening a business account with you?
- Do you offer business debit cards?
- Do you offer overdraft protection on business accounts?
- If I need a loan, what are your policies for lending to small businesses?
- Do you offer small business credit cards?

Business Credit Cards

Speaking of credit cards, in addition to having a business bank account, most small business accountants and financial planners will recommend that you apply for a business credit card. Yes! Can you believe it? They actually encourage you to get credit. It's an excellent way to track your business expenses, earn rewards, and have more purchasing power than you would using a personal credit card. Remember, though, to keep *all* sales receipts for purchases made with your business credit card; your accountant may ask to see these. Also, resist using the card for anything other than your business purchases—no cross-purchasing. I know the temptation can be intense! But you'll be happy you didn't mix business with pleasure in the long run.

• • •

And while we're on the subject of banking, get to know your banker in person rather than trying to do everything online. I'm still kind of old school, so I like to go to the bank to drop off my deposits. Over the years, when I would see my banker, I'd say things like, "Hey, come on down and get your hair done!" Because of the informal relationship I built with her and the fact that she knew I kept my accounting in good order, she didn't hesitate to automatically send me an application for financial relief when COVID hit. I didn't even have to ask.

BUYING VERSUS LEASING EQUIPMENT

Whether you're just getting started or upgrading your existing space, you'll likely need to purchase or lease furniture and equipment. The good news is even if you have a history of bad credit or are just starting to build it, most wholesalers will extend some type of credit or payment plan for you to purchase big-ticket items like dryers or furniture.

Buying Equipment

The benefit of using credit or cash to **buy** equipment is that it's yours for as long as you want it. If you get color on it or it gets damaged, no problem. It's yours! Plus, you can get a tax credit for purchasing equipment (see chapter seven). You can also sell it when you're ready to upgrade. On the flip, even though a wholesaler (who buys and sells large quantities of items) may look the other way at your bad credit, a retailer (who buys and sells smaller quantities of items) may not, so it may be hard to get a loan with low enough interest rates to afford the payments if your credit is bad.

Leasing to Own Equipment

Another option for getting the equipment you need is **lease to own**, where a percentage of the money you pay to rent the equipment is applied toward the purchase price at the end of the term. The drawback here, though, is that the equipment might be outdated by the time you've paid off the lease.

Short-Term Leasing Equipment

You can also get a **short-term lease** for equipment you may need, which works similarly to leasing a car. The payments are smaller, more manageable, and in this scenario, you have the option of trading in older equipment to get the newest thing. But just remember, under this model, you have no ownership rights to the inventory.

PRICING

When it comes to pricing in any small business, there are two critical rules:

1. Never overcharge.
2. Never undercharge.

Sounds simple, right? Well, not really. So many of us beauty professionals have a problem with one or both of these rules. I struggled with this for years until I learned to consider four key things when setting my prices:

1. What is the going rate for the service?
2. How much time will I spend on the service?
3. What are my costs to provide the service?
4. How experienced am I to offer the service compared to my competition?

What Is the Going Rate for the Service?

What are other stylists charging in your area for the same services? What are your clients willing to pay? Set goals for what you ultimately want to charge. It's OK to start with one price and increase as you build your portfolio and reputation. Keep your base price competitive and upsell (see chapter eleven for more on upselling) compatible services to make those bonus bucks.

How Much Time Will You Spend on the Service?

Remember, time is money! You absolutely have to factor in your time when you're deciding your rate. How long does it take you to do lash extensions, a facial, a weave, color, or styling? If it takes six hours to do a weave and a takedown, you should think about what you would want to make per hour for your service, then set a price based on time served. It takes me four to six hours to do a full hair weave (takedown, brush out, shampoo, color, braid up, etc.) depending on whether my assistant works with me. If I don't factor in color or cut or anything extra, that time equates to a base fee of around $140 an hour for six hours, or $850 total.

Another way to decide your rate against the value of your time is to think about what you would be willing to pay someone else for doing your job. That will help you decide if you're charging too much or too little.

What Are Your Costs to Provide the Service?

How much does it cost you to purchase the products you use for your services, including shampoo, color, relaxer, hair, etc.? Make sure these expenses are comfortably covered when calculating your rate. And don't forget to factor in sales tax and shipping, if necessary.

What Is Your Experience in the Industry for the Service?

You may think charging $850 is a lot for a weave—maybe you only charge $250. But your platform, including your years in the business, clientele, awards, and other accolades, factor into how much someone is willing to pay for your services. I never set my prices arbitrarily; I base them, in part, on the fact that I've been in the business for over twenty-five years. Combine that with the honors, recognition, portfolio, and experience I have, and I've earned the right to charge what I do.

Never Underprice Yourself

As you think about what you should be charging, make sure you don't *underprice yourself*. Start fair, then leave room for small yearly increases. You are doing your clients and yourself a disservice if you stay too low. Don't charge thirty-five dollars when you're spending three hours on somebody's head; you can't sustain that. Your time is your money. Don't worry about whether your customers will walk away because you're charging too much. If they appreciate the value of your service and they leave your chair feeling satisfied and looking beautiful, they *will* pay your rate. Think about it: if a customer goes to Gucci or Louis Vuitton, they're not going to walk away once they see what they want, and they're not going to ask for discounts. They're going to pay the rate. So take a lesson from those luxury brands and charge what you're worth.

Once you're more established, it's natural that you'll want or need to raise prices. Just make sure that the value to the customer justifies the new price point.

Depending on how long you've been in the business and the amenities you offer, like champagne, water, candles, candies, flowers, etc., it's OK for your base rate to go up 5 to 10 percent every three to five years. In other words, for your weaves, colors, and rinses, you can go up ten to one hundred dollars. You can go higher or lower depending on the market value of where you're located. Just always be considerate of your client because, after all, this is a customer service–driven business.

PAYING YOURSELF

There is no set rate for independent hairstylists to pay themselves, but after talking to many beauty professionals about their approach, I found that most of them use one of two methods:

- **Fixed weekly dollar amount.** Some decide how much they want to be paid per week. At the end of the week, they take out their $200, $500, or $1,000—whatever amount they decide is their guaranteed weekly income. Anything that's left over goes back into the business. For me, about 25 to 45 percent goes into my pocket and the rest goes to the business.
- **Percentage of weekly earnings.** Quite a few beauty professionals pay themselves by holding onto a percentage of everything they take in from a client. For instance, if a client pays them $120 for a service and they take 20 percent of every ticket, they will pocket twenty-four dollars plus any tips from that client as their guaranteed pay. The rest of the money goes back into the business. Income can be less consistent this way; the amount they earn will vary each week based on how many clients they have and how much they pay for services.

Regardless of which method you choose, be sure to keep careful track of your income and do all your accounting in the same system for consistency.

CHECKLIST FOR START-UPS

(Start Small. Think Big)

* Secure a beauty license.
* Get proper permits and licenses. This may include a salon retail seller permit, salon business operation license, and/or a certificate of occupancy.
* Secure insurance. Health and disability insurance are must-haves. Public liability, product liability, and employer liability are also important, depending on your situation.
* Apply for a fictitious name (optional).
* Apply for an EIN.
* Set up a business bank account. Both checking and credit accounts are a good idea, if possible.
* Secure the proper equipment for your space (lease or purchase).
* Set your prices (remember: time is money!).
* Determine your salary and how to pay yourself (fixed weekly dollar amount versus percentage of weekly earnings).

ADDITIONAL RESOURCES

Domain Searches (for Your DBA):

* Domains.Google.com
* Namecheap.com
* Instantdomainsearch.com

Business License Application:

Visit sba.gov, then type in "Apply for licenses and permits." From there, you can see the requirements for federal and state applications, with instructions on how to apply.

EIN (Employer Identification Number) Online Application:

You can find the EIN application online by visiting irs.gov, then selecting EIN.

PHOTO BY CHERYL FOX

CHAPTER 5

Marketing, Part 1: The Basics

If your business **ISN'T** on the internet,

then your business will be *out of business.*

—Bill Gates, founder of Microsoft

Marketing is a broad term used to encompass everything you'll do as an entrepreneur to attract—and retain—customers and boost profits. This includes advertising, sales and promotions, social media, PR events, websites, word of mouth, and more. Marketing yourself and your business is an essential part of the job; when done right, it can be one of the most effective ways to promote your services and boost your revenue.

There are so many marketing strategies available to us, I could write a whole book on the topic. But before you can fully take advantage of all these strategies, you need to start with the basics. In this chapter, I'll lay out the five things every beauty professional should do to promote themselves and their business.

- Develop a Marketing Plan
- Create a Winning Website

- Utilize Email Marketing
- Set Up Advertising
- Customer Experience: Embrace Promotion, Customer Service, and Loyalty Programs

It can be tempting to think of these things as nice-to-haves, but these days, they are absolutely must-haves. Luckily, it's not as complicated as you might think to put effort into marketing yourself, and the payoff is huge.

DEVELOP A MARKETING PLAN

First, you'll need to create a marketing plan that nails down who you want to reach, how you can reach them, and your budget. Having a written-out marketing plan will help you assess your target market and prioritize your efforts to reach them with the highest impact. To create your marketing plan, write down your answers to the following questions:

- What is your *why*—the reason you do what you do?
- What is your brand image? What kind of tone do you want to get across through your brand?
- Who are you trying to reach? What is your target market?
- What activities do you want to pursue (paid or otherwise) to reach them, and how often?
- What incentives can you offer your target audience to attract their business?
- What's your budget? This can be determined daily, weekly, monthly, or whatever time frame is best for you.
- What makes your services the best choice for your potential customers?

One of the first points of contact you can make with your target audience is through a website, which is crucial for any business owner these days.

CREATE A WINNING WEBSITE

Everyone in business, whatever your business, *must* have a website. The average internet user spends 144 minutes on social media sites every day.[8] When they do, you want them to discover you! Creating a website will build your legitimacy and professionalism and provide your customers with information about who you are and the services you offer. It will be most people's introduction to you, so you want to make a good first impression.

You don't have to invest a lot of money or be a techie to create a website, especially with so many low-cost hosting companies, design templates, and tutorials available. Here are a few tips for getting started:

Choose a Domain Name

If it's available, the domain name you use for your website should be the same as your company name. If your exact company name isn't available, make sure your website is a variation of your company name. You can use tools like Leandomainsearch.com, GoDaddy.com, Domains.Google.com, or Namecheap.com to see if the domain you want is available. Once you've decided on and cleared your domain name, make sure you do an internet search to see if anyone else is using your chosen name, then *register it*. Domain name fees are usually paid annually and can vary from ten dollars to twenty dollars per year.

Find a Hosting Service

Hosting companies like GoDaddy.com, Bluehost.com, and InMotion.com, among many others, lease you space on their servers to upload and store the files used to create your website. Sometimes these companies are turnkey, meaning they'll not only host your website but also lease you a domain name and help you design your site. Hosting plans can vary between five dollars to forty dollars per month, depending on how much storage you need (to post pictures, videos, etc.) and any other services you purchase. Be sure that your hosting service offers you free email accounts and a content management system (CMS) for your website so you can make changes and updates yourself rather than having to rely on the host company to make even the smallest changes for you every time. And call them once a year or so to make sure you aren't missing out on any discounts.

Invest in an SSL Certificate

Make sure your domain has an SSL (secure sockets layer) certificate. This will ensure that your website is encrypted and safe for anyone browsing or purchasing anything there, and it'll protect sensitive information like credit card and social security numbers, login credentials, and birth dates. Some people won't even visit your site without SSL. They'll know you don't have it if they see "unsecured" pop up after entering your URL (or if they see "http" instead of "https" at the beginning of your URL), which can affect your sales. Protecting your customers is critical as well. Sites like Hubspot, Let's Encrypt, and Cloudflare can help you obtain and install the SSL certificate.

Design Your Website

If you choose to design your website yourself, there are many inexpensive website builders and templates out there to lead you in the right direction:

- **WordPress** is one of the most popular, used for 42.4 percent of all the websites on the internet[9]—but it can be technical.
- **Wix** is easy to use and more friendly when you want to make changes. It offers great templates as well.
- **Squarespace** is another popular and user-friendly option.

· · ·

No matter which website builder you use, it's pretty easy to create your site if you follow these steps:

1. Start with a basic design template that you can customize with your own graphics, images, and other content. Beautiful pictures are *essential* for a successful website, and these days, high-quality videos are helpful, too.

2. Ensure the design you select looks good in both a **vertical** and **horizontal** format because many of your customers may check you out on their phones.

3. Have your logo designed professionally if possible and include photos of your work, clients, or salon that are appropriately cropped and edited. Nothing crooked or out of focus.

4. Include client testimonials if you have any.

5. Include some type of "call to action" that leads visitors to make an appointment, stop by, or leave their contact information, whether it's a contact form, scheduling system, etc.

6. Include your contact information (address, email, phone number, hours of operation, etc.). Also include prices if you feel comfortable doing that. Keep it easy for your customers because they won't want to search for anything when browsing your site.

Launch Your Website

Even if you have just one page, get it up as soon as you can. If you have more than one page—and you eventually should—make sure it's easy for users to navigate between pages with enough interesting content and images to make clients want to stay on your website, come back to visit it often, and make an appointment to see you.

Invest in Search Engine Optimization (SEO)

I know you've heard this term a lot and maybe never quite knew what it meant. I sure didn't! Well, in a nutshell, SEO is a process that places your website in the top position when people search for it online through Google, Bing, Yahoo, Safari, etc. You can hire a company to optimize your SEO for you. It's a great add-on, but it can be a bit costly. Still, it's something I highly recommend, especially when you're starting on your own and want to build brand awareness fast on a broader level.

Find Relevant Keywords

What use is a website if no one visits it? Adding relevant keywords to your website content can increase your visibility over the internet (and can help optimize your SEO, leading potential customers more easily to your website). Use keywords that support the ideas and topics that define what your content is about, such as #haircare, #makeupartist, #healthyskincareregimen, #lacefrontwigcelebritystylist, #lastylist, or #memphishairstylist.

Monitor Your Statistics

Your website traffic can help you build your online credibility, and monitoring certain statistics will help you understand consumer behavior. Watch for things like the number of page views per visitor, the average time spent on your website and each page, bounce rate for emails sent, information about where your visitors found you, and your most popular landing pages. Understanding these statistics can help you improve your website content and attract more traffic to your website.

UTILIZE EMAIL MARKETING

You may think emails are old school. Yep, they are! The first ones were sent back in the 1970s. Yet, to this day, emails are still considered one of the most effective marketing tools for entrepreneurs. For just the cost of your time and maybe small fees for using services like Mailchimp, Zoho, or Mailjet to handle the distribution, you can get a very high return on your investments (ROI).

Here are a few tips to consider with email marketing:

- **Keep it simple.** Your email messages should be simple, skimmable, and informative, using just one topic in the subject line that's short, precise, and catchy to ensure it will get opened. Here's a sample of one of my most read emails:

PHOTOGRAPHY BY TYREN REDD

My customers who received this email got the facts about my message in just a few lines of copy. It was also customized with each customer's name and included high-end graphics, a call to action, and all the information I needed to get across.

- **Send test emails before launching a campaign.** Whether you're creating a new email from scratch or using a predefined template, it's always important to test the email before sending it out to your customers. Send it to yourself and a few of your colleagues first to make sure the email opens correctly across all devices. Visit websites like Short-stack.com, Vyper.ai, and Rafflecopter.com to help with this process.

- **Optimize for mobile.** It's worth repeating: when creating your website, make sure it will be displayed correctly for reading on mobile devices.
- **Follow-ups.** Sending reminder emails can be effective if they are not overdone. There's no general rule about how many times you should send reminders, but consider this: would you want to get the same reminder about a special offer more than twice within a single week? And when you do resend an email, be sure to switch it up with different pictures and headlines!

SET UP ADVERTISING

Advertising is the process of communicating with the users (or potential users) of a product or service and persuading them to come to you rather than your competition.

There are multiple options at our disposal to advertise to potential customers, including radio, TV, online, newspapers, flyers, posters, etc. Marketing experts recommend staying geographically local with advertising when you're just starting out. For the beauty industry specifically, I recommend focusing on three areas: Instagram ads, Google Ads, and print media.

Instagram Ads

For Instagram, prioritize quality over quantity. You want Instagram followers who are interested in your content and will engage with your brand, click through your stories, and visit your website. You want users to click an ad that leads them to your Instagram page and encourages them to follow you.

Google Ads

Google Ads is an online advertising platform from Google that allows businesses to show ads to potential customers based on what they search for. It's a great way to reach customers who are searching for beauty services or products that you offer. Google Ads allows you to target specific keywords and create customized advertisements for these keywords. Each time a user searches for a term or phrase that you have added to your list, Google can display your ad above the organic search results. This will improve your chances of being found by new consumers.

Note: Bing ads, run by Microsoft, are similar to Google Ads, but they help you reach customers who are searching on Bing and Yahoo sites. The cost for placing ads on Bing is lower than Google, but the reach tends to be smaller.

Print Media

Print media may seem old school in this digital media age, but trust me, it's still very effective wherever there is physical consumer presence. Print is a target-specific medium that allows you to reach a broad yet relevant audience. Advertising in niche blogs and magazines will help you reach your target market and efficiently increase brand awareness. Print media also has a longer shelf life. Translation: your ad will live on for as long as that magazine sits in a salon.

CUSTOMER EXPERIENCE: EMBRACE PROMOTION, CUSTOMER SERVICE, AND LOYALTY PROGRAMS

Promotional marketing refers to using a special offer to pique a customer's interest and encourage them to purchase from you. There are many ways we in the beauty business can take advantage of this.

Seasonal and Timely Marketing

Occasionally, and for short periods, create special offers like introducing new treatments, products, or seasonal discounts that are timed to coincide with holidays like Valentine's Day, Easter, Mother's Day, etc. The sky's the limit as to what you can offer:

- **BOGO deals** (Buy one product or treatment, get one free or half price)
- **Add-on incentives** (Free brows with lashes or free paraffin wax with a pedicure)
- **Time-of-day deals** (10% off all treatments before noon)

- **Sales for specific groups** (Half-price treatments for "Ladies who Lunch" on Mondays)
- **Contests and competitions** (Enter to win a free haircare kit or facial)

Two strategies that have worked particularly well for me are free trials and contests.

Offer Free Trials

A free product trial can be a win-win for both you and your customers: you're investing money by offering free product trials, and your customer is investing time by learning more about your product. When I launched my Last Look Hairspray into the marketplace, I not only used the product on my clients, but I offered free samples to give them a chance to see how the product worked outside of the salon. It worked! Clients came back wanting to buy full sizes.

Experience is always a great way to reduce aggressive selling efforts and increase customer satisfaction. A great product or service will sell itself and attract more customers with word-of-mouth marketing.

Start Contests

Contests are a great way to generate buzz about your business and increase your online fan base as well as your email list. People get excited about the possibility of winning something! You don't have to offer prizes that will break your bank. Just offer enough that will make your customers and potential clients want to get in on the chance of winning. Maybe it's a gift basket that includes products you want to promote or free services. You can pull together a contest in five easy steps:

1. **Decide the goal of your contest,** that is, increase Instagram followers or reach more people or build your email list.
2. **Finalize your budget for the prizes** and decide how many prizes you can give away within that budget.
3. **Build your contest.** Think of an exciting idea that people would like to talk about or something that may also help your business. Maybe

you're offering free products or services, or a unique, exclusive experience—don't be afraid to get creative!

4. **Create your promotion plan.** Do you want to limit the contest to visitors of your website? Print media? Social media? Or all of the above?

5. **Decide the basic ground rules** and the timelines for the contest.

Years ago, I launched a "Win a MuzeHair Beauty Kit" contest with great success! The kit was a total beauty maintenance package filled with my favorite hair extensions, razors, brushes, hairspray, and other styling and maintenance products.

I sent emails to all my customers and posted the announcement on social media, encouraging people to invite their friends to sign up. "The more friends you sign up, the closer you'll be to getting the ultimate prize!" I asked people to follow me on social media and sign up for my email list. Here's one of the graphics I used to promote the contest on social media:

Once your contest is over, you can measure the results by checking your social media analytics pages and/or email list to see your ROI. I tend to see significant increases in email signups and social media followers after these contests.

Marketing is essential for any business to grow, but don't put so much energy into getting new customers that you risk losing the loyal ones you have. Once you do get new clients, you want to keep them coming back.

Client Retention

I am a salon girl at heart and I love the everyday woman—twenty-eight years later and I still love it. The average business loses about 10 to 25 percent of its customer base per year—not because of its prices or location but due to poor customer service. Twenty-five percent is a lot! You might not think of it this way, but quality customer service is one of the best ways you can promote yourself and your business. If your clients have a great experience with you, they *will* recommend you to their friends (and vice versa if the customer service isn't good). Here's my best advice to beef up your customer service practices so your new and loyal customers will never want to leave you:

MY *Wright* CUSTOMER SERVICE TIPS

- **Create and maintain a comfortable and welcoming atmosphere.** I don't have blaring music, stained smocks, hair all over the floor, dirty stations, or inappropriate music in my salon. I don't even use bad language around my customers. My long-time and new clients have told me how much they appreciate that. If this is already how you operate, maintain that level of customer service. If it's not how you operate, then strive to improve so you can deliver the environment your customers expect.
- **Listen and learn.** Some clients share their private lives with me, while others like to get in and out of my chair with minimal

conversation. Know the mood of your clients. Show an interest when they want to share and take their lead when it seems like they just want to close their eyes and relax. Listen to them when they make references to birthdays, anniversaries, or promotions. Offer discounts or even freebies to celebrate those occasions. Even a simple "congrats" note from you on their special day can go a long way.

- **Treat them well.** Can you offer champagne, juice, or wine while clients are under the dryer, in your chair, or in the waiting area? Can you validate their parking? When I worked at Warren Tricomi in Los Angeles, the only parking available was metered. But clients didn't have to worry: we had assistants ready to feed their meters so they wouldn't get ticketed when the meters expired. I thought that was excellent customer service.

- **Handle your complaints.** If a client doesn't like their hair, waited too long for service, or hated a product you used, how would you handle their complaint? If you say anything to them other than "How can I fix the problem?" then you've got a problem with customer service. Always listen to the customer, remain calm as they explain the issue, offer an apology, discount the service, or do whatever you need to fix the problem. If you decide you don't want the customer to come back because they disrespected you, your staff, other clients, or for any other zero-tolerance reason, you have the right to refuse service next time.

- **Offer a personal touch.** My clients like that I know their names and remember how long they've been with me or other things they've shared with me over the years. Asking about that vacation they were excited about or that job promotion or graduation goes a long way.

- **Be reachable.** Some clients want to talk to you and not your assistants. If they leave a message for you to call, email, or text them, try to find time to do it. Again, it's that personal touch that keeps loyal clients loyal.

- **Stay on time.** I know staying on time is tough for a lot of beauty professionals, but not surprisingly, punctuality is the number one concern for a lot of customers. I'm always pretty busy, but I do my best not to be late. If I can do it, you can do it. At least have an assistant move your clients along with shampooing, hair steaming, nail gel removing, etc. Being on time is professional. By doing this regularly, you'll find that you will not only retain clients, but you might pick up a few more in the process.

Loyalty Rewards

Return customers appreciate feeling valued, and feeling valued will keep them coming back. It's a good idea to reward loyal customers who are there for you time and time again, and there are a ton of ways you can do that:

- **Gifts.** Maybe it's a swag gift like a pocket comb, a headscarf, a lash brush, skin moisturizer, or a coupon for money off one of your services.
- **Referral Discounts.** Big businesses do this all the time—you can, too! Give your clients discounts for referring new customers to you. I do it all the time. It's kind of like their "commission" for bringing me business. I make extra money on the new client, my loyal client makes extra money or gets discounts, and my new clients get my outstanding service.
- **Exclusive Invitations.** When my TV series *Love in the City* on Oprah Winfrey's OWN aired, I invited my clients to join me for a private screening of the premiere episode. We had food and drinks, and they were able to mingle with celebrities. They felt special that I wanted them there. Maybe you can hold an appreciation event at the salon to announce a new service or remodel, celebrate a holiday, or host a "just because" event.

• • •

What I've covered in this chapter are **basic marketing strategies** for you to attract more customers, keep your existing ones happy, and increase your profits. Check out chapter ten and chapter sixteen for more advanced strategies on how to **target niche clients**, **build brand awareness through social media**, **convert prospects into customers**, and **optimize sales**.

KEY TAKEAWAYS

Marketing your business doesn't have to be complicated if you start with the basics:

Develop a Marketing Plan:

* ✳ Who are you trying to reach? What's your target market?
* ✳ What activities do you want to pursue (paid or otherwise) to reach them, and how often?
* ✳ What incentives can you offer your target audience to attract their business?
* ✳ What's your (weekly or monthly) budget?
* ✳ What makes your services the best choice for your potential customers?

Create a Winning Website:

* ✳ Choose a domain name, find a hosting service, and invest in an SSL certificate
* ✳ Design and launch your website
* ✳ Invest in Search Engine Optimization (SEO), find relevant keywords, and monitor your statistics

Utilize Email Marketing:

* ✳ Keep it simple
* ✳ Send test emails before launching a campaign
* ✳ Optimize for mobile
* ✳ Follow up with reminder emails

Set Up Advertising:

- ✳ Instagram, Google, or Bing ads
- ✳ Print media

Embrace Promotion:

- ✳ Special offers
- ✳ Free trials
- ✳ Contests

Client Retention:

- ✳ Create and maintain a comfortable and welcoming atmosphere
- ✳ Listen and learn
- ✳ Treat them well
- ✳ Handle your complaints
- ✳ Offer a personal touch
- ✳ Be reachable
- ✳ Stay on time
- ✳ Reward loyalty
- ✳ Include them at invitation-only events

CHAPTER 6

The Bigger the Dream,
the Bigger Your Team

Great things in business are
NEVER done by one person.
They're done by a *team* of people.
—Steve Jobs, cofounder of Apple

ou may have heard the saying, "The bigger the dream, the more important the team." I agree with this wholeheartedly, but for us beauty professionals, I like to switch the adage up a little: "The bigger the dream,
the bigger your team."

So many beauty service entrepreneurs think they can go it alone. They
want to keep overhead down and profits high. And there is nothing wrong
with that if they want to remain stagnant.

But big dreamers with big success goals will need one or more key people on their side and their team:

- Salon assistant
- Personal assistant (optional)
- Receptionist (optional)
- Accountant or bookkeeper (mandatory)

Each of these roles is intended to fill a certain need, and you'll want to make sure you know what to look for when hiring for each position.

HIRING A SALON ASSISTANT

Before I hire a salon assistant, I want to see their work experience. I want to know they can complement my strengths or make up for my weaknesses. During the interview, I'm continually observing their demeanor and wondering, *Am I going to be able to work with you? Are you patient? Do you love haircare? Do you pay attention to details like I do?*

Some people just do the hair, but I have trained my assistants to *care* about hair. They spend more time with the client than I do sometimes. My job is to make sure the client feels and looks pretty, then get them out the door feeling fab. My assistant's job is to be like my left hand: make sure my clients are shampooed, conditioned, and getting pampered for the few hours they are with us.

When hiring an assistant, make sure you clearly define their duties up front so there's no question about what's expected of them. Also, let them know their pay rate, work schedule, and time off up front—and make sure you put all those terms in writing.

I'm a real stickler when it comes to my customers, so I want to make sure my assistants have the same priorities. Whoever works for me has to have the following qualities:

- Clear about their goals
- Good at multitasking
- Passionate about their business
- Gives their best daily!

If you and your assistant are aligned and share the same goals, your work will go more smoothly and your customers will have a better experience.

Fit the Image

When I started working at Warren Tricomi in Los Angeles with my own chair in 2006, my concern wasn't how well I'd fit in there—I knew I had that on lock. I had the look, experience, upscale clientele, right attitude, and image for success. I wondered more about how my assistant would fit in.

I hate to generalize, but in some instances, many of the salon assistants I met were soulful sistahs from the hood who were incredibly talented and had everything it took to be great but didn't necessarily fit the "elite" salon image. My assistant at that time was no exception, but I didn't care; my assistant and I were a package deal. I decided I didn't want to go anywhere, including the predominantly white Warren Tricomi salon, without her, so I suggested she change her wardrobe and shift her mindset. I made sure she fit the image she needed to portray.

Getting an assistant with a "sacrifice before success" mindset who can maintain a specific image and standard that you determine should be your priority when hiring. I know it sounds a bit shallow, but that's a reality. In this business, you need to know the clientele you're working with and what they'll expect from their salon experience. It's important that both you and your assistant are able to adapt to the environment you're in. Remember: your assistant is representing you!

"Sacrifice Before Success" Mindset

After killing it for years, I ended up with three chairs at Warren Tricomi, Los Angeles. When I'd get into the salon each day and start working, it was a whirlwind. Some days were more relaxed, but a lot of days were out of control. My assistants were working their butts off! I would be styling a client, while they were at the back bowl, prepping clients for me.

From day one, I set high expectations for my assistants because I throw them into the fire right away and they needed to be able to keep up. I'd say, "You have to be able to multitask and always on be time. If I have to be here at 10:00 a.m., you should be here by 9:30 a.m., salon ready. You've got the steamer ready, the needles are threaded, you've eaten, and you've gotten your mind right for the day because it's going to move really quick."

Whoever helps me has to balance anything that could take them away from their job, whether it's family, kids, pets, whatever. I tell them, "Have babysitters in place. Have somebody to walk your dog. Take care of your business before you come to work because this job will require a lot of time!" Clients don't care what's keeping you from focusing on your job; they want their hair done!

Whether you're doing hair, nails, or facials, make sure you hire assistants who have the stamina to keep up with your pace. Let them know your expectations up front. If they're not there yet, they need to step up their game!

Passion and Loyalty

Fitting the image and having endurance are vital traits to expect of every salon assistant, but if you can find one who also has a passion for what they do and can have your back, too, then you'll want to do whatever is necessary to keep them!

I still remember my very first assistant back in DC, Eric. We worked really well together. He was mild-mannered yet assertive, had a great work ethic, and was a true example of loyalty! He was also super talented. He helped me out with shampooing and washing, and he was self-taught with color, which was his best talent. With that kind of help, I could pump out clients quickly.

In the winter of 1997, when I decided to move to another state, I knew the transition might not be smooth and I would need help. So I asked Eric if he wanted to come with me to New York.

"Heck yeah!" he said.

Eric supported my decision and dropped everything to go with me to New York City, so there was a lot on the line for me to make it all work. Luckily, even though Eric and I had a wild start in New York—the salon we were about to start working in was robbed shortly before we got there, thankfully hurting no one, but understandably scaring off a lot of stylists there—we stuck together, and inherited a full clientele in the meantime. Thank God Eric was entirely on board.

One year into my career in New York, I started touring with Puffy's Bad Boy Records artists. As I expanded my work and toured, I agreed that Eric could work with one of the other stylists at the salon while I was on the road. Eventually, after five short years together we parted ways when he ventured out on his own and got a job at an insurance company to make more money. Earning under $500 a week was too little for a thirty-year-old living in New York anyway. It was time for him to move on and evolve. Thankfully, he loved New York City, and I'm glad I was instrumental in helping him get there.

If you currently have an assistant, ask yourself if they are devoted to their job and *you*. They don't have to move with you to another state like Eric did to show their loyalty, but when they show that they have talent, passion, and belief in you, keep them!

What to Pay Your Salon Assistants

Expect to pay an excellent hair assistant around $300 to $500 a week, plus tips and incentives, or a little higher, depending on where you're based.

As another added perk, I let some of my assistants work on my celebrity clients, where they could make extra money at a commissioned price. I try to build in ways they can make extra money.

People always ask me, "Aren't you worried about your assistants stealing clients away from you?"

I tell them, "Look, if you're a good stylist and confident in your work, you never have to worry about that." If my assistant takes one of my clients by chance, I know it's not because I'm not good; it's most likely because I am not available or for a lower cost or other personal reasons. The key is not to take anything personally. You don't own your clients. I can't be in the salon all the time, and I recognize that some clients want consistency. Sometimes they bond with my assistants and want to have them tend to their hair while I'm away, just doing the basic stuff. I'm cool with that, and actually, the fact that I can trust my assistants to do this well is part of how I know they're great. I am not worried about losing clients to them permanently; my assistants are there to support me and learn from me, and they are usually very loyal. For that reason, I treat them right and compensate them well.

Where to Find a Good Salon Assistant

A perfect assistant can be hard to find. More often than not, I rely on word-of-mouth, other stylists, and friends because hairdressers all know each other, and they can help put the word out to find people who fit your vision.

Of course, the whole hiring game has changed with the rise of social media. You can put ads on Craigslist, Instagram, Facebook, and other media platforms. Here are a couple examples of social media ads I've posted in recent years when hiring an assistant:

The nice thing about social media is that it theoretically targets people who are already interested in and following your work. I've had good luck hiring talented assistants through ads there.

Salon assistants are crucial to have. But depending on your schedule and work, a personal assistant can be really useful, too. For me it's always been mandatory.

WHEN DO YOU NEED A PERSONAL ASSISTANT?

Personal assistants aren't necessary for everyone, but they can be lifesavers, particularly if you need help handling the day-to-day administrative duties of your business. If you're working a show or are constantly on the road, your business can get lost in the mix, which can negatively affect your finances. Ever since I stepped away from working on the *Tyra Banks Show* back in 2007, I've had a personal assistant who handles all of my administrative business so I can go full throttle on the business management side.

My first personal assistant worked part-time for just a few hours a week when I was only doing salon and freelance work. Now that I've added more business opportunities to my plate, I've expanded my personal assistant's hours and role to full-time operations manager, with responsibilities that now go beyond administrative. They now earn commissions on bookings, negotiate rates for me, answer client questions, and more. It's important that your personal assistant is able to play many roles in your small business.

When your team stays year after year and believes in your brand, it's really important to take total care of them, and if you can, salary bumps or other creative incentives are also appreciated to keep them on board long term.

Here are a few things to consider that will help you decide if and when you may need a personal assistant:

- Can you afford to take this step? Are you bringing in enough revenue to sustain paying someone weekly, biweekly, or monthly for the long haul, including expenses and taxes?
- Do you need support full-time or part-time? The best way to determine this is by writing down all the tasks you want the assistant to accomplish regularly.
- Interview several candidates to be sure you find the right fit. Don't settle because you're desperate for help right away. Ask for references. Find out why they are interested in working with you.
- Are they responsible in their own lives and with their personal responsibilities?
- Once you hire someone, be sure to do a trial run. Start with three days, and if that works out, extend to three months. Put the deal terms and their duties in writing so there is no question about their role, responsibilities, or payment structure. And be sure to have them sign an NDA (nondisclosure agreement), for the privacy of any celebrity clients.

With my schedule as busy and unpredictable as it is, I need someone who I can really trust to handle the details of my business and career. Here are some traits I look for in a personal assistant:

- A background in marketing so they're able to talk confidently to publicists and PR people or celebrities.
- Excellent writing skills to write for our blog and newsletters or send an email to a client.
- A comfort level to go out and confidently pitch projects, concepts, and opportunities to vendors, buyers, and potential partners.
- The ability to manage my schedule while I'm on the road, in the salon, or tending to my other income streams.

My administrative assistant/operations manager also has to cross-check everybody else on the team—like my bookkeeper and salon assistant—to ensure invoices and schedules are aligned. It takes a village.

When looking for a personal assistant or operations manager, I recommend finding someone who thinks like you. My current operations manager has been with me for five years. Sometimes, when I'm feeling doubtful, I ask, "Do you believe we can do this?" She says, "Oh, God, yes! I see it, Kiyah." That's what I like to hear! Even when she's annoyed with me or we're working our butts off with the same passion and are feeling exhausted, I make sure she feels like she's a valuable part of my team by including her in some of my critical decisions. Our mutual respect makes us a great team.

HIRING A RECEPTIONIST

The receptionist position is becoming somewhat obsolete in smaller independent salons. It's fairly common these days for salon assistants to take on receptionist duties like scheduling and checking in clients. Online booking is also very common these days (Salon Iris, Mindbody, and StyleSeat are a few common scheduling platforms). I recommend getting a dedicated receptionist only if you have your own salon and want to grow your business, sell products, or give a better customer experience. Some clients appreciate that one-on-one experience over booking online or relying solely on apps. Here are a few questions to ask yourself before you decide whether to hire a receptionist:

- Can I afford to pay a part-time or full-time receptionist (along with a salon assistant)?
- Do I have enough work for a receptionist to justify the salary?

- What value will they add to the salon?
- Do they have a customer service background as well as an understanding of sales?
- Do I have space for them to work and the tools they need to make appointments and tend to clients' needs?
- Will hiring a receptionist help me make more money? If so, when will I see a return on my investment?

GETTING THE MOST OUT OF YOUR SUPPORT TEAM

Once you commit to bringing someone new onto your team—whether it's a salon assistant, personal assistant, or receptionist—remember that they're not the only ones who will need to step up. You have some responsibilities to them as well.

Take care of them. Richard Branson, founder of Virgin Airlines and many other successful businesses, said it best, "Clients do not come first. Employees come first. If you take care of your employees, they will take care of the clients." When you care about the people who work for you, they will help you take care of and grow your business.

Cultivate passion. The people who work for you are motivated to work even harder when you identify their strengths, help them grow in their goals, and give them pats on the back for doing exceptional things.

Show tough love when necessary. Your employees need to know when they are not cutting it in their role. Maybe their attitude isn't right. Maybe they're neglecting their overall duties. Maybe they have to work on their customer service skills. If they have a weakness, address it! Try to help them overcome the issue. If they can't step up, you have to keep the ship moving and let them go. You are not doing them or your business any favors by keeping them on if they are a bad performer.

Be a mentor. Help your team members move outside their comfort zones and grow by teaching them new skills or offering them opportunities to take classes or attend workshops. I've always tried my best to be a mentor to whoever is working for me. I take a real interest in their professional and personal goals. I don't do it for accolades or for a "best boss" trophy, but I do often get feedback from my mentees that they appreciate our mentor-mentee relationship. Take the job of being a mentor seriously—you may be influencing greatness!

Of course, paying salon assistants, personal assistants, and receptionists can eat at your financial resources, but if you can make it work, it's well worth the cost. I'd rather pay a great team fairly than not get the work done. I just don't have time to be on set with a celebrity while juggling all my other businesses. I need someone to focus and be invested in every part of my brand and help keep me sane.

Having these kinds of employees can be game changing for your productivity. Similarly, having an accountant or bookkeeper on board to manage payroll for you and your team, as well as pay bills and manage your other finances, will automatically up your chances of success.

BUILDING YOUR FINANCE TEAM

I travel a lot for work, and sometimes I'm out for long periods. I need to know that the financial side of my business is still running smoothly and being handled correctly. This is why I use a **bookkeeper** who handles payroll and my personal bills, keeps me in line, and provides me with weekly and monthly financial reports, including profit and loss statements because I sell products and have several streams of income.

I hired my first bookkeeper in 2004 when I started really touring. She was like a mama bear. Anytime I was running out of money or things were getting tight, she'd rein me in, saying, "Hey, you gotta slow up!" If I wanted to go on a spending spree, she'd say, "Kiyah, you're too low right now" or "Kiyah, you gotta start saving more" or "Here's your balance, now tighten up." We agreed that I'd get a $200 weekly allowance, and I had to learn to live with it. Boy, was that hard! But she, and all the bookkeepers I've had since, have been invaluable in terms of keeping my finances on track and giving me peace of mind that everything was being handled smartly.

Any beauty professional who's serious about amassing wealth—whether they want to be a millionaire or just successful—should also have a **certified public accountant (CPA)** on their team to keep them abreast of changes in the industry that affect their financial matters. They don't have to be full-time; in fact, it's OK if you only see them during tax season. But try to find a CPA who understands business deductions and our industry in particular because the problem with some generic tax preparers or the friend of a friend who's good at math and does your taxes as a side hustle is that they'll probably miss some deductions that can benefit you, and they might not be up on all the proper tax codes. Trust me, I've heard some stories.

Good CPAs and bookkeepers will help you stay on top of your registrations, licenses, and permits, and they'll make sure your fees are paid. They can ensure that you maintain your books at least monthly and keep you up to date on the latest business standards in our industry.

My biggest caution here is to make sure that *you* understand all the reports your accountant or bookkeeper gives you, especially your profit and loss (P&L) reports, which lay out all your income and expenses. Hiring a professional and trusting them to do a good job doesn't mean that you shouldn't also understand the ins and outs of your own business.

It may not be easy to find a professional accountant who understands our business, so ask other professional colleagues if they have referrals. Or go online to Aicpa.org, where you can find CPAs and verify their licenses. You can also check out chapter seven, where my team and I offer information and insights about tax deductions for the hair and beauty industry, which you can pass on to whoever does your taxes to help you get back some of your hard-earned money and get you closer to your financial goals.

BIGGEST TAKEAWAY

Don't go it alone. Self-employed doesn't mean working solo. Set out to put together the best support team you can that's confident, committed, and believes in *you*! My team consists of a salon assistant, personal assistant, bookkeeper, and CPA, but your team may look slightly different depending on your needs. No matter the size, you should be able to trust your team fully and work together to achieve your mutual goals. If budget is an issue, start small. Hire wisely, and don't be afraid to ask for references.

Top Traits to Look for When Hiring Support Teams:

* ✳ Organized
* ✳ Responsible
* ✳ Multitasker
* ✳ Passionate
* ✳ Loyal

Greatest Lesson Learned:

If an assistant wants to leave, let them, especially if they are unhappy. Offering more money and more perks to someone with one foot out the door will only extend the inevitable.

Resources:

Need to find a good CPA who knows the beauty industry?
Ask colleagues for references or check out Aicpa.org.

CHAPTER 7

Taxes, Tips, and Tough Lessons

... in this world, *nothing* is certain

EXCEPT death and taxes.

—Benjamin Franklin

To be a successful entrepreneur in the beauty industry, you don't necessarily have to hire an assistant, full-time accountant, or bookkeeper, or even work in a traditional salon. But what you *must* do is *pay taxes*.

I was in my early twenties, working in New York, when my career really started to take off. I didn't know anything about taxes, deductions, managing money, reporting my tips, or anything that had to do with finances. They didn't teach me any of that in hair school. So, when I say I'm a "self-made entrepreneur," I really mean it!

Back in the nineties, the beauty industry was a cash business. I'd tell a client, "That'll be $200," and they'd hand me the cash. A lot of the time, they'd also say, "Oh, and here's a $25 tip! See you in two weeks!" Every single dime of that money, including the tip, went into my pocket. It never occurred to me that I had to pay taxes on the cash tips either. I honestly didn't know any better. But don't think my naivete and the IRS didn't eventually catch up with me.

At that time, I was on the road touring with Puffy's Bad Boys Records artists. I was also freelancing on photo shoots and in the salon. By the end of the year, I was easily making $200,000, plus tips. Needless to say, I thought I had it made. And despite my lack of knowledge about taxes and finance, over the years, I was smart enough to stash away about $80,000 with the goal of buying my own home.

I found a beautiful brownstone on 131st in Mount Morris Park, the most prominent area in Harlem, long before it became the "New Harlem." Most of the four-level brownstones there were selling for around $250,000. I had the down payment, and I knew I could easily make the monthly note. So, I was grinning from ear to ear as I sat in front of the loan officer, ready to buy my first piece of property. Then, *bam*! He said, "Ms. Wright, your taxes aren't in order."

"Huh?"

"Where are your financial statements?" he asked. "Are you paying taxes? Are you doing your quarterlies?"

"*Huh*?" I repeated. I didn't know what else to say.

The more he talked, the more my ears went numb. I left with my head hanging down, feeling like my dreams were squashed. It was the most hopeless I had felt in years.

Oh, no. I gotta get my shit together! I gotta get my finances in order!

After that defining moment, I made it a priority to take the "business" of being an entrepreneur seriously. That's also what led me to add a CPA and bookkeeper to my team to help align all of my finances. My CPA helped me get on track financially, paying all my back taxes and penalties, and took the time to teach me everything I needed to know about entrepreneurial finances—specifically those things relevant to the hair and beauty industry.

Not everyone has the luxury of finding a CPA who knows our industry, but it's their job to keep you abreast of all the new laws. In this chapter, my team and I have pulled together key information you can pass on to whoever does your taxes to help you get organized and closer to financial success.

We've broken down the tax advice and information into five key areas:

1. Understanding Your Tax Status
2. Top Tax Deductions for Beauty Professionals
3. What the IRS Already Knows About Your Tips
4. Tax Rules for Mobile Payment Apps
5. Research and Development Credits

UNDERSTANDING YOUR TAX STATUS

The rules are pretty simple: If you work under the control and direction of someone else, whether it's a salon owner or someone in your freelance world, then you are an **employee**. Someone else establishes your hours or shifts. That someone else—not you—purchases the supplies you use. They determine the prices charged to customers. They set up the appointments for you. They are responsible for expenses and, at least, some of the insurances.

On the other hand, if you run your own salon or you work out of someone else's salon but control when you work and how you run your business; you have a key to the building, your own phone number, and business name; you purchase your own products; and you determine your own price structure, the IRS says you're a **self-employed business owner**. And yes, this applies to independent contractors like booth renters.

Employee/Commission Worker

Suppose you're working in a salon where your employer makes deductions that include social security and unemployment. In that case, they will issue you an **IRS Form W-2** in January based on your income and deductions from the prior year. It looks like the one below and can be found online at https://www.irs.gov/pub/irs-pdf/fw2.pdf.

22222	a Employee's social security number		
	OMB No. 1545-0008		
b Employer identification number (EIN)		1 Wages, tips, other compensation	2 Federal income tax withheld
c Employer's name, address, and ZIP code		3 Social security wages	4 Social security tax withheld
		5 Medicare wages and tips	6 Medicare tax withheld
		7 Social security tips	8 Allocated tips
d Control number		9	10 Dependent care benefits
e Employee's first name and initial Last name Suff.		11 Nonqualified plans	12a
		13 Statutory employee Retirement plan Third-party sick pay	12b
		14 Other	12c
			12d
f Employee's address and ZIP code			

15 State Employer's state ID number	16 State wages, tips, etc.	17 State income tax	18 Local wages, tips, etc.	19 Local income tax	20 Locality name

Form **W-2** Wage and Tax Statement   **2021**   Department of the Treasury—Internal Revenue Service

Copy 1—For State, City, or Local Tax Department

W-2 Form (Wage & Tax Statement)

Chances are this form may be familiar to you, and is fairly straightforward. Self-employed business owners, on the other hand, have a few more tax considerations to keep in mind.

Self-Employed Business Owners

If you are a self-employed business owner (see criteria above) or work as an independent contractor, you are issued a W-9 tax form if you have earned more than $600 that year. This helps whoever issued it accurately prepare your 1099-NEC form and report payments they've made to you that year exceeding $600. It's a record of how much you've made when paying your income tax and self-employment tax. These contributions are based primarily on three things:

- How much you earned each year
- Your marital status
- The state where you operate

Remember, the more you make, the more they take! So if you think you'll owe $1,000 or more in taxes at the end of the year, you may need to make estimated tax payments to the IRS during the year (quarterly, to be exact) to cover any tax liabilities.

Form **W-9**	**Request for Taxpayer**	Give Form to the
(Rev. October 2018)	**Identification Number and Certification**	requester. Do not
Department of the Treasury Internal Revenue Service	▶ Go to *www.irs.gov/FormW9* for instructions and the latest information.	send to the IRS.

1 Name (as shown on your income tax return). Name is required on this line; do not leave this line blank.

2 Business name/disregarded entity name, if different from above

3 Check appropriate box for federal tax classification of the person whose name is entered on line 1. Check only **one** of the following seven boxes.

☐ Individual/sole proprietor or single-member LLC ☐ C Corporation ☐ S Corporation ☐ Partnership ☐ Trust/estate

☐ Limited liability company. Enter the tax classification (C=C corporation, S=S corporation, P=Partnership) ▶ _____

Note: Check the appropriate box in the line above for the tax classification of the single-member owner. Do not check LLC if the LLC is classified as a single-member LLC that is disregarded from the owner unless the owner of the LLC is another LLC that is **not** disregarded from the owner for U.S. federal tax purposes. Otherwise, a single-member LLC that is disregarded from the owner should check the appropriate box for the tax classification of its owner.

☐ Other (see instructions) ▶

4 Exemptions (codes apply only to certain entities, not individuals; see instructions on page 3):

Exempt payee code (if any) _____

Exemption from FATCA reporting code (if any) _____

(Applies to accounts maintained outside the U.S.)

5 Address (number, street, and apt. or suite no.) See instructions.

Requester's name and address (optional)

6 City, state, and ZIP code

7 List account number(s) here (optional)

Print or type.
See Specific Instructions on page 3.

Part I   **Taxpayer Identification Number (TIN)**

Enter your TIN in the appropriate box. The TIN provided must match the name given on line 1 to avoid backup withholding. For individuals, this is generally your social security number (SSN). However, for a resident alien, sole proprietor, or disregarded entity, see the instructions for Part I, later. For other entities, it is your employer identification number (EIN). If you do not have a number, see *How to get a TIN*, later.

Note: If the account is in more than one name, see the instructions for line 1. Also see *What Name and Number To Give the Requester* for guidelines on whose number to enter.

Social security number

or

Employer identification number

Part II   **Certification**

Under penalties of perjury, I certify that:

1. The number shown on this form is my correct taxpayer identification number (or I am waiting for a number to be issued to me); and
2. I am not subject to backup withholding because: (a) I am exempt from backup withholding, or (b) I have not been notified by the Internal Revenue Service (IRS) that I am subject to backup withholding as a result of a failure to report all interest or dividends, or (c) the IRS has notified me that I am no longer subject to backup withholding; and
3. I am a U.S. citizen or other U.S. person (defined below); and
4. The FATCA code(s) entered on this form (if any) indicating that I am exempt from FATCA reporting is correct.

Certification instructions. You must cross out item 2 above if you have been notified by the IRS that you are currently subject to backup withholding because you have failed to report all interest and dividends on your tax return. For real estate transactions, item 2 does not apply. For mortgage interest paid, acquisition or abandonment of secured property, cancellation of debt, contributions to an individual retirement arrangement (IRA), and generally, payments other than interest and dividends, you are not required to sign the certification, but you must provide your correct TIN. See the instructions for Part II, later.

Sign Here

Signature of U.S. person ▶   Date ▶

W-9 Form (Request for Taxpayer Identification Number and Certification)

Estimated Tax Payments

Estimated tax payments are how many self-employed workers pay taxes on earnings that aren't automatically subjected to withholding (i.e., withheld by an employer). When you commit to paying the estimated taxes, you must do so by January 18 of the following year (unless you file your upcoming tax return by January 31 and pay the entire balance due to your return at that point).

These estimated tax payments are made each quarter using **Form 1040-ES**, which looks like the one below and can be found by visiting IRS.gov and searching for "Form 1040-ES."

Form **1040-ES** Department of the Treasury Internal Revenue Service	20**21 Estimated Tax**	Payment Voucher **4**	OMB No. 1545-0074

	File only if you are making a payment of estimated tax by check or money order. Mail this voucher with your check or money order payable to **"United States Treasury."** Write your social security number and "2021 Form 1040-ES" on your check or money order. Do not send cash. Enclose, but do not staple or attach, your payment with this voucher.	Calendar year—Due Jan. 18, 2022

Amount of estimated tax you are paying by check or money order. | Dollars | Cents

Pay online at www.irs.gov/ etpay	Print or type	Your first name and middle initial	Your last name	Your social security number
		If joint payment, complete for spouse		
Simple. Fast. Secure.		Spouse's first name and middle initial	Spouse's last name	Spouse's social security number
		Address (number, street, and apt. no.)		
		City, town, or post office. If you have a foreign address, also complete spaces below.	State	ZIP code
		Foreign country name	Foreign province/county	Foreign postal code

For Privacy Act and Paperwork Reduction Act Notice, see instructions.   Form 1040-ES (2021)
-9-

Form 1040-ES (Estimated Tax Form)

Not all of us make the estimated payments quarterly, but if you don't and you owe too much the following year, the IRS can hit you with a tax penalty that accrues over time. Per the IRS, you can avoid estimated tax penalties if:

- You owe less than $1,000 in taxes after subtracting withholdings and credits.
- You paid at least 90 percent of the tax owed for the current year through withholding.
- Or you paid 100 percent of the tax shown on the return for the prior year, whichever is smaller.

Visit the IRS website for more information about estimated tax payments.*

---

* https://www.irs.gov/newsroom/heres-how-and-when-to-pay-estimated-taxes

Booth Renters and Independent Beauty Professionals

If you're renting space at someone's salon, the owner should also provide you with a **1099-NEC** before filing your taxes (in addition to the 1040-ES). Likewise, if you have your own shop, use this form to report nonemployee compensation, including fees, commissions, prizes, awards, and other forms of compensation for services. This 1099-NEC Form replaces many former instances where 1099-MISC was previously applicable.

This form looks like the one below and can be found on the IRS website at https://www.irs.gov/pub/irs-pdf/f1099nec.pdf.

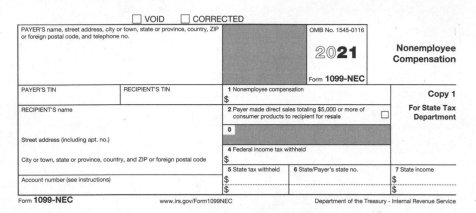

Form 1099-NEC (Replaces 1099-MISC in many cases)

Other Forms for Employers

In addition, if you hire an assistant or other employee, including an accountant, you are required to deduct social security, Medicare, and federal income taxes from their pay. This involves filing **Form 940 (filed annually) and Form 941 (filed quarterly)**. You can view samples of these forms here, and they can also be found online by visiting IRS.gov and searching "Form 940."

Form **940 for 2020:** Employer's Annual Federal Unemployment (FUTA) Tax Return

Department of the Treasury — Internal Revenue Service

850113

OMB No. 1545-0028

Employer identification number (EIN)

Name *(not your trade name)*

Trade name *(if any)*

Address

Number   Street   Suite or room number

City   State   ZIP code

Foreign country name   Foreign province/county   Foreign postal code

Type of Return
(Check all that apply.)

☐ **a.** Amended

☐ **b.** Successor employer

☐ **c.** No payments to employees in 2020

☐ **d.** Final: Business closed or stopped paying wages

Go to *www.irs.gov/Form940* for instructions and the latest information.

Read the separate instructions before you complete this form. Please type or print within the boxes.

Part 1: Tell us about your return. If any line does NOT apply, leave it blank. See instructions before completing Part 1.

1a If you had to pay state unemployment tax in one state only, enter the state abbreviation . **1a**

1b If you had to pay state unemployment tax in more than one state, you are a multi-state employer . . . . **1b** ☐ Check here. Complete Schedule A (Form 940).

2 If you paid wages in a state that is subject to CREDIT REDUCTION . . . . **2** ☐ Check here. Complete Schedule A (Form 940).

Part 2: Determine your FUTA tax before adjustments. If any line does NOT apply, leave it blank.

3 Total payments to all employees **3**

4 Payments exempt from FUTA tax **4**

Check all that apply: **4a** ☐ Fringe benefits   **4c** ☐ Retirement/Pension   **4e** ☐ Other

4b ☐ Group-term life insurance   **4d** ☐ Dependent care

5 Total of payments made to each employee in excess of $7,000 . . . . **5**

6 Subtotal (line 4 + line 5 = line 6) **6**

7 Total taxable FUTA wages (line 3 – line 6 = line 7). See instructions **7**

8 FUTA tax before adjustments (line 7 x 0.006 = line 8) **8**

Part 3: Determine your adjustments. If any line does NOT apply, leave it blank.

9 If ALL of the taxable FUTA wages you paid were excluded from state unemployment tax, multiply line 7 by 0.054 (line 7 × 0.054 = line 9). Go to line 12 . . . . **9**

10 If SOME of the taxable FUTA wages you paid were excluded from state unemployment tax, OR you paid ANY state unemployment tax late (after the due date for filing Form 940), complete the worksheet in the instructions. Enter the amount from line 7 of the worksheet . . **10**

11 If credit reduction applies, enter the total from Schedule A (Form 940) **11**

Part 4: Determine your FUTA tax and balance due or overpayment. If any line does NOT apply, leave it blank.

12 Total FUTA tax after adjustments (lines 8 + 9 + 10 + 11 = line 12) **12**

13 FUTA tax deposited for the year, including any overpayment applied from a prior year . **13**

14 Balance due. If line 12 is more than line 13, enter the excess on line 14.
- If line 14 is more than $500, you must deposit your tax.
- If line 14 is $500 or less, you may pay with this return. See instructions **14**

15 Overpayment. If line 13 is more than line 12, enter the excess on line 15 and check a box below **15**

▶ You **MUST** complete both pages of this form and **SIGN** it.   Check one: ☐ Apply to next return.   ☐ Send a refund.

Next ▶

For Privacy Act and Paperwork Reduction Act Notice, see the back of the Payment Voucher.   Cat. No. 11234O   Form **940** (2020)

Form 940 (Employer's Annual Federal Unemployment Tax Return), page 1

850212

Name *(not your trade name)*	Employer identification number (EIN)

Part 5: Report your FUTA tax liability by quarter only if line 12 is more than $500. If not, go to Part 6.

16 Report the amount of your FUTA tax liability for each quarter; do NOT enter the amount you deposited. If you had no liability for a quarter, leave the line blank.

16a **1st quarter** (January 1 – March 31) . . . . **16a** [.   ]

16b **2nd quarter** (April 1 – June 30) . . . . **16b** [.   ]

16c **3rd quarter** (July 1 – September 30) . . . . **16c** [.   ]

16d **4th quarter** (October 1 – December 31) . . . . . . **16d** [.   ]

17 **Total tax liability for the year** (lines 16a + 16b + 16c + 16d = line 17) **17** [.   ] **Total must equal line 12.**

Part 6: May we speak with your third-party designee?

Do you want to allow an employee, a paid tax preparer, or another person to discuss this return with the IRS? See the instructions for details.

☐ **Yes.** Designee's name and phone number [   ] [   ]

Select a 5-digit personal identification number (PIN) to use when talking to the IRS. [ ] [ ] [ ] [ ] [ ]

☐ **No.**

Part 7: Sign here. You MUST complete both pages of this form and SIGN it.

Under penalties of perjury, I declare that I have examined this return, including accompanying schedules and statements, and to the best of my knowledge and belief, it is true, correct, and complete, and that no part of any payment made to a state unemployment fund claimed as a credit was, or is to be, deducted from the payments made to employees. Declaration of preparer (other than taxpayer) is based on all information of which preparer has any knowledge.

✗ Sign your name here [   ]

Print your name here [   ]

Print your title here [   ]

Date [/   /   ]

Best daytime phone [   ]

Paid Preparer Use Only Check if you are self-employed ☐

Preparer's name	[ ]	PTIN	[ ]
Preparer's signature	[ ]	Date	[/ /]
Firm's name (or yours if self-employed)	[ ]	EIN	[ ]
Address	[ ]	Phone	[ ]
City	[ ] State [ ]	ZIP code	[ ]

Form 940 (Employer's Annual Federal Unemployment Tax Return), page 2

Form **941 for 2021:** Employer's QUARTERLY Federal Tax Return
(Rev. June 2021)   Department of the Treasury — Internal Revenue Service

951121

OMB No. 1545-0029

Employer identification number (EIN) ☐☐ – ☐☐☐☐☐☐☐

Name (not your trade name)

Trade name (if any)

Address

Number	Street		Suite or room number

City	State	ZIP code

Foreign country name	Foreign province/county	Foreign postal code

Report for this Quarter of 2021
(Check one.)

☐ **1:** January, February, March

☐ **2:** April, May, June

☐ **3:** July, August, September

☐ **4:** October, November, December

Go to *www.irs.gov/Form941* for instructions and the latest information.

Read the separate instructions before you complete Form 941. Type or print within the boxes.

Part 1:   Answer these questions for this quarter.

1   Number of employees who received wages, tips, or other compensation for the pay period including: *June 12* (Quarter 2), *Sept. 12* (Quarter 3), or *Dec. 12* (Quarter 4) . . . . . .   **1** ☐

2   Wages, tips, and other compensation . . . .   **2** ☐

3   Federal income tax withheld from wages, tips, and other compensation . . . . . .   **3** ☐

4   If no wages, tips, and other compensation are subject to social security or Medicare tax   ☐ Check and go to line 6.

	Column 1		Column 2
5a Taxable social security wages* . .	☐	× 0.124 =	☐
5a (i) Qualified sick leave wages* .	☐	× 0.062 =	☐
5a (ii) Qualified family leave wages* .	☐	× 0.062 =	☐
5b Taxable social security tips . . .	☐	× 0.124 =	☐
5c Taxable Medicare wages & tips. .	☐	× 0.029 =	☐
5d Taxable wages & tips subject to Additional Medicare Tax withholding	☐	× 0.009 =	☐

*Include taxable qualified sick and family leave wages for leave taken after March 31, 2021, on line 5a. Use lines 5a(i) and 5a(ii) only for wages paid after March 31, 2020, for leave taken before April 1, 2021.

5e   Total social security and Medicare taxes. Add Column 2 from lines 5a, 5a(i), 5a(ii), 5b, 5c, and 5d   **5e** ☐

5f   Section 3121(q) Notice and Demand—Tax due on unreported tips (see instructions) . .   **5f** ☐

6   Total taxes before adjustments. Add lines 3, 5e, and 5f . . . .   **6** ☐

7   Current quarter's adjustment for fractions of cents . . . .   **7** ☐

8   Current quarter's adjustment for sick pay . . . .   **8** ☐

9   Current quarter's adjustments for tips and group-term life insurance . . . . . .   **9** ☐

10   Total taxes after adjustments. Combine lines 6 through 9 . . . .   **10** ☐

11a   Qualified small business payroll tax credit for increasing research activities. Attach Form 8974   **11a** ☐

11b   Nonrefundable portion of credit for qualified sick and family leave wages for leave taken before April 1, 2021 . . . .   **11b** ☐

11c   Nonrefundable portion of employee retention credit . . . .   **11c** ☐

▶ **You MUST complete all three pages of Form 941 and SIGN it.**   Next ▶

For Privacy Act and Paperwork Reduction Act Notice, see the back of the Payment Voucher.   Cat. No. 17001Z   Form **941** (Rev. 6-2021)

Form 941 (Employer's Quarterly Federal Tax Return), page 1

951221

Name *(not your trade name)*	Employer identification number (EIN)

Part 1: Answer these questions for this quarter. *(continued)*

11d Nonrefundable portion of credit for qualified sick and family leave wages for leave taken after March 31, 2021 . . . . **11d** [_____.__]

11e Nonrefundable portion of COBRA premium assistance credit (see instructions for applicable quarters) . . . . **11e** [_____.__]

11f Number of individuals provided COBRA premium assistance [_____]

11g Total nonrefundable credits. Add lines 11a, 11b, 11c, 11d, and 11e . . . . **11g** [_____.__]

12 Total taxes after adjustments and nonrefundable credits. Subtract line 11g from line 10 . **12** [_____.__]

13a Total deposits for this quarter, including overpayment applied from a prior quarter and overpayments applied from Form 941-X, 941-X (PR), 944-X, or 944-X (SP) filed in the current quarter **13a** [_____.__]

13b Reserved for future use . . . . **13b** [▓▓▓▓▓▓.▓▓]

13c Refundable portion of credit for qualified sick and family leave wages for leave taken before April 1, 2021 . . . . **13c** [_____.__]

13d Refundable portion of employee retention credit . . . . **13d** [_____.__]

13e Refundable portion of credit for qualified sick and family leave wages for leave taken after March 31, 2021 . . . . **13e** [_____.__]

13f Refundable portion of COBRA premium assistance credit (see instructions for applicable quarters) . . . . **13f** [_____.__]

13g Total deposits and refundable credits. Add lines 13a, 13c, 13d, 13e, and 13f . . . . . **13g** [_____.__]

13h Total advances received from filing Form(s) 7200 for the quarter . . . . **13h** [_____.__]

13i Total deposits and refundable credits less advances. Subtract line 13h from line 13g . . . . **13i** [_____.__]

14 Balance due. If line 12 is more than line 13i, enter the difference and see instructions . . . **14** [_____.__]

15 Overpayment. If line 13i is more than line 12, enter the difference [_____.__] Check one: ☐ Apply to next return. ☐ Send a refund.

Part 2: Tell us about your deposit schedule and tax liability for this quarter.

If you're unsure about whether you're a monthly schedule depositor or a semiweekly schedule depositor, see section 11 of Pub. 15.

16 Check one: ☐ Line 12 on this return is less than $2,500 or line 12 on the return for the prior quarter was less than $2,500, and you didn't incur a $100,000 next-day deposit obligation during the current quarter. If line 12 for the prior quarter was less than $2,500 but line 12 on this return is $100,000 or more, you must provide a record of your federal tax liability. If you're a monthly schedule depositor, complete the deposit schedule below; if you're a semiweekly schedule depositor, attach Schedule B (Form 941). Go to Part 3.

☐ You were a monthly schedule depositor for the entire quarter. Enter your tax liability for each month and total liability for the quarter, then go to Part 3.

 Tax liability: Month 1 [_____.__]

  Month 2 [_____.__]

  Month 3 [_____.__]

 Total liability for quarter [_____.__] Total must equal line 12.

☐ You were a semiweekly schedule depositor for any part of this quarter. Complete Schedule B (Form 941), Report of Tax Liability for Semiweekly Schedule Depositors, and attach it to Form 941. Go to Part 3.

▶ You MUST complete all three pages of Form 941 and SIGN it.   Next ▶

Page **2**   Form **941** (Rev. 6-2021)

Form 941 (Employer's Quarterly Federal Tax Return), page 2

951921

Name (not your trade name)

Employer identification number (EIN)

Part 3: Tell us about your business. If a question does NOT apply to your business, leave it blank.

17   If your business has closed or you stopped paying wages . . . .   ☐ Check here, and

      enter the final date you paid wages   [/ /] ; also attach a statement to your return. See instructions.

18a   If you're a seasonal employer and you don't have to file a return for every quarter of the year . . .   ☐ Check here.

18b   If you're eligible for the employee retention credit solely because your business is a recovery startup business   ☐ Check here.

19   Qualified health plan expenses allocable to qualified sick leave wages for leave taken before April 1, 2021   19 [.]

20   Qualified health plan expenses allocable to qualified family leave wages for leave taken before April 1, 2021   20 [.]

21   Qualified wages for the employee retention credit . . . .   21 [.]

22   Qualified health plan expenses for the employee retention credit . . . .   22 [.]

23   Qualified sick leave wages for leave taken after March 31, 2021 . . . .   23 [.]

24   Qualified health plan expenses allocable to qualified sick leave wages reported on line 23   24 [.]

25   Amounts under certain collectively bargained agreements allocable to qualified sick leave wages reported on line 23 . . . .   25 [.]

26   Qualified family leave wages for leave taken after March 31, 2021 . . . .   26 [.]

27   Qualified health plan expenses allocable to qualified family leave wages reported on line 26   27 [.]

28   Amounts under certain collectively bargained agreements allocable to qualified family leave wages reported on line 26 . . . .   28 [.]

Part 4: May we speak with your third-party designee?

Do you want to allow an employee, a paid tax preparer, or another person to discuss this return with the IRS? See the instructions for details.

☐ **Yes.** Designee's name and phone number   [   ]   [   ]

         Select a 5-digit personal identification number (PIN) to use when talking to the IRS.   ☐ ☐ ☐ ☐ ☐

☐ **No.**

Part 5: Sign here. You MUST complete all three pages of Form 941 and SIGN it.

Under penalties of perjury, I declare that I have examined this return, including accompanying schedules and statements, and to the best of my knowledge and belief, it is true, correct, and complete. Declaration of preparer (other than taxpayer) is based on all information of which preparer has any knowledge.

✗   **Sign your name here**   [   ]   Print your name here [   ]

                                                      Print your title here [   ]

           Date   [/ /]   Best daytime phone [   ]

Paid Preparer Use Only   Check if you're self-employed . . . ☐

Preparer's name [   ]   PTIN [   ]

Preparer's signature [   ]   Date [/ /]

Firm's name (or yours if self-employed) [   ]   EIN [   ]

Address [   ]   Phone [   ]

City [   ]   State [ ]   ZIP code [   ]

Page **3**   Form **941** (Rev. 6-2021)

Form 941 (Employer's Quarterly Federal Tax Return), page 3

TOP TAX DEDUCTIONS FOR HAIRSTYLISTS

Tax deductions are an excellent way for salon owners and other beauty professionals who work as independent contractors to put money back into their pockets.

Before I got with my current CPA, I wasn't informed about tax write-offs that benefit hairstylists. I had no idea how many things I could've been deducting for all those years I'd been working. Things like gifts, laundry, bank charges, and even client refreshments could have been written off, putting money back in my pocket to the tune of *tens of thousands of dollars!*

Now that I know better, I can do better!

My team and I compiled the following list of more than fifty hair and beauty industry items that you may or may not know are legitimate tax deductions that can reduce your annual tax liability.

Haircare Products and Tools. Did you know you can write off client refreshments? You can! You can also write off the cost of haircare supplies like shampoo, conditioner, hair dyes, blow dryers, and other styling tools like foil, towels, caps, clips, shears—you get the idea.

Cell Phone Bills. Cell phone bills are a deduction a lot of us stylists forget about. I did! If you use your phone exclusively for business, you can deduct the phone's cost and 100 percent of the monthly bills. If you use it as both a personal and business phone, you'll have to estimate how much you use the phone *just* for business and claim only that percentage of the bill as a deduction.

Car, Mileage, Parking, and Travel Expenses. You cannot write off your mileage driving to and from home and work because that's a regular commute. But driving from a home office to a salon counts. Driving between client appointments counts. Driving on work-related errands like picking up supplies counts. Also, if you traveled to attend classes or salon-related functions, you can deduct unreimbursed transportation, meals, mileage, and hotel expenses. Even parking can be deducted with the proper receipts. And no, that doesn't mean parking tickets! And you cannot deduct for gas, oil changes, car repairs, or insurance. In some cases, you can only deduct mileage, which you have to keep track of by taking down the odometer readings before and after each trip.

In addition to the standard mileage rates, you can deduct the toll costs you accrued while using your vehicle for one of the approved purposes. These are separate deductions. However, if you have claimed vehicle depreciation, you cannot deduct tolls and parking fees.

Ooh, and you'll like this—even the purchase of your car can be seen as a legitimate expense. But only the percentage that's related to your work is deductible. For instance, if you only drive your car 25 percent of the time for work, you can only deduct 25 percent of the car's expense. If you do not lease the car's payments and instead purchase it, the portion that is deductible as a business expense is the interest—not the principal loan payment. The depreciation expense is also a tax deduction. As of 2020, the standard mileage rate for business is 57.5 cents per mile. You can read more about this on the IRS website at https://www.irs.gov/taxtopics/tc510. And you'll like this too—you can even deduct a portion of public transportation, like that bus pass, Uber, Lyft, and even your limo, if you've got it like that!

Office Expenses and Utilities. Since our business relies heavily on the telephone and internet, we can deduct a percentage of these utilities, as well as gas, electricity, water, and anything else needed to keep the salon running, including rent if you lease a space. The same goes for if you do hair out of your home; you can deduct a portion of these same utilities, along with a portion of your homeowners insurance and rent. Your answering service and booking service can also fall into this category as an approved deduction.

Repairs and Maintenance. You can deduct the cost of repairs and maintenance on any service you rely on to keep your business running smoothly, like sharpening scissors, equipment maintenance, and even salon cleaning services.

Insurances. As I mentioned back in chapter four, if you don't have professional insurance, I highly recommend you get some. You never know if a customer who isn't happy with their hair will want to take action against you. Or sue you if you use a photo of their hair in an ad. Or want to take action if you break something in their house when you go there to do their hair, or if they fall while in your salon. My point is *you need insurance*! Review chapter four for a complete list and breakdown of the insurances you should consider.

Need even more incentive to get insurance? Here's some good news: you can deduct your insurance premiums from your taxes. And as long as you don't get your health insurance from a spouse or employer, you can deduct 100 percent of those monthly premiums. But understand that health insurance is a personal expense, *not* a business expense. And for the record, the one insurance the IRS considers to be nondeductible is life insurance.

Retirement Plans. Even though you can't deduct life insurance premiums on your taxes, you can deduct your retirement plan, which is a double benefit. Because while you're planning for your future, you're potentially putting money back in your pocket at the same time. See chapter twenty for information about retirement and other long-term investment options.

Licenses. Hopefully, you're keeping up with the renewal of your business and professional licenses. All of these renewals are approved tax deductions.

Advertising. Your business cards and any expenses associated with advertising your business in trade magazines, flyers, online ads, print ads, and videos are deductible. Plus, any associated printing and copying costs, social media, and website hosting expenses are also deductible.

Clothes. No, you can't write off your everyday glam streetwear; however, things like beauty smocks and salon uniforms—things that can't be worn off the job—are deductible.

Training, Personal, and Professional Development. The IRS recognizes online courses, like the ones I teach about "Perfecting Your Weave" and "Color Techniques," and any other educational investment you make to perfect your craft as approved deductions. Also, registrations to trade shows you attend and your subscriptions to hair magazines, journals, and membership dues are deductible as long as you can justify that they help you improve your business.

Gifts. If you give gift cards to your clients for their birthdays, Christmas, or some other occasion or provide a gift to someone who is sending you a lot of referral business, then the IRS will let you deduct up to twenty-five dollars per person or entity that you give to per year.

Bank Charges. Here's another deduction that many third-party accountants miss: you can deduct bank charges and merchant fees for your business bank accounts. And if you borrowed money for your business, you can deduct the interest incurred on loans and credit cards.

• • •

The following three categories are **limited**, meaning there's only so much you're allowed to deduct within a single tax year.

Meals and Entertainment—Limited. The following are deductible at 50 percent of their costs, as of October 2020 final IRS regulations:

- Business meals with clients
- Office snacks (including coffee, soft drinks, bottled water, donuts, and similar snacks or beverages) and other food items provided to employees on the business premises:

    Any meals provided on the employer's premises for the convenience of the employer are also partially deductible. For example, if you are providing meals to employees to keep them working late or further compensate them for working during the weekend or being on call, it is for your convenience to have them at work, and the meal is a means of enticement.
- The cost of meals while traveling for work
- Meals at a conference that aren't included in the price of the ticket
- Lunch out with fewer than half of your company employees
- Food for company holiday parties
- Food and beverages given to the public for free

Be sure to keep detailed records if the costs are over seventy-five dollars. Include the amount spent, the place, the people attending, and the business purpose. Often, I write details on the back of the receipt and put them in a file. Some people scan receipts and save them on a computer. Whichever way you choose to keep track, just remember that **no documentation = no deduction**. One easy way to keep track of your business expenses is by using a business credit card to pay for them so all of your receipts are recorded on that one card. And a word of caution: if you bring a friend or companion along on a business meal, you can't deduct their portion of the check—only your portion and the clients'.

As for entertainment? The IRS has gotten strict with this one over the years. The list of what you can no longer deduct is too long to print. For our purposes, what they *will* accept as deductions include expenses related to attending business meetings or conventions of specific exempt organizations, such as business leagues and chambers of commerce, professional associations, etc.

Charitable Deductions—Limited. Some charities, community organizations, and even Hollywood event organizers often ask me to donate gift certificates for my services, product line, or celebrity wigs, which, most of the time, I don't have a problem doing. If you do the same, the good news is these gifts are probably at least partially deductible. What's tricky is understanding how much you can deduct. Say, for instance, I donate one of my $1,200 custom wigs to a charity. If I paid $300 for that wig, I already deducted that cost when I bought it, so I can't deduct it again. The same holds if I donate my services, such as if I'm doing a makeover at an event for cancer survivors or making a monetary contribution to the organization.

Salon Furniture and Equipment—Limited. Chairs, stools, carts, trays, waiting room furniture, magazines, computers, iPads in reception, credit card processors, and hardware are all deductible. In fact, some of these "capital expense" items that you buy when you're starting up or making improvements to things like the furniture, salon equipment, scanners, computers, copy machines, or printers might wear out or "depreciate" over time. So you can write them off over three to five years, depending on the item. For example, if you buy a shampoo chair for $1,800, you can deduct one-fifth of that cost, or $360, every year for up to five years. Or, if you go for what's called a Section 179* deduction, you can deduct the entire $1,800 in the first year as long as your total Section 179 deductions don't exceed $1,000,000.

• • •

Remember, this list of deductions for beauty professionals isn't comprehensive, but it features legitimate write-offs that can put a lot of money back in your pocket if you know about them.

Ensure that you, your CPA, or another tax preparer stays on top of the IRS changes that could make a difference between what deductions are

* "IRS Issues Guidance on Section 179 Expenses and SECTION 168(g) Depreciation under Tax Cuts and Jobs Act." Internal Revenue Service, www.irs.gov/newsroom/irs-issues-guidance-on-section-179-expenses-and-section-168g-depreciation-under-tax-cuts-and-jobs-act.

accepted or not. And if you want to learn about your tips and taxes (trust me—you do!), keep reading for some valuable information about those.

TAX INFO YOU NEED TO KNOW ABOUT YOUR TIPS

I remember when I hooked up with my first accountant and asked, "Do I have to pay taxes on my cash tips?" She was like, "Uh, yeah!" Then she quoted IRS tax law: "All tips are taxable income and must be reported and taxed."

Dang! Really?!

She explained that it doesn't matter whether the tip is received in cash, included in a charge, or paid through Cash App or Venmo; it is subject to federal income tax, Social Security, and Medicare taxes—and in some places, it may be subject to state income tax as well. Don't be slick trying to pretend you didn't get what you got. The IRS knows that tips for most of us in the beauty industry are usually 10 to 15 percent of the bill. They expect you to report your tip income on **IRS Form 4070** on the tenth day of the following month that tips are received—every month. A sample form is below. You can also find the form on the IRS website by visiting IRS.gov and searching "Employee's Report of Tips." You'll find a sample form with instructions on how to complete it.

Form **4070** (Rev. August 2005) Department of the Treasury Internal Revenue Service	**Employee's Report of Tips to Employer**	OMB No. 1545-0074
Employee's name and address		Social security number
Employer's name and address (include establishment name, if different)		1 Cash tips received
		2 Credit and debit card tips received
		3 Tips paid out
Month or shorter period in which tips were received from , , to ,		4 Net tips (lines **1 + 2 - 3**)
Signature		Date
For Paperwork Reduction Act Notice, see the instructions on the back of this form.	Cat. No. 41320P	Form **4070** (Rev. 8-2005)

Form 4070 (Employee's Report of Tips to Employer)

Credit card receipts can also be accepted as proof of your tips. And just know that if you have an ATM in your salon, the IRS can use it to compare against what you reported. So be honest!

At first, I hated that I had to report my tips, but then I learned that one of the biggest benefits of reporting them is that it increases my overall income, which can mean the difference between getting approved or denied for a home mortgage or car loan.

TAX RULES FOR MOBILE PAYMENT APPS

It used to be that hair, nails, and many other beauty services were a cash business. But then people started paying with checks, then credit cards. Once COVID-19 came into our lives, getting paid became more of a cashless and altogether contactless process. Cash App, Apple Pay, Zelle, Google Pay, Venmo, and PayPal all became more popular methods for customers to pay for our services. The question I get a lot is: can the IRS track these kinds of payments?

☐ VOID ☐ CORRECTED			
FILER'S name, street address, city or town, state or province, country, ZIP or foreign postal code, and telephone no.	FILER'S TIN	OMB No. 1545-2205	**Payment Card and Third Party Network Transactions**
	PAYEE'S TIN	2021 Form **1099-K**	
	1a Gross amount of payment card/third party network transactions $		
	1b Card Not Present transactions $	2 Merchant category code	**Copy 1 For State Tax Department**
Check to indicate if FILER is a (an): Payment settlement entity (PSE) ☐ Electronic Payment Facilitator (EPF)/Other third party ☐	Check to indicate transactions reported are: Payment card ☐ Third party network ☐	3 Number of payment transactions $	4 Federal income tax withheld $
PAYEE'S name	5a January $	5b February $	
	5c March $	5d April $	
Street address (including apt. no.)	5e May $	5f June $	
	5g July $	5h August $	
City or town, state or province, country, and ZIP or foreign postal code	5i September $	5j October $	
PSE'S name and telephone number	5k November $	5l December $	
Account number (see instructions)	6 State	7 State identification no.	8 State income tax withheld $ $

Form **1099-K**   www.irs.gov/Form1099K   Department of the Treasury - Internal Revenue Service

Form 1099-K (Payment Card and Third Party-Payment Transactions)

According to the IRS, the answer is yes! All payments on "peer-to-peer" mobile payment apps need to be reported if they are more than $600 per year. The reporting is on you! But if you have receipts that total more than $20,000 in a year through a given mobile payment app, the platform you use will automatically send you a **1099-K** for tax filing purposes. See the sample form, or go online at IRS.gov then search "1099-K" to find the form and filing instructions.

RESEARCH AND DEVELOPMENT CREDITS

I'll end this chapter with a huge piece of advice I got from my accountant, who put *a lot* of money back into my bank account.

As a result of placing all my businesses, including my freelance work, under my MuzeWorld, LLC, umbrella, I could be taxed separately for each one, meaning the income and losses of each business is reported as income for my LLC and can be reported as pass-through income on my tax returns. I also was able to get a research and development (R&D) tax credit for the product line I developed.

Here's how it works: the R&D tax credit is a government-sponsored tax incentive that rewards companies for conducting research and development in the United States. It's available for all sizes of companies that develop new products or enhance or improve products that they previously created (see more on developing and selling a product line in chapter eleven). It requires a lot of documentation, like payroll records, development notes, and expense records that go back as far as four years and credit forward as far as twenty years, but it's worth the effort. This tax credit worked in my favor big time, earning me credits worth about $8,500.

A company must have less than $5 million in gross receipts (income) for the credit year and no more than five years of gross receipts to be eligible. But new businesses that don't qualify for research and development tax credits should still track all business organization and startup expenses because the IRS allows (one-time) deductions for up to $5,000 in credits for organizational expenses and up to $5,000 for startup expenses.

See below for a sample of the **IRS Form 6765** to file or visit https://www.irs.gov/pub/irs-access/f6765_accessible.pdf.

Form **6765** (Rev. December 2020) Department of the Treasury Internal Revenue Service	**Credit for Increasing Research Activities** ▶ Attach to your tax return. ▶ Go to *www.irs.gov/Form6765* for instructions and the latest information.	OMB No. 1545-0619 Attachment Sequence No. **676**
Name(s) shown on return		Identifying number

Section A—Regular Credit. Skip this section and go to Section B if you are electing or previously elected (and are not revoking) the alternative simplified credit.

1	Certain amounts paid or incurred to energy consortia (see instructions)		**1**
2	Basic research payments to qualified organizations (see instructions)	**2**	
3	Qualified organization base period amount	**3**	
4	Subtract line 3 from line 2. If zero or less, enter -0-		**4**
5	Wages for qualified services (do not include wages used in figuring the work opportunity credit)	**5**	
6	Cost of supplies	**6**	
7	Rental or lease costs of computers (see instructions)	**7**	
8	Enter the applicable percentage of contract research expenses. See instructions	**8**	
9	Total qualified research expenses. Add lines 5 through 8	**9**	
10	Enter fixed-base percentage, but not more than 16% (0.16) (see instructions)	**10**	%
11	Enter average annual gross receipts. See instructions	**11**	
12	Multiply line 11 by the percentage on line 10	**12**	
13	Subtract line 12 from line 9. If zero or less, enter -0-	**13**	
14	Multiply line 9 by 50% (0.50)	**14**	
15	Enter the **smaller** of line 13 or line 14		**15**
16	Add lines 1, 4, and 15		**16**
17	Are you electing the reduced credit under section 280C? ▶ Yes ☐ No ☐ If "Yes," multiply line 16 by 15.8% (0.158). If "No," multiply line 16 by 20% (0.20) and see the instructions for the statement that must be attached. Members of controlled groups or businesses under common control, see instructions for the statement that must be attached		**17**

Section B—Alternative Simplified Credit. Skip this section if you are completing Section A.

18	Certain amounts paid or incurred to energy consortia (see the line 1 instructions)		**18**
19	Basic research payments to qualified organizations (see the line 2 instructions)	**19**	
20	Qualified organization base period amount (see the line 3 instructions)	**20**	
21	Subtract line 20 from line 19. If zero or less, enter -0-		**21**
22	Add lines 18 and 21		**22**
23	Multiply line 22 by 20% (0.20)		**23**
24	Wages for qualified services (do not include wages used in figuring the work opportunity credit)	**24**	
25	Cost of supplies	**25**	
26	Rental or lease costs of computers (see the line 7 instructions)	**26**	
27	Enter the applicable percentage of contract research expenses. See the line 8 instructions	**27**	
28	Total qualified research expenses. Add lines 24 through 27	**28**	
29	Enter your total qualified research expenses for the prior 3 tax years. If you had no qualified research expenses in any one of those years, skip lines 30 and 31	**29**	
30	Divide line 29 by 6.0	**30**	
31	Subtract line 30 from line 28. If zero or less, enter -0-	**31**	
32	Multiply line 31 by 14% (0.14). If you skipped lines 30 and 31, multiply line 28 by 6% (0.06)		**32**
33	Add lines 23 and 32		**33**
34	Are you electing the reduced credit under section 280C? ▶ Yes ☐ No ☐ If "Yes," multiply line 33 by 79% (0.79). If "No," enter the amount from line 33 and see the line 17 instructions for the statement that must be attached. Members of controlled groups or businesses under common control, see instructions for the statement that must be attached		**34**

For Paperwork Reduction Act Notice, see separate instructions. Cat. No. 13700H Form **6765** (Rev. 12-2020)

Form 6765 (Credit for Increasing Research Activities), page 1

Section C—Current Year Credit

35	Enter the portion of the credit from Form 8932, line 2, that is attributable to wages that were also used to figure the credit on line 17 or line 34 (whichever applies)	35
36	Subtract line 35 from line 17 or line 34 (whichever applies). If zero or less, enter -0-	36
37	Credit for increasing research activities from partnerships, S corporations, estates, and trusts . . .	37
38	Add lines 36 and 37	38
	• Estates and trusts, go to line 39.	
	• Partnerships and S corporations not electing the payroll tax credit, stop here and report this amount on Schedule K.	
	• Partnerships and S corporations electing the payroll tax credit, complete Section D and report on Schedule K the amount on this line reduced by the amount on line 44.	
	• Eligible small businesses, stop here and report the credit on Form 3800, Part III, line 4i. See instructions for the definition of eligible small business.	
	• Filers other than eligible small businesses, stop here and report the credit on Form 3800, Part III, line 1c.	
	Note: Qualified small business filers, other than partnerships and S corporations, electing the payroll tax credit must complete Form 3800 before completing Section D.	
39	Amount allocated to beneficiaries of the estate or trust (see instructions)	39
40	Estates and trusts, subtract line 39 from line 38. For eligible small businesses, report the credit on Form 3800, Part III, line 4i. See instructions. For filers other than eligible small businesses, report the credit on Form 3800, Part III, line 1c	40

Section D—Qualified Small Business Payroll Tax Election and Payroll Tax Credit. Skip this section if the payroll tax election does not apply. See instructions.

41	Check this box if you are a qualified small business electing the payroll tax credit. See instructions ☐	
42	Enter the portion of line 36 elected as a payroll tax credit (do not enter more than $250,000). See instructions	42
43	General business credit carryforward from the current year (see instructions). Partnerships and S corporations, skip this line and go to line 44	43
44	Partnerships and S corporations, enter the smaller of line 36 or line 42. All others, enter the smallest of line 36, line 42, or line 43. Enter here and on the applicable line of Form 8974, Part 1, column (e). Members of controlled groups or businesses under common control, see instructions for the statement that must be attached	44

Form **6765** (Rev. 12-2020)

Form 6765 (Credit for Increasing Research Activities), page 2

I know this tax conversation gets really confusing, so check out this summary to make all this tax stuff a little easier to navigate:

KIYAH'S OVERVIEW OF TAXES THAT AFFECT BEAUTY PROFESSIONALS: Independent Contractors/Self-Employed		
Form	**What's it for?**	**Timetable to Submit**
W-9 Form https://www.irs.gov/pub/irs-pdf/fw9.pdf	Common for freelancers and independent contractors. The business or person paying you will send you a W-9 with your personal information, so you can get paid and can be issued a 1099 with the total paid to you during the calendar year.	The business or person paying you generally sends this at the beginning of a service.

Form	What's it for?	Timetable to Submit
Form 1099-NEC (Replaces 1099-MISC in most cases) https://www.irs.gov/pub/irs-pdf/f1099nec.pdf	For nonemployees who receive compensation from a business or person, including fees, commissions, prizes, awards, etc.	Should be received prior to filing. If you're an employer, you must provide a copy to the IRS and the taxpayer/recipient no later than January 31.
Form 1099-K https://www.irs.gov/pub/irs-pdf/f1099k.pdf	Remember all those Cash App transactions? Form 1099-K is used by credit card companies and third-party processors to report the payment transactions they process for retailers or other third parties.	You should receive any 1099-K forms by January 31.
Form 1040-ES https://www.irs.gov/pub/irs-pdf/f1040es.pdf	Estimated tax payments for self-employed individuals whose income isn't automatically subject to withholding by an employer.	Filed to the IRS quarterly (four times a year)

KIYAH'S OVERVIEW OF TAXES THAT AFFECT BEAUTY PROFESSIONALS: Employees		
Form	**What's it for?**	**Timetable to Submit**
Form 940 https://www.irs.gov/pub/irs -pdf/f940.pdf	If you've paid an assistant or any employee on your team $1,500 or more in a year or paid them for more than twenty weeks of the year, you must file this federal unemployment tax form.	Filed annually (one time a year)
Form 941 https://www.irs.gov/pub/irs -pdf/f941.pdf	For employers to report wages they've paid and tips their employees have reported to them, as well as employment taxes.	Filed to the IRS quarterly
Form 4070 https://www.irs.gov/pub/irs -pdf/p1244.pdf	If you earn tips, you need to report them on this form if they total more than twenty dollars per month.	Filed to the IRS monthly

Form	What's it for?	Timetable to Submit
W-4 Form https://www.irs.gov/pub/irs-pdf/fw4.pdf	This form you receive from your employer includes information that helps them determine how much to withhold from your paychecks. It requests your marital status and number of dependents.	Usually provided to you by your employer before you receive your first payment
W-2 Form https://www.irs.gov/pub/irs-pdf/fw2.pdf	Issued by your employer to show how much taxes have been withheld from your paycheck for the year. You'll want to show this when you file your federal and state taxes.	Your employer generally issues it to arrive by January 31 of each year for the previous tax year.

ADDITIONAL RESOURCES

Here are a few other resources that will help you when filing:

* IRS Tax Tips for the Cosmetology and Barber Industry: Visit IRS.gov, then search "Tax Tips for the Cosmetology and Barber Industry." You'll find a publication that instructs you on employer tax responsibilities and tip responsibilities, how to define an employee, and the forms for all the necessary filings.
* Tax Guide for Small Business: Go to IRS.gov and search "Publication 334."

Check Out This Video:

Scan the QR code to watch a video where I talk more about the importance of understanding the business side of beauty, especially your taxes.

CHAPTER 8

The *Wright* Ways to Manage Your Money

We don't *build* services to make **MONEY**;

we *make* money to **BUILD** better services.

—Mark Zuckerberg, founder of Facebook

When you first start making real money, there's a natural tendency to *spend it*, right? You see something in the window or online that you can't quite afford, but you convince yourself, *I work hard. I need to do something for myself. I'm going to buy it now and worry about how I'm going to pay for it later.* Don't be ashamed—it happens to all of us.

I had only been working at my first salon just outside of DC for about four months when I made my first major purchase. There was an auto mechanic shop right next door to the salon where I worked. I saw it every day as I walked into work from the bus stop. And every day, my eyes were drawn toward this cute, white stick shift 1989 Pontiac LeMans sitting in the driveway. It had a big For Sale sign right on the front windshield. Finally, I decided to check it out.

The mechanic said, "For $3,500, you can have it."

I was just starting to make good money, so the price seemed OK. I had heard before that you should have a car-repair person check out your car if you buy it used. I figured since a mechanic was selling it, it must be in good shape. So, I bought it right on the spot—*in cash*!

I was so excited and proud of myself!

As soon as I got inside the salon, I called my girlfriend. "Hey, can you come to get me when I get off work and teach me how to drive?"

There I was again, getting ahead of myself. Not only did I *not* know how to drive, but the car was a stick shift! My friend had me driving around that parking lot in circles for hours until I finally got it.

Luckily, this impulse purchase turned out OK, but my spending habits continued long after that first investment I made in transportation.

While working and living in New York and later, when I first moved to LA, it was nothing for me to spend money on clothes and my image in general—whether it meant fulfilling some of my childhood wants, like pulling up in a Mercedes Benz or Cadillac Escalade or stepping out in designer labels, from Gucci to Louis Vuitton to Versace.

And while looking the part is important, it gave me an air of credibility with my clients; they took my advice more readily and my tips were even better. Regardless, it can be easy to take your spending too far.

The deeper I got into debt for the sake of my image, I realized my spending habits had to change. As my accountant once told me, "What you do with your money is your business—as long as you take care of business so you don't lose your business."

Managing my spending became easier for me once I had a handle on these four **money management basics** every beauty entrepreneur needs to know:

- Managing Cash Flows
- Planning for Slow Seasons
- Understanding Credit Scores
- Understanding Good Debt versus Bad Debt

MANAGING CASH FLOWS

Take any business 101 class, and you'll learn that poor cash flow can kill a business. Knowing where your money is coming from and going out is the key to controlling cash flow. It also gives you a good indication of how healthy your business is and how much you can allocate for yourself to spend at any given time.

If you have a good sense of your business's cash flow, you'll know in advance the times of the month where there will be a "cash crunch," and you'll be able to prioritize what expenses need to be paid before then. There's no feeling worse than knowing you have $2,000 worth of bills due on the first of the month but only $1,200 in the bank. Knowing your cash flow can help prevent these situations, as you'll have time to develop a plan to cover these expenses. This is especially helpful for those annual expenses we tend to forget about, like insurance premiums and license renewals that pop up just when we think we have extra cash to spend.

I've pulled together the following step-by-step guide for preparing a cash flow that has worked well for me.

Step One: Expenses. Go through a typical month or year and list all the predicted expenses that will come out of your bank account. The good thing is your credit card companies itemize these for you. These may include things like rent, assistant's salary, products, your salary, utilities (personal and business), and license renewals. Be sure to note when those expenses must be paid, so you can easily see the slow periods. Here's an example of four months' worth of expenses a beauty professional may face:

EXPENSES: APRIL THROUGH JULY			
	APRIL	**MAY**	**JUNE**	**JULY**
Rent	$1,200	$1,200	$1,200	$1,200
Assistant	$1,200	$1,200	$1,200	$1,200
Products	$400	$250	$400	$250
Fees, Etc.	$0	$250	$0	$0
Your Salary	$2,400	$2,400	$2,400	$2,400
Utilities	$450	$450	$450	$450
TOTAL:	**$5,650**	**$5,750**	**$5,650**	**$5,500**

Total up all your expenses for a given period for a bird's-eye view of what's due.

Step Two: Projected Income. Estimate how much money you think you'll bring in during that same period.

PROJECTED INCOME: APRIL THROUGH JULY (before taxes)				
	APRIL	**MAY**	**JUNE**	**JULY**
Book Clients	$6,240	$6,240	$4,000	$2,000
Weaves	$1,600	$800	$0	$0
Braids	$200	$500	$0	$0
Upsells	$1,200	$300	$0	$0
Tips	$1,200	$1,000	$200	$200
TOTAL:	**$10,440**	**$8,840**	**$4,200**	**$2,200**

Again, total up all of this projected income to see what you can expect to make.

Step Three: Determine Your Net Cash Position. Subtract your projected taxes from your projected receipts, then subtract your projected expenses to determine your *net cash position*.

NET CASH POSITION: APRIL THROUGH JULY				
	APRIL	**MAY**	**JUNE**	**JULY**
INCOME	$10,440	$8,840	$4,200	$2,200
TAXES (20%)	$2,088	$1,768	$840	$440
TOTAL:	**$8,352**	**$7,072**	**$3,360**	**$1,760**
EXPENSES	$5,650	$5,750	$5,650	$5,500
NET TOTAL:	**$2,702**	**$1,322**	**$-2,290**	**$-3,740**

This allows you to see how your income and expenses will balance out, so you can plan ahead for leaner times accordingly.

Step Four: Adjust as Needed. If your net total shows you anything in the red (negative), it's time to make adjustments. See if there is something you can do without. Maybe you had budgeted to offer champagne for your clients. Well, rethink that and offer water and juices. Or, instead of premium cable service, maybe invest in a Firestick for your waiting area. Do whatever you have to do to minimize expenses while still maintaining a positive experience for your customers. Then look at what you can reasonably do to increase your income during those expected slow periods.

PLANNING FOR SLOW SEASONS

For most of us beauty professionals, there's a lull in business during the summer because people are traveling and often don't keep their regular appointments. The January/February appointments right after the holidays are sometimes even worse because people have spent lots of money during those times. When our clients spend less, we tend to get stressed.

Instead of panicking, start **saving money** during the profitable months to cover the shortfalls during the slow months, then use the slowdown period to rejuvenate and reevaluate where you're at in your business.

Another option is to offer **seasonal promotions** to boost income during the slower months. This might include discounts on premium conditioning services for extra sun protection for the hair or skin, seasonal trend items, gym maintenance products, etc.

Here's an example of something I've posted ahead of the slow seasons:

PHOTOGRAPHY BY TYREN REDD

I also sent out newsletters and monthly marketing emails reminding clients when to return. These notices attracted more business for me *before* the slowdowns so I could coast a little when my clients weren't booking as often.

These are strategies I rely on to plan for slower seasons. But since my schedule can be unpredictable, I also need to think ahead for times when I'm not in the salon.

Create a Winning Formula for Long Absences

Whenever you take a leave of absence longer than a few weeks—either due to illness, maternity leave, bereavement travel, or on tour—you risk losing regular clients. This happened to me for the first time when I finished working my first Bad Boy tour. I had been away for a few months, so I anticipated I might have lost some of my regular clients. As soon as I got settled back in New York, I jumped on the phone and called every one of my clients and sent out mailer cards (this was long before texting and social media were popular).

I wrote, "Hey, I'm back in the salon and would love to catch up with you!"

Sometimes I'd use email marketing incentives to encourage my clients, like 15 percent off their next weave, color, or cut, as a courtesy for being inconvenienced. Twenty-five years later, I'm doing the same thing; only now, I also use social media, newsletters, and blogs. And though, over the years, I would inevitably lose some clients when I was away from the salon for long stretches, my regular ones who didn't take my absence personally would eventually book appointments with me again because I always gave them a satisfying experience.

Since I work with a lot of celebrities who have regular gigs on TV series or came to me only during awards season, there was always a lull in my schedule when the season ended. So, I started targeting more clients who worked year-round or worked on movies, toured, or did other work outside of the heavy production seasons.

Remember this: Loyal clients will come back if you strive to show them a level of professionalism and passion for their hair when they are in your chair. They feel it, miss it when you're gone, and come back every time!

Just as important as planning ahead with promotions, however, is planning ahead financially and understanding your credit and debt.

UNDERSTANDING CREDIT SCORES

Managing your credit is just as important as managing your cash flows. One of the most important parts of understanding your credit is understanding your credit scores. A credit score helps lenders see your history of repaying debts. Personal credit card debt and credit scores are identified and calculated based on your social security number. These scores average between 300 and 850, with 711 being the average. A banker once told me that if your business score is over 650, you're doing good!

Business credit card debt and credit scores are calculated based on your EIN (see chapter four for more on EINs). There was a time when our personal credit scores didn't matter when we applied for a business credit card or loan, but as of 2020, the model for FICO business credit scores has changed. They will now also look at your personal credit history when determining your business credit score. So, think twice before you apply for that increase on your retail or gas card. By expanding the amount of money you borrow on your personal cards or by making late payments, you risk lowering your business credit score by as much as twenty points.

FICO is the industry standard for credit reporting, and it's utilized by the three major bureaus for consumers—Transunion, Equifax, and Experian—and the major bureau for businesses, Dun & Bradstreet. By law, the credit bureaus are required to give consumers one free credit report annually, so if each quarter, you ask just one credit bureau to provide you with a report, you can essentially get a total of four credit reports per year. Some banks will also offer free monthly credit score as a perk for having an account with them, such as Chase Bank.

There are quite a few things you can do to keep your credit in good standing. Here are some tips to stay on track:

- **Pay your debts on time.** Most credit bureaus report outstanding debts on the fifteenth of the month, so try to make all of your payments before the eleventh to ensure a more favorable report.
- **Manage credit wisely.** Just because you have a $1,500 credit limit doesn't mean you have to use it all. Banks like to see at least 50 to 70 percent of available credit on your cards or loans when considering lending you money. In other words, make sure your debt is no more than 30 percent.

- **Diversify your credit.** Just like we like to diversify our incomes, try to diversify your credit. Credit bureaus base their calculations on the type of credit you have, whether it's revolving debt on credit cards or installment loans like mortgages, car loans, and student loan debt. Having multiple accounts of different types shows that you can manage your credit, which can work in your favor (versus, say, having many retail cards).
- **Minimize hard inquiries.** When *you* check your credit rating, that's a good thing! When *someone else* checks your credit (aka a "hard inquiry") when approving you for a loan or credit card, it could be harmful. So, unless you're shopping around for something like a car where multiple dealers may check your credit within a short time frame—which counts as one inquiry—try to limit the number of lenders checking up on you within a forty-five-day cycle. Your safest bet? Avoid applying for multiple loans or credit cards within a short period.
- **Keep credit accounts open.** Even if you pay down your credit card, don't close the account; it could reduce your score by up to twenty points. Now, if you had something like fifteen retail cards, then yes, you *do* need to shut half of them down *completely*. That is way too much "bad" credit.

UNDERSTANDING GOOD DEBT VERSUS BAD DEBT

In chapter four, I offered the advice to open a bank account and get a credit card once you file for your DBA. I know it sounds crazy, but yes, financial planners encourage us to get business credit cards. It's almost a rite of passage for entrepreneurs to have (reasonable) credit card debt for their business.

When you apply for a business credit card, the lender will expect you to provide a physical business address for their files—not a home address, not a PO box. They'll also want to know your business phone number, website, email address, and license number to confirm that you are a legitimate "business."

When you get business credit, it's important to also understand the difference between good debt and bad debt:

- **Good Debt:** Credit card debt is "good" when you have low interest rates and use the funds to buy items for your business that appreciate in value. When you keep up with the payments, you're increasing your chances of getting loans, raising your credit score, and improving your long-term financial standing.
- **Bad Debt:** Credit card debt is "bad" if it's used to purchase depreciating items, that is, those that lose value over time like chairs, sinks, heat lamps, fixtures, and any other items that can't generate income in the long term or can't be quickly repaid. And credit cards are absolutely bad news when you use them to make cash advances.

CREDIT CARD INSURANCE

My last piece of credit advice is to do whatever you have to do to protect your finances from credit fraud on your cards and bank accounts. I speak from experience!

When I first moved to LA, I stayed with a girlfriend until I found this beautiful two-story duplex apartment on Hauser Street in the historic Hancock Park. When I arrived to sign the lease, the landlord told me there was a problem with my credit check. *What? Really?!* I knew I had over $80,000 in my account—it was what I'd saved to buy my Harlem brownstone years before.

After making some calls, I got the news that the bank had frozen all of my accounts because of credit card fraud.

Are you freaking kidding me?

Not only could I not write a check to secure the apartment, I also couldn't buy a car, rent a car, buy clothing—nothing! I sat in the garage of what was to be my new apartment, having my first meltdown ever.

Things got worse when I realized that my furniture and everything else I had in New York was on its way across the country and I didn't have an address for them to deliver it to because I didn't have a place to live.

Thankfully, two days later, I got a call from the bank and learned it was all a big mistake; this wasn't a case of credit card fraud after all, and my bank account hadn't been hacked.

Everything worked out, and the experience led me to a few lessons, like don't put all your money in one bank. If it had turned out that my account had been compromised, at least they wouldn't have had access to all of my money. Secondly, it taught me to invest in **credit card protection**.

There are several third-party identity theft and credit monitoring services like LifeLock, but when you're looking at getting basic **credit card insurance** (which is intended to minimally cover identity theft but is mostly there for when you're not able to earn an income), make sure the coverage is extended to the **self-employed**. More often than not, the small print in these policies states their insurance only protects those who receive W-2s from their employers—not self-employed folks. So, look closely or ask questions if you're not sure.

• • •

If you're just now starting your career, a lot of this finance talk might not seem important. But trust me, *it is*! Understand it now so you can manage your wealth as you grow, which you will be doing by leaps and bounds as soon as you **find your niche**!

KEY TAKEAWAYS

Only when you develop methods to manage the money you make can you put yourself on the path to success. Practice prioritizing the following:

* Managing your cash flow
* Planning for slow periods and long absences
* Understanding credit scores

* Managing your credit
  - Paying your debts on time
  - Keeping credit accounts open
  - Diversifying your credit
  - Avoiding too many "hard inquiries"
* Understanding good versus bad debt
* Investing in credit insurance

RESOURCES

The Consumer Financial Protection Bureau is a US government agency that provides valuable information about credit scores, how to dispute an error on your credit report, what to do if you've been a victim of fraud or identity theft, and more. Visit their website at Consumerfinance.gov for more information.

Principle 3

Find Your *Niche*

CHAPTER 9

Find Your Niche and Build Your Brand

Put in the **TIME** to become

an *expert* in whatever you're doing.

—Mark Cuban, billionaire entrepreneur

nderstanding the fundamentals of finance is essential to making money—not just in the beauty business but for any entrepreneurial venture. But once you've grasped those basics, if you want success to really flow for you in this field, the most crucial step you can take is to **find your niche**—your signature thing only you do. That one thing you want people to know you for. The talent you mastered that sets you apart from the rest. It's great to be good at a lot of things, but in this case, you don't want to be a "jack of all trades and a master at none."

So, what is your niche?

Whatever area of the beauty industry you work in, find your specialty within that area. Maybe that means you're an excellent colorist, go-to wardrobe stylist, trendsetting braider, or local glam makeup artist. Maybe it means you're a master at shaping eyebrows. What are you most passionate about, and what makes people want to come to you instead of someone else?

Don't worry if you haven't identified your niche yet. Sometimes finding your niche can take time, and your niche can change and evolve as you grow.

My niche has developed over time into makeovers. My gift is giving a woman instant beauty solutions that will leave her looking and feeling her best and a maintenance regimen that keeps it practical and achievable for every day. I've also had the chance to utilize my makeover abilities with certain celebrity clients, like the short cut I gave to Gabrielle Union, Jennifer Hudson's makeovers for *American Idol* and the *Dreamgirls* and *Aretha* press tours, and of course, supermodel and talk show host (and my former boss) Tyra Banks, who did the big chop into a cute pageboy cut when she had her *FABLife* show.

I had so much fun transforming Tyra from wearing her long, signature extensions to a cropped pixie cut with multidimensional hues of blonde and brown. At first, Tyra was skeptical and didn't think the cut would translate to her new show, but I had confidence in my skills, and as I predicted, it was a hit!

Tyra loved it. Her audience loved it, too. It got over 100,000 likes when she posted a picture of her chicer, more modern look on Insta.

For me, no amount of money could ever compare to that feeling of mission accomplished! It was satisfying to be known for a skill I had worked so hard to cultivate.

Before makeovers, my niche was color. Before color, it was cut and styling. I have tried to master all sides of this business. But finding my niches didn't happen overnight. It has been a several-years-long journey.

FINDING MY NICHE(S)

The area I worked in at Imagine This in DC had a reputation for being trendsetting. During that time, it was all about short cuts like Nia Long and Halle Berry—even Anita Baker and Salt-N-Pepa before them. Cutting was new for me, but I caught on fast because I've always been a look-and-learn type of stylist; when I see a look on someone or see a person's style in a magazine, I can easily model it.

To perfect my haircutting skills, I studied my mentor, the amazing David Dior. He was so good and so fast, we all had a hard time trying to keep up. They would literally pick on me every day about how slow I was.

"You're too slow, Kiyah!" he used to say. Or "Kiyah, aren't you done yet?"

The other guys in the shop would fall to the floor, being funny, to show how long I would take with my cuts, curls, and styles.

"You still workin' on her, Kiyah?"

"Kiyah, you're too damn slow!"

I felt the pressure! David was pumping out about six to seven people in eight hours. This was much faster than me—a new stylist in the making—who was taking my time trying to perfect every single curl.

In hindsight, their picking on me made me faster, gave me more confidence in my abilities, and taught me to work well under pressure. But it was tough to take at first. Eventually, I understood that the more time you spend on a client, the less money you make. If you take three hours on one person, that means you're only going to be able to get one more in on a given day. So, speed was the magic to making money. And that's what I wanted to do: make lots of money doing what I love.

I did my best to pick up speed around the guys. I got better fast, but I had to work my butt off! I was at the salon five days a week from 10:00 a.m. to 10:00 p.m., working twelve-hour days only to get in maybe six people.

Before long, though, I was stacking curls, spiking hair, and poppin' a few tracks in the front with my razor and asymmetric cuts. I was doing so many clients that I ultimately had to become great at cutting. I perfected it, excelled at it, and it became the one thing I was recognized for. Cutting and styling had become my niche. In fact, it was my style that first caught the eye of Sean "Puffy" Combs.

• • •

Back then, in 1994, Puffy was this hip, fly dude from Harlem, New York, and I met him while hanging out on the Howard College scene. We first met when he'd come down to DC to splash a little flavor by throwing parties that attracted other music artists like Guy, Heavy D, and Slick Rick.

After I moved to New York, we became reacquainted during his many visits to the salon where I worked. One day, he approached me about doing hair for some of his Bad Boy Records artists, including Faith Evans, the first female artist on his label.

Puffy said, "I want her hair to look just like yours."

"All right," I said. "Cool!"

Faith was a writer who had become a recording artist. Super light-skinned, she had dark hair and a sultry urban voice with a great tone. She was a little shy and mild-mannered, but she wrote and sang her butt off. I had never worked on an artist before, so I had something to prove. After all, it's Puffy— his taste on all levels was over the top and elaborate with a great sense of style. He had also just gotten a $27 million record deal from Universal Records, so I knew his artists' music *and* images had to be on point. Once I grasped the magnitude of all he expected, I was like, *Oh, shit. I gotta do this right.*

With Faith's personality and her look, I knew I had to go big. I wanted to do something bold and courageous, something that would make more noise than I knew her mild-mannered temperament would let off. Aside from her voice, her hair would have to be her most significant accessory—the biggest part of her brand image.

I experimented with a lot of different looks and colors—blond, platinum, weaves, extensions, cuts.

"Yeah, I like that," Puff said. "But what else you got?"

I'd show him something else.

"Naw, I don't like that!"

As I mentioned, Puffy was from Harlem, where the guys were known to be sharp, fly, and trendsetting. He knew what he wanted, and he wasn't afraid to tell you. A "shiny suit guy" is what everyone knew him as. And Faith, his First Lady of Bad Boy Records, had to represent that same image.

When I stepped back to think about Faith's look, I asked myself, "What kind of image does he want her to have? What are her songs like? What is her sound about? How can we maintain her look on the road?"

Everybody knows me for switching it up and giving her that hot copper-red hair look she rocked on her second and third albums, but I actually started her out blonde.

I gave her a feathery bob with a layered bang like rap artist Pebbles's hairdo, which was popular during that era of Babyface and Jodeci. When Puffy saw her, he was like, "That's the look! That's it!"

I was so excited that Puffy was happy with the look I created. I knew his word meant everything. I observed so much about imaging, artistry, and management by being on tour and a part of the Diddy years.

By working with Puffy, I had advanced from being an expert at cutting and styling to really understanding how the overall image (hair, makeup, and wardrobe) matters to the artists, which came in handy when I started to do editorial work. All I needed was the client to tell me what image they were going after, and I could create that look.

It wasn't until I moved to LA and worked at Warren Tricomi, thirteen years into my career, that I shifted and added the art of coloring to my palette.

. . .

I didn't want just to know how to color. I wanted to master it!

At one point, I had considered taking color classes, but they weren't online like they are now. Time was always a factor. I had too much on my plate. And since I was on the road touring a lot, I didn't have time to be in a classroom.

Being at Warren Tricomi LA was a new experience for me. I got to work alongside young, talented, and creative stylists and colorists like Kaz Amor, Kristin Ess, and Stacy Heitman. I learned a *ton* from all of them. But I wasn't trying to stand over anybody's head all day. I'd walk to the back of the salon and quietly watch and learn how they mixed color. They taught me new techniques, formulas, and the *science* behind toners and maintenance products, which were products that led to higher sales tickets.

In those days, most of us Black hairstylists weren't really into color like that. Color can be technical, and like any science, it can be complex. But by watching and asking a lot of questions, I learned how mixing colors and toners are critical to the quality of the final result. It's not just about the base color; sometimes it's a three-step process to finish.

A lot of times, I would practice what I learned on myself, and my clients would look at me and say, "Ooh, Kiyah, I love that color of your hair! I want that same thing."

The most rewarding thing about color is that it can have a huge impact on a woman's look. But it's also a big-ticket item. A good color typically involves three steps, so clients who want the look have to be willing to spend the money because if you cheat on a step, you can compromise the integrity of their hair.

Not only did this little addition to my styling plate add to my resume, it expanded my niche, my clientele, and ultimately got the attention of Procter & Gamble, who made me a celebrity ambassador and colorist for their Clairol Professional Hair Color brand. Now that's what I'm talking about when I tell you that finding your niche can bring you career-changing success!

TIPS ON FINDING YOUR NICHE

Having a hard time finding your niche? Use your answers to these questions as your guide to narrow your focus:

- What unique skills do I have?
- What part of fashion, beauty, skin, hair, etc., am I most passionate about?
- What do I want to be known for?
- What more do I need to know about what I'm best at doing?
- What classes can I take to hone that craft I'm most passionate about?
- Who can I shadow that is an expert at what I am most passionate about?
- How can I get the best hands-on experience doing what I'm best at?

Once you get a handle on your niche, spend at least three to five years perfecting it so you can set yourself apart from the competition. In doing so, try to stay connected with current trends.

After defining your niche, you'll be better able to brand your services to a niche market and make some serious cash!

KEY TAKEAWAYS

No one is good at absolutely everything. Identify what you're best at doing—color, cuts, weaves, braids, brows, lash extensions—whatever that may be. As you grow, your niche will change, or you may develop more than one niche.

* ✳ Define your niche.
* ✳ Continue to hone those skills.
* ✳ Stay up on the trends.
* ✳ Strive not just to be good, but the best.

CHAPTER 10

Marketing, Part 2: Define Your Niche

Everyone is **NOT** your customer.

—Seth Godin, author and master marketer

Once you identify your niche—that one thing that sets you apart from the competition—it's time to focus on getting the word out to a targeted, rather than a mass, audience. In other words, **niche marketing**.

I love the niche marketing strategy. It's popular with many prominent business retailers, from Saks Fifth Avenue and Neiman Marcus that target upscale clientele to Ross and Walmart that target cost-conscious customers to luxury consignment retailers that target people like me who favor high-end merchandise at a value price.

To take full advantage of niche marketing, start by creating a niche market vision statement, in which you identify your niche audience, list five traits of your ideal client, and craft a mission statement.

CREATING A NICHE MARKET VISION STATEMENT: THE *WRIGHT* STEPS

Step One: Identify your niche audience. The first step of creating your niche market vision statement is identifying the customer base you want to target. To do that, answer these key questions:

- What is your niche?
- Who can benefit most from your niche? Is it older or younger women? Affluent women? Young kids? Don't get comfortable and say your demographic is "everyone." This exercise is about identifying your *target* niche customer, so being specific is important.
- What message do you want to communicate to your customers through your niche?
- Who are your competitors, and what can you offer your target demo better than they can? Is it lower pricing? More bang for the buck? Flexible hours?
- How are you using your niche to fill the unique needs of a market? Are you the only one offering the service in your area? Are you offering discounts for seniors and kids? Perhaps you're targeting college students or businesswomen/men?

Step Two: List the top five traits of your ideal client. Be specific and consider factors like gender, age, tastes, spending habits, and loyalty level.

Step Three: Create a one-paragraph vision and mission statement. Write a paragraph that incorporates your responses from Steps One and Two to describe your niche audience. Use as few words as possible.

• • •

I'll show you how to use these steps to create your own niche market vision statement using myself as an example. With twenty-five years in the business, I currently have four niches: makeovers, color, styling, and weaving. But for this exercise, I'll focus on just one: makeovers. Following my own *Wright Steps* laid out above, here's how my answers checked out:

• • •

STEP ONE: Identifying my niche audience

Q: *What is my niche?*

A: I'm a celebrity hairstylist. My gifts are cutting, coloring, and wig application. My niche is makeovers and total imaging, including tips on how to maintain hair.

Q: *Who can benefit most from my niche?*

A: Business bosses who invest in themselves. These are the women and men who want that polished, tailored look along with beauty solutions that inspire them to look and feel their best. They typically make good money and don't mind investing in themselves.

Q: *What message do I want to communicate with my target customers?*

A: Invest in yourself. If I can inspire you to change your look, it can change your life.

Q: *What advantage do I have over my competition?*

A: My experience doing celebrities' hair and makeovers sets me above a lot of my competition. I've won two Emmy Awards for my work, and I'm regularly quoted in magazines and online. I'm a sought-after TV personality and influencer for my expertise. I offer instant beauty solutions for the everyday woman or man, selling hair, extensions, wigs, and products. For over thirteen years, I've been an ambassador for P&G Beauty Brands.

Q: *How am I using my niche to fill the unique needs of a market?*

A: The everyday women I'm targeting want the same glam looks I offer my celebrity clients, so I'm providing them with makeovers to help them look and feel beautiful and have that feeling of a red-carpet experience if that's what they desire.

(continued)

STEP TWO: Top five traits of my ideal client

1. Comes regularly.
2. Is a trendsetter who loves to experiment with different looks and is willing to go out of her comfort zone.
3. Trusts my judgment when I recommend a new look or product purchases.
4. Wants to feel and look beautiful.
5. Open to change.

STEP THREE: My vision and mission statement

I'm a two-time Emmy Award–winning celebrity hairstylist who has styled the hair of some of the biggest celebrities in the entertainment industry. While I enjoy working with celebrities, my passion is to help the everyday woman achieve her dream look while inspiring her to "change your hair, change your life." That is my motto!

See, that was simple! Now it's your turn. Try using my *Wright Steps* to do the exercise for yourself. Then do it a second time as if you were your competitor to see if that leads you to change your answers.

Once you've defined your niche and know your target audience, you can use niche marketing strategies to reach them and set yourself apart from your competitors and increase your income.

NICHE MARKETING STRATEGIES

The biggest benefit of targeting customers who want your specialized services versus targeting a mass audience is that there's less competition, greater customer retention, and more opportunities to sell products. This doesn't mean ignoring those who just want the basics, but rather taking advantage of that unique group of customers who may be willing to pay more for the specialized services you offer. Here are some niche marketing strategies I've had success with:

Study your competitors. Check out what your competitors are *not* offering. If the salon on the next block only does natural hair and your niche is press and curl, make sure you lead with that service in all of your promotions, especially if you see a demand for that service in your area.

Collaborate with colleagues who complement your niche. Look to partner with other professionals who are not your competition to offer a total beauty experience. For instance, my colleague Damone Roberts, aka "The Eyebrow King," throws me a few of his clients. He'll do their brows, then send them my way to complete their look. Maybe you know someone who offers complementary beauty services like lashes, nails, or facials and has clients who want a total beauty experience. Even if you don't have a personal relationship with them, but you know their work and they are in the same vicinity, set up a time to meet with them and talk about how you can merge synergies. This cobranding concept works exceptionally well if you're in a salon suite with other beauty professionals in the complex.

Hold specialty events. If cuts are your thing, schedule a day or weekend reserved for just doing cuts. Think about it—no washing, no coloring, only cuts. Think of how many clients you can move through your salon during that time, mainly new clients who are coming because they are interested in what you've identified as your niche.

Become the resident expert. When you do interviews for magazines, radio, podcasts, or online, get in the habit of talking up your niche. Better yet, become an expert by hosting a webinar or posting a DIY video that targets clients who would be interested in your expertise.

Solve your customer's hard-to-solve problems. Present yourself as a problem solver for your clients. Maybe your niche is that you know the *science* of hair. Put it out there that you can help them reduce shedding or hair loss by treating their condition and recommending products you sell in the salon that they can use at home.

Keep niche clients nearby. Location is everything! If you're not where your niche market can get to you, then rethink your location. My niche market is celebrities and women who tend to be boss women and don't mind spending money on looking and feeling good. Be where your potential clients can easily get to you. Don't move around from salon to salon. People like consistency—period! For the entire time I've lived in LA, I've worked at salons in trendy upscale locations like West Hollywood and Beverly Hills. And no matter what, when your location offers the following attributes, you can charge a higher ticket:

- Comfort
- Aesthetics
- Relaxation
- Great customer service
- Professionalism

• • •

Using your niche to attract new clients is smart business, but don't forget your existing loyal clients. My clients mean everything to me. Going through COVID-19 made that extra clear; I missed every one of my clients.

Remember this: *customers matter.* Use your niche marketing strategies to attract them and use your best customer service practices to keep them. And if you're looking for even more tips and strategies for utilizing niche marketing to its full potential, scan the QR code to check out my exclusive bonus ebook:

RECAP

Before you can sell *it*, you have to know what you're selling. Create a one-paragraph mission statement about your professional talents that draws attention to your niche.

Create a Niche Marketing Vision Statement:

* ✳ Identify your niche audience
* ✳ List the top five traits of your ideal client
* ✳ Incorporate your responses to create a one-paragraph vision and mission statement

Niche Marketing Strategies:

* ✳ Study your competitors
* ✳ Collaborate wIth colleagues
* ✳ Hold events
* ✳ Become the resident expert
* ✳ Solve your customers' problems
* ✳ Keep clients nearby

Principle 4

Diversify with
Multiple Streams of Income

CHAPTER 11

Secrets of Upselling

If you're going *to play* the game properly,
you'd better know **EVERY RULE**.

—Barbara Jordan, civil rights activist

One of the most impactful lessons I learned by studying the paths of insanely wealthy entrepreneurs is that six- and seven-figure success is practically guaranteed if you **diversify** your income with four to seven ongoing streams of income that don't veer you too far away from your business. I am living proof!

Even if you don't want to reach millionaire or billionaire status, having multiple streams of income is almost a necessity for us beauty entrepreneurs to amass wealth, fill voids when we have slow seasons, or, worst case, supplement when a natural disaster forces us to shut down. When COVID-19 hit, I got *a lot* of financial assistance to help pay bills and keep my team in place, but that kind of aid is only there to assist when your flow gets low. Had it not been for my multiple income streams, like my ambassadorship with

Procter & Gamble, my online marketing efforts, and the online wig sales, I'd have been in much worse shape.

I urge every stylist, esthetician, nail pro, brow pro, and every other beauty professional looking to build up revenue to seriously look into opportunities to diversify their incomes. In the following chapters, I'll cover a number of great options to diversify with multiple incomes:

- Upselling services at the salon
- Freelance work (touring, on-location, and editorial)
- Working on TV & film with actors
- Sponsorship/brand ambassadorships
- Creating/selling product lines
- Teaching/speaking engagements

In this chapter, I'll focus on something any professional can do—upsell.

UPSELLING SERVICES AT THE SALON

Upselling is one of the most simple, organic, and effective sales tools we beauty professionals have to make extra money on top of our base fees. This is where we offer clients an added service or products that benefit them. In turn, we end up making a larger sale.

I know some beauty professionals don't like the process. They think it's not very honest, but that simply isn't true. Not only is it honest, it's also good business! The big guys upsell all the time. Have you ever been to a fast food place where they ask you if you want to supersize your order or get a combo meal with an added drink? Have you ever been on a flight where the airline says, "You can have more legroom for an extra price?" They call it upgrades. We call it *upselling*.

I can honestly say that upselling accounts for $50,000 a year of my added income. Yes! Here's how:

Since my niche is makeovers, when I have a client who says, "I want something different today," I say, "How about color?" Or I say, "How about a weave or a couple of extensions?" Adding services and products gives the client greater value, making them feel more beautiful, special, and trendsetting. Meanwhile, I make extra money on the sale. It's a win-win for both of us.

Think about it. If you see two hundred clients a month and convince each of them to make a small ten-dollar upgrade, you're getting an extra $2,000 a month, or $24,000 in extra income per year. It doesn't sound like such a bad idea after all, does it?

If you're a nail care professional and offer mani/pedis, you can upsell the service by simply asking, "How would you like to try a paraffin wax? We have it on sale today." That's not taking advantage of the customer. That's called giving the client added value at an excellent cost to them and an extra sale for you. Plus, it costs you little to no more money and no more time.

If you're not upselling, you're missing out on many opportunities to boost your revenues. One of those opportunities is through bundling.

Bundling

Cable companies figured out a long time ago that they can upsell more services when they are bundled. The same strategy works in our field. If you usually charge $400 for a weave, and you want to upsell by adding color for $225 and a cut for eighty dollars, the customer might balk at paying $705 when they had only intended to pay $400. But by bundling the upsell with a 10 percent discount, the client may jump at the savings. Meanwhile, you increase your sales of all services in the bundle.

The trick with upselling, though, is to be sure you come out on top. So, if it costs you more time and money than what you saved, then you need to make the discount for the bundle a little lower. The incentive has to be of value to the customer, with profits still going in your pocket.

Another effective bundling strategy involves the marketing "rule of three," also called "price anchoring." Studies show that if a customer is offered three price levels, they most often go for the middle level. So, let's say you decide to offer three beauty packages. Ensure that the middle item in your bundle is attractive enough for the customer and set to yield a more-than-satisfactory profit for you.

In the following example, the prices are better as a package than as a la carte services and attractive enough for customers to see the value and splurge a little on what they may not have otherwise tried.

LASH EXTENSIONS	LASH & BROW PCKG	LASH, BROW, FACIAL
Lash Extensions	*Lash Extensions*	*Lash Extensions*
3–4 week fill	*3–4 week fill*	*3–4 week fill*
(mink upgrade)	*(mink upgrade)*	*(mink upgrade)*
	Plus Brow Shaping	*Plus Brow Shaping*
		Plus Facial
$99	**$129**	**$210**

Pre-booking

Another subtle but effective upsell strategy is encouraging new satisfied customers to book a second appointment *before* leaving the salon. The pre-booking would give you the committed funds you may not have otherwise gotten from the client once they returned home.

UPSELL DOS & DON'TS

There are so many organic and creative ways to upsell in our industry, but they come with a set of unofficial rules to follow if you want a win for your client and your bank account.

DO: Stand by what you upsell. If you tell your client, "This will hide your gray and make you look ten years younger," be prepared to back your claim. You may want to show before and after pictures from some of your other clients who tried the color and look ten years younger. Or, if you're tech-savvy, take a picture of your client and use imaging to show the simulated results. If you've used the product yourself and like it, then say so. Or you could offer testimonials from others who've used it. However you do it, be able to back your claim.

DO: Be honest. Don't just sell extra services because you want to meet a profit goal. Understand your client's lifestyle so you can give a style or service that works for them and their self-esteem.

DO: Make recommendations, not scare tactics. If your client's hair is shedding and you think they can benefit from a premium conditioner or steam treatment, don't say, "If you don't do something about this shedding, you're going to lose all your hair." Consider saying, "I have a conditioner that I believe will help with your shedding. It costs a little more than the generic ones, but it will slow the shedding and give your hair a shinier look in the long run. Is that something you think you'd want to try?" Or you could offer a steam treatment with high-end protein treatments.

DO: Offer complete transparency up front. If you're upselling color, be up front about how much longer your client will have to be at the salon for the treatment and how much more it will cost. They may not have the time to be there for an extra hour, or they may not have the additional sixty-five dollars. Be fully transparent *before* the sale or upgrade. If they don't have the time or money, suggest they do it on the next visit.

DO: Listen and *act*. If a client in your chair is getting a wash and blow-dry for seventy-five dollars but talks to you about going to the Caribbean or somewhere else with beachy vibes for vacation in two weeks, you may want to suggest braids or a protective style weave or extensions. They'll cost a little more, but they can swim with confidence and be cute without worrying about sweating out their curl.

DON'T: Be a bully. Never take advantage of a customer. If they say, "No, I can't afford it" or "No, I don't want it," let it go! No means no! Upselling only works when it's a two-way street that benefits your client's needs *first*.

• • •

The best kind of upsell you can have is the kind where everyone benefits and is happy.

RECAP

When looking to diversify your income, **upselling** is one of the easiest methods for beauty professionals. Using any one or more of the following strategies will easily increase your revenue:

* ✳ Add-ons
* ✳ Bundling
* ✳ Practice the "rule of three"—offer three beauty package options, knowing the middle option will likely be the one your client selects
* ✳ Pre-book new clients for return visits

Rules of Upselling:

* ✳ **DO** stand by what you upsell
* ✳ **DO** be honest
* ✳ **DO** make recommendations. **DON'T** insist or force a service
* ✳ **DO** offer full transparency up front
* ✳ **DO** listen and act
* ✳ **DON'T** be a bully. No means no!

CHAPTER 12

Getting Freelance Work

A *side hustle* is the
new Job **SECURITY**.

—Forbes

'm a salon girl at heart. But standing behind a chair all day isn't what got me to my financial goals. So, what's my million-dollar secret?

I'll say it again: multiple streams of income! And one of my most lucrative streams of income comes through my freelance work.

Between concert tours and movie and TV press tours, virtual consultations, product sales, brand endorsements, affiliate program offers, photo shoots, promotional junkets, red carpets, and celebrity appearances, my freelance work accounts for over $200,000 of my annual earnings. Some of these freelance gigs pay more than others. Some are more rewarding than others, but most of all, they are fun and lucrative. In this chapter, I'll lay out two of the most common types of freelance work you might encounter as a beauty professional: promotional and concert tours and editorial work.

PROMOTIONAL AND CONCERT TOURS

A promotional tour is when an artist casually meets major media—like TV, radio, and journalists—in various locations to promote a current project like a film, TV show, album, or concert.

My first promo tour ever was in 1994 with recording artist Faith Evans when she released her first album on Sean Puffy Combs's Bad Boy Records label (right after I'd given her that iconic platinum blonde look!).

When you're gearing an artist up to promote an upcoming release, you have to prep them for promo pictures so they're ready when their single drops. For Faith, that meant doing her hair for photos, packaging, morning shows, clubs, press—basically all media events.

We started off doing promo tours for radio; Wendy Williams, Ed Lover, Angela Martinez, 97.1 radio, and Dr. Dre were the popular ones at the time. Then we'd go over and do the print shoots with *Essence, Vibe, XXL*, and any other magazines and print press, including cover photo shoots, which took anywhere from six to ten hours.

The days were long and exhausting for me, but I hung in there. This was my first go-round with a tour. I was starting to get my rhythm down. I had Faith's image down. After rocking small, local events for a few weeks, we were ready to go on tour when, *boom*, Puffy comes to me and says, "I got an issue, Kiyah."

While Puff was prepping Faith to go on tour, he was also managing Mary J. Blige. When she and her hairstylist got into a disagreement, Puffy said to me, "I'm switching you guys. I need *you* to go on the road with Mary."

After all I had been through with Faith, I was like, "What?!"

This was a lesson in switching gears and staying flexible. So just like that, I was doing hair for Mary J. Blige, a rising star with Uptown Records. She was this edgy, urban girl with tomboy swag from Mount Vernon, New York, who was really at the beginning of her career. But everyone knew she was about to be *big*.

Even though I had gotten to know Faith really well, I was cool with making the switch, plus she would be on the same tour, so I could still see her from time to time. I had never been on a music tour before, so I didn't know what to expect. All I knew was that it would be a history-making event with Biggie Smalls, 112, Faith Evans, Mary, Total, Lil' Kim, Craig Mack,

Mase, and other legendary performers. I'm so proud to have been asked to be a part of it!

Mary's team told me I would be making $2,500 a week for hair, which included four days of hair and three days off. It was less money than I was making on commission at the salon where I was working in New York at the time, but more than I would've made working with Faith. In addition to the $2,500 per week doing Mary's hair, the record label agreed to cover my food, per diem, and hotel stays. Nothing else would come out of my pocket, so I figured it would all even out.

On Mary's tour bus, I was assigned one bunk bed out of nine that felt like a casket on wheels when I was inside it. There was no privacy, limited space, and for hours, there'd be no cell service for long pockets of the drive. It was quite an adjustment!

Mary was a relatively new artist, so there'd be listening parties and maybe an after-party at night. Sometimes I had a 3:30 a.m. call time for a radio show. Our schedules were nonstop, brutal, every day. And I'd have to stick with Mary the whole time. There were often long days where I had to be dressed from day to night to be ready at a moment's notice. "Let's go, let's go, let's go," Puffy would always say. "Can't stop, won't stop" was his mantra.

Trust me, we never stopped!

All that hustling and bustling taught me early in my freelance career how to *stay* ready so I never had to *get* ready. I learned to have everything I needed with me at all times: combs, hairspray, brushes, set bag. Nobody wanted to hear excuses. There was never time to go back to get something from a trailer. You had to be ready! Your artist had to look on point. Whatever style I did for Mary had to last from day to night, so I kept a touch-up kit with me at all times. That was key—no slipping on the job!

That tour also taught me how to live out of a suitcase so I could be the first one ready to roll at the drop of a dime. Even today, people are like, "Wow, Kiyah, you get ready so fast!" It takes me less than an hour to be packed and out the door—without any advance notice—depending on how long I'll be gone.

Beyond having to keep up with schedules and the inconveniences of being on the road for weeks at a time, I had to work around many personalities. One time, I was forced to call Puffy, who was back in New York, to tell him about an incident on the road that had me stressed out. "Kiyah, don't even worry," he said. "Don't get caught up in anything. Just stay focused on the goal. You are there to work. You are there to do your job. Get in. Get out. Don't get caught up in anyone's mess."

It was good advice but tough to follow because a lot of times, you become the artists' friend and confidante when you're doing their hair. You're the person who spends the most intimate moments with the celebrity, so it's not an easy act to balance. But I heeded his advice and stayed focused on the job at hand.

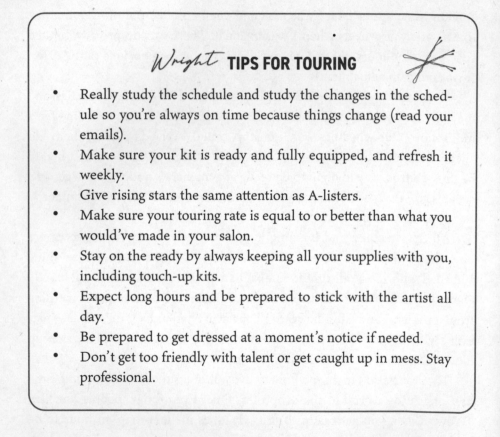

Wright TIPS FOR TOURING

- Really study the schedule and study the changes in the schedule so you're always on time because things change (read your emails).
- Make sure your kit is ready and fully equipped, and refresh it weekly.
- Give rising stars the same attention as A-listers.
- Make sure your touring rate is equal to or better than what you would've made in your salon.
- Stay on the ready by always keeping all your supplies with you, including touch-up kits.
- Expect long hours and be prepared to stick with the artist all day.
- Be prepared to get dressed at a moment's notice if needed.
- Don't get too friendly with talent or get caught up in mess. Stay professional.

My Mary J. Blige tour was my first. Now, flash-forward about six years later to 2003. I had only been living in Los Angeles for a short time when I was riding down Sunset Boulevard one really beautiful afternoon in my new Lexus RX 300 truck. That's when I looked up and saw this huge movie poster for *Bad Boys II*, with big pictures of the stars, Martin Lawrence, Will

Smith, and Gabrielle Union. I was like, "Wow, Gabrielle Union! She's dope! She's so pretty!"

Gabrielle was the new sexy "Black girl" actress in Hollywood. I had seen her in *Bring It On* and *Deliver Us from Eva*, and in my mind, she was someone who could easily be my friend. Plus, people said we kind of looked alike. As I drove past that poster in what seemed like slow motion, my mind drifted and manifestation set in.

God, I really want to do her hair!

I couldn't wait to call my agent later that afternoon to tell her what I wanted. After we talked, I decided to let it go, and I went about my business of doing hair. I knew that if I was meant to work with Gabrielle Union, then God would open doors.

My agent called just a few days later. "Kiyah, I've got great news," she said. "They want to know if you can do hair . . . *and* makeup for Gabrielle Union on the *Bad Boys II* European press tour?"

"What?! Hair *and* makeup?!"

I had done some makeup with Mary J. Blige and Faith Evans and on the Lauryn Hill tour, but no way was I a professional makeup artist. But when they asked me if I did both, I was like, "Yeah, of course!" not feeling the most confident. But I knew I could do it. Besides, I really wanted to do that press movie tour—bad!

I knew working with Gabrielle Union would put me at that next level of celebrity hairstyling. I'd be doing *Hollywood A-list celebrity hair*! That had been my goal since as early as I could remember.

Once my agent told me everything was a go, I was so hyped!

The press tour for the movie was next-level fun. It was still a whirlwind, but unlike my first tours on the road in buses, this time I was flying on private jets and staying in Mandarin Oriental hotels all over Europe with some of the biggest stars in Hollywood, including the director Michael Bay, producer Jerry Bruckheimer, and Will Smith. I had never been on tour at that level before, mingling with Hollywood A-listers and high-power directors and actors. I felt totally out of my element, but I loved every minute of it. I started to think, *I could get used to this!* I could actually see myself doing celebrity hair full-time, living large and flying all over the world to places I had never been.

Every day on tour, I did Gabrielle's hair and makeup for TV, radio, print, you name it. Then afterward, we'd go to dinner or sometimes a party.

The tour lasted for nearly two-and-a-half weeks, and I made really good money—$5,000 a week or more for just three or four days of work each week. It was a crazy, exciting time for me and the turning point in my career as a celebrity hairstylist.

Over the years, I've done a lot of music, TV, and movie press tours with talents like Kerry Washington, Tyra Banks, Jennifer Hudson, and so many more. They were all great and sometimes humbling experiences. But they were all *a lot* of hard work! If this is a route you want to take to create that extra stream of income, here are a few things to consider before you accept any gig:

- What's the time commitment?
- Is your rate hourly, daily, weekly, or by tour?
- Will the money you make be equal to, better, or more beneficial than what you would've made in the salon?
- Is there a pay guarantee?
- Are all of your expenses covered, including travel, meals, per diem, kit fee?
- What exactly are you required to do?
- Are you working with a team or solo?
- Are you comfortable traveling, living out of a suitcase, and working long hours?
- Is there a hair or supply budget?

Promotional tour work isn't for everyone, but it can be a great learning experience and a lot of fun if you're willing to work hard.

EDITORIAL OR SESSION WORK

Doing editorial hair and makeup is another excellent freelance opportunity to earn an extra income stream that complements your salon work. In this setting, you are essentially creating dedicated looks for magazine photo shoots and ad campaigns.

Just like touring, doing editorial work can sound glamorous, but that's not always the case. The pay can be lackluster, but a huge benefit is that you can get good images for your portfolio.

Many factors go into determining your rate, such as your experience, the project, the location, and the term of the gig. A day rate for a hairstylist or makeup artist can be as high as $3,500+. If you can do hair *and* makeup, you can add a rate onto your rate. For a TV show or production, the average hourly rate goes up to around fifty-five dollars to $110 if you're in the union (more on unions in the next chapter).

When I first explored editorial work on magazines back in the early nineties, most of my initial bookings came through referrals from photographers who knew me or artists I'd worked with on tour. Since then, I've done hundreds of cover shoots throughout my career for magazines like *Elle*, *Essence*, *Ebony*, *Vogue*, *Vanity Fair*, and *InStyle*. I've worked photo sessions with Nia Long, Tyra Banks, Kerry Washington, Laverne Cox, Taraji P. Henson, Gabrielle Union, Jennifer Hudson, and Ciara. And I've done photo campaigns for Clairol Professional, Sally Beauty, Neutrogena, Pantene, Head & Shoulders, Olay, and many more!

Editorial shoots have their own rules that are very different from doing salon hair. I had to learn how to make styles that were soft, pretty, and had movement, rather than being "neat" or styled with a lot of hairspray, crunch, and grease.

I also had to learn how to be compatible with makeup artists who are very particular about which side they work on when the talent is in the chair facing the mirror—it may seem silly but trust me, we artists can be particular. Most of the time, they prefer to work on the right side, so I had to learn how to work on the left. It's the little things you have to do in the name of teamwork!

But thanks to the lessons I learned early in my career and from Puffy about imaging, I knew to ask questions from the creative directors before my photo shoots like, "What are they going to be wearing?" That's a very important detail because the clothes typically lead the direction for the talent's hair and makeup. Are they going to have a high collar? OK, then I'll put their hair up. A drop-back dress sometimes meant hair down the back. The goal is to customize each look according to the talent's wardrobe. Unless guided otherwise, everything must be considered as part of one cohesive package.

When the referrals I was getting for editorial work started to dry up, I knew I needed more help finding the really good gigs. So, I pulled together a portfolio that had attracted my first agent, Timothy Priano, early on when I lived in New York City. I'd done enough looks for celebrities since then that my portfolio was pumping. My images had great cinematography, good lighting, and quality makeup. It was strong enough for my agent to land me my first magazine covers.

Every time I got new editorial work, I updated my portfolio, including tear sheets from the original magazine covers. Early on, I didn't know what to add to my portfolio; I was just putting stuff in there with no focus. Today, hard copy portfolios are pretty much a thing of the past. Most stylists are using their Instagram pages and personal websites as well as various apps to show off their work and skills, which is cool, but a word of caution: if you want to be seen as a professional, you need to keep your work images on separate social media pages from your personal ones. Devote a file, media press kit, page, website, or account to specifically show your work.

Here are some tips for creating an impressive portfolio:

Wright TIPS FOR CREATING YOUR PORTFOLIO

- **Keep it current.** When your portfolio is digital, you have the luxury of easily swapping out images, so there's no excuse not to keep it up to date with relevant looks and styles. Stay on trend.
- **Showcase your best work.** It's not necessary to include everything you've done since graduating from hair school. Ensure the images of your work are as clear, crisp, beautiful, and stunning as possible because a picture truly is worth a thousand words.
- **Show variety** to showcase your versatility and diversity. Even if your niche in the salon is color, show us beautiful color on all hair textures. It would be good to show the finished cut and style as well.

- **Include background detail.** A portfolio is more than pictures. Give a little detail about your background and training.
- **Include testimonials** from people who have loved your work and commented on it.
- **Credit photographers and makeup and hair teams** who provided the images.
- **Organize the images** so the presentation is easy on the eye. Keep all studio or on-location work together. It's nice to see the most current photos at the top of the feed, or maybe you have an area with before and after images. You can even mix in a bit of video as well.
- **Be proud.** Whenever I finish a project that I'm proud of or think would be impressive in my portfolio, I post it online—especially the behind-the-scenes photos and videos. Archive all your images as well.

Scan the QR code to see some of my favorite images from my current celebrity portfolio.

Another great thing about freelancing on photo shoots is that you have the opportunity to learn about lighting, production, and doing hair on television versus in a salon. I dabbled in producing my own hair shows early in my career when I lived in DC, but as my career expanded to NYC, I worked side by side with some of the industry's best photographers, which made me even more in demand and better as an editorial hairstylist. That knowledge about lighting and what worked for the camera also came in handy when I started to produce shoots for my brand and product lines.

Wright **TIPS FOR EDITORIAL WORK**

- Ask photographers and colleagues for referrals to get your foot in the door. Let them know you are interested and available.
- Be adaptable to sharing the workspace with other beauty professionals. Collaboration is key.
- For hair and makeup artists, understand the differences between salon looks versus editorial looks versus TV hair.
- Create a portfolio or media/press kit to attract an agent. It should include your best and most current work. Show variety.
- Consult with the creative director of your shoot to determine wardrobe and other specifics about the talent so you can tailor your service to that look.
- Understanding lighting is a big bonus for securing more work and getting the job done right.

Editorial work isn't limited to people living in LA or New York. Ad agencies in your town are often hiring for their commercial productions and print ad shoots. Magazines hire hairstylists for their cover shoots. There are many opportunities out there if you have the talent, a rocking portfolio, and passion for getting the job done. Here are a few more tips to help you thrive in the editorial world once you get your foot in the door:

- If you're regularly working in a salon on commission, be sure you have an arrangement with the owner so you can do freelance work that will sometimes take you away from your chair.
- Do your homework. The more you know about the celebrity or other talent and their project, the more you can help with their imaging.
- Be up on the latest trends and know your history in the event you're asked to do a period look.

- Have your work kit in order. Be prepared to tailor your gear to the talent you're working with, and always be prepared with extra hair, nails, lashes, or other accessories.
- Network with photographers and makeup artists who do session/editorial work and let them know you're interested in working together.

Scan the QR code to watch a video with more advice for anyone living outside of LA or New York:

A FINAL WORD ON EDITORIAL/TOURING/FREELANCING

Lastly, if you want to freelance on a photo shoot or promotional tour, heed this advice: *do not do it just for the money*! Yes, it's a great additional stream of income, and the experience is awesome! Yes, sometimes it can be exciting and glamorous. But it can also be tiring, trying, and often not even profitable. Sometimes you have to ask yourself, "What am I interested in? What *don't* I enjoy doing? Can I do this long term?" That is how I decided how I would lay out my goals. But don't put too much pressure on yourself because sometimes the answers come to you along the journey.

KEY TAKEAWAYS

* Be prepared for long days.
* Be prepared on set or on location by keeping all your tools with you or within arm's reach. There may not be time to go back to the studio, car, or dressing room to get them.
* You're a professional. Don't get too friendly with the talent—at least prove yourself first.
* Learn to be a team player and work well with other beauty or fashion pros who are sharing the same space.
* Constantly update your portfolio, including online.

CHAPTER 13

How to Break into TV and Film

Success is never a
STRAIGHT LINE.

—Tyra Banks

The early days of my career as a celebrity hairstylist—doing Angela Bassett's hair for a few *What's Love Got to Do with It* press dates, followed by a gig touring all over Europe with Gabrielle Union and the *Bad Boys II* stars—were only the beginning of what turned into a long and satisfying journey working with Hollywood A-listers. But as much as I loved freelancing on the road, I was always happy to get back to the salon to service the *everyday women* I favor at this point in my career. These clients are *loyal*, and even when all else fails, they need their hair done. Clients love consistency, so even though I was freelancing on the road a lot, I always went back to my base as a salon stylist. By around 2003, I had built up over four hundred clients in the two years since I left New York and moved to LA. I was fully booked in the salon when I got a call from the famous makeup artist Jay Manuel.

"Hey, Kiyah," he said. "I got a client for you. Tyra Banks is starting a new TV show. She wants to work with you. I think you two would be good together."

"Tyra wants *me*?!"

"Yeah, she's gonna call you."

Even though I had an agent, celebrities sometimes called me directly because everything was about the referral business. Before Tyra even called, I was skeptical about doing hair for TV. Everybody had been telling me since I first arrived in Hollywood, "You're not gonna make any money doing TV!" This was back in 2003, when the hourly pay for working on a TV talk show was around forty-five dollars to sixty-five dollars an hour—maybe a little more for a key stylist. Today, it's something like sixty-five dollars-plus an hour. There are no tips, no extra side cash like in a salon, and no flexible hours. There are ways to make extra money outside of the show when the talent does billboards, talk shows, editorial shoots, events, and other media to promote their show, but for the most part, everything is set.

I knew that if I took the job working with Tyra on her TV show, my salon and freelance work would pretty much come to a halt. I would just be getting a weekly paycheck based on every counted hour I worked. I was making between $2,000 and $4,000 a week in the salon at that point and got a minimum day rate of $2,500 for my work on music videos and photo shoots. My career was flourishing. In one day, I earned a hell of a lot more than I would make in a week on a TV talk show. The TV job would be a long-form gig, which would be a mental adjustment. On the other hand, everything in my salon world was quick money. Why would I set aside all that to work on some TV show? I kindly turned down the offer when Tyra called.

Then her team called a second time.

I admired their persistence and liked the idea of getting to work with her. But I also worried that working in TV would keep me from being creative, which I've always thrived on. The back and forth in my mind went on for a couple of days. As I weighed all the pros and cons, I thought about when I put my salon work on hold to go on the road with Puffy's Bad Boy artists for years.

Hmmm. Everything worked out back then! I thought. If anything, going on the road helped boost my notoriety among other music talents and, frankly, helped me get to a place where somebody like Tyra would even notice me. I asked myself, *Should I just do it?* I prayed to God about it and also asked my agent at that time for her advice.

"I'll negotiate a higher rate for you," my agent said, "and I'll get you in as key hair so your sole responsibility would be to do Tyra."

Most keys are responsible for pulling together the team, managing them for the show, and creating the entire look for the show or film. They are in charge of the hair department, which works with the director, production designer, and key makeup artist to set the tone for the whole production. But I was set to do Tyra's hair only.

Despite some of my peers telling me not to do it, I thought long and hard about it, prayed, and decided to take the plunge. The next day, I called my agent and said, "OK. Let's do it!"

Once I committed, I got really pumped about working with Tyra. She had already made a name for herself as the first Black supermodel to walk the runways in Paris and grace the covers of *GQ*, *Vogue*, *Sports Illustrated*, and the *Victoria's Secret* catalog. She was also the creator and host of the hit show *America's Next Top Model*. With *The Tyra Banks Show*, she was looking to do something new and unique. The program was so innovative in its day, focusing on fashion and lifestyle makeovers along with topical issues that empowered young women to reach their goals and achieve their dreams.

Joining a Union

Joining Tyra's team also meant joining the Makeup Artists and Hair Stylists Guild Local 706. This is important because it's like getting your master's as a hair, makeup, or wardrobe stylist. Being in the union protects you as an employee when working for film and television. They offer great health insurance, burial insurance, and security for your long-term goals, which is especially awesome if you have a family. There were only a few ways to get in at that time: you had to be brought in by a star request, go through a grueling backlog of paperwork, or get referred by a hairstylist who's already in the union. So, I got in at Tyra's request.

Union rules vary depending on your state, but most local unions require you to show verification of thirty days' worth of union-qualifying employment—usually through pay stubs or employment records—in the county where you'll be working before you can join. In some cases, they dig deep for references and your work history. Then all you have to do is fill out your application and pay your initiation fee and dues.

The fees associated with joining a union can be significant. When I joined, it ended up being around $6,000! Half was due upon signing and the other half was due later. After the initial payment, there are yearly verification renewals with dues running about $180 every quarter for the contract's life or the rest of my life if I choose to keep my membership in the union. Today, if I maintain at least four hundred to six hundred hours a year working in TV, I get universal insurance, which means I'm in it for life!

The Logistics of Working in the Film and TV Business

Once I got the business affairs out of the way, I had to learn the process of working in TV. That meant clocking in and out every day and keeping up with my weekly time card. I didn't have a clue about those kinds of things, so in the beginning, I just followed the leader and asked a lot of questions.

In terms of the work itself, I quickly started to see how doing TV hair was quite different from doing salon hair. For instance, the curls are not the same. The everyday woman wants her hair to last, so you make the curls a little bit tighter, knowing they'll fall throughout the evening. But those same tight, spirally curls can look too old-school on television. The hair had to be moveable and not greasy because television picks up every little detail, angle, and mistake. I had to learn the importance of those small "TV hair details" and make the necessary adjustments on the spot.

Once I found my groove, I started experimenting with a lot of different looks on Tyra. She wore weaves and wigs for years, but she trusted me to be bold with the hair, and we even rocked her edgier *Top Model* hair on her talk show sometimes. I liked that she was always open to something new. Setting Tyra's look for the show is what excited me most, and the fact that I could see my work showcased to millions of people every single day was nice, too.

What I liked the least about TV were the three twelve- to fourteen-hour-long days I had to spend in the dark, cold studios filming two shows a day. Every day I went through the same routine: I arrived at 7:00 a.m. to set up. I grabbed a bite at craft services while I waited for Tyra to finish her debriefing with the producers. By 7:45 or 8:00 a.m., I'd finish getting her ready for the 10:30 a.m. taping. Sometimes we did press right after the show, which meant that, more often than not, my days didn't end until 6:30 or 7:00 p.m.

It was grueling, but the biggest saving grace for working under those conditions was Tyra. She inspired me with her work ethic, business acumen, patience, and creative mind. She was killing it in the business world and was always taking things to the next level. Tyra was the ultimate professional! Even after she had worked hours and hours on her talk show then went over to edit *Top Model*, she still came in the next day with her face on and a positive attitude.

What I had learned from Puffy about branding and image was invaluable, but Tyra took me to a whole other level. From working on her show, I learned how to produce my own photo shoots, understand TV lighting and poses, and have confidence on camera, as well as perfect her well-known *smizing* techniques, body angles, and all the other *Top Model* secrets.

Although my work in-studio on *The Tyra Banks Show* was exhausting on its own, I still found time to get in two twelve- to sixteen-hour days at the salon a week and go on quick weekend tours. I pretty much put a family, kids, a man, and a social life all the way to the side.

The TV world looks glamorous, but before you take the plunge into pursuing work in this field, think about whether it's right for you.

DO YOU HAVE THE *Wright* STUFF FOR TV?

- **Time commitment.** Do you have the freedom to be away from your bread-and-butter clients while you put in potentially long hours on TV sets or on location? Remember, a series production can span weeks, months, or even years.
- **Willingness to join the union.** Are you prepared to join the union? Most TV gigs look for union workers. Dues can be quite pricey up front, then quarterly for the life of your membership. There are significant insurance benefits, though, if you maintain enough hours per year.
- **Available to travel.** Just because you agree to work on a TV set doesn't mean there won't be times you have to do location work. Are you flexible with your time and resources?
- **Disciplined.** Are you disciplined and organized enough to punch a time clock every day or regularly invoice for your services?
- **Adaptable.** Are you up on or willing to learn the techniques for doing hair and makeup for TV cameras and lighting, which differ from salon styles?
- **Focused.** Maintaining continuity is critical in TV. Are you adept at recreating the same looks for the cameras when there are multiple "takes" or for each episode?

Just as I was starting to burn myself out working the grueling TV schedule, maintaining my other work, and wondering if it was all worth the exhaustion, I got a sign that my hard work had paid off. On February 8, 2006, during an episode of *The View*, the cohosts, Barbara Walters, Meredith Vieira, Star Jones, Joy Behar, and Elisabeth Hasselbeck, announced that I had been nominated for a Daytime Emmy Award for my work as Tyra's personal stylist, alongside Theresa Broadnax, who was the lead hairstylist on the show.

What?! Look at me! I'll never forget that day. I was super excited.

Nothing was cooler than learning that I was in the running for a Daytime Emmy Award with other morning show hairstylists who worked on *Dr. Phil*, *The Oprah Winfrey Show*, *The Price Is Right*, *Full Frontal Fashion*, and *The View*.

The awards for Outstanding Achievement in Hairstyling, Production, and Lighting—all the behind-the-scenes categories that are part of what the Television Academy calls the Creative Arts—were presented during a huge sit-down dinner in Hollywood.

With little family, my sister Jalannia flew in from DC to join me at the ceremony. I think she was even more excited than I was. When we pulled up to the event, we saw a long red carpet lined with photographers, press, and even some fans looking on from the street. I had gotten so comfortable doing hair for A-listers before the Primetime Emmys, Grammys, Oscars, or one of the other awards shows, but now that it was my time to shine, I didn't know how to act. It was all too *freakin' surreal*!

Once my sister and I entered the ballroom, I remember fumbling through the dim-lit space, making my way to the reception table. We got our name tags, then were escorted to our table, where my excitement turned into anxiety. Then, because it was so dark and the show was so long and kind of boring, I guess I started to nod off. My sister kept poking me. "Wake up!" she whispered.

Another thirty minutes or so had gone by when my sister shoved my arm again and said, "Your category is coming up."

I was still taking a quick doze when I heard, "And the winner is . . . *The Tyra Banks Show*!"

My sis was like, "Kiyah, Kiyah. You won!"

I'm like, "Wait! What? What?!" I honestly thought I was dreaming.

I bolted straight out of my seat and ran toward the stage all frazzled. Theresa Broadnax (key stylist for the talent on the show) and I met at the podium. It's hard to describe how I felt in that moment when they passed the gold Emmy trophy over to me. I couldn't believe it was ours.

I was so excited, I didn't even read the notes I had prepared. I just improvised and said what was on my heart. But I did remember the important parts: thanking Tyra, the Academy, and, most importantly, God.

One person I didn't thank publicly but had in my heart to thank was my mom. I knew that if she could've seen me at that moment, she would've been so proud of her baby girl and that $150 investment she made for me to go to hair school at Edison Career Center in Maryland, which is no longer around. She not only brought me into the world but equipped me with the armor I needed to be a success.

As I stood backstage with the photographers snapping away at me holding my Emmy, I flashed back to when I was a kid, watching Anita Baker and Madonna thank their hairdressers on national TV and imagining myself on that stage getting recognition. Twenty-five years later, I was living my Cinderella moment.

Here's my journal entry from April 6, 2006:

> Hey God, guess what? I won the award, dude! I really won!! The last time I wrote in this book, I prayed I would win the Emmy, and guess what? I really won. I even feel a little numb too! Like I am too proud even to get excited. And I pray to embrace the moment. Every moment, because in my mind, I am all ready for the next "what's next?"

Little did I know that day when I grabbed my Emmy, I was also grabbing a piece of history as the first African American to win an Emmy for Outstanding Hairstyling. Winning that Emmy was a humbling moment and one of the happiest in my life. It affirmed for me that there is power in hard work and manifestation.

About a month after I got my Emmy at the Creative Arts Awards ceremony, the big Primetime Emmys Show came on TV, and Tyra was going to be one of the presenters. I did her hair that afternoon and went back to my apartment to catch the show on TV. I had the sound blasting so I could hear it from the kitchen while I was cooking. Who knew that not even five minutes into the show, Tyra would say, "My hairstylist Kiyah Wright won! Check out the clip!"

I was like, "What? Did she just say my name?!" Then, I heard my voice. I made a quick dash into the living room.

"Oh, my God!" I said. "I'm on national TV!"

They were running my entire acceptance speech. I watched with my mouth hanging wide open. *This is really crazy!* Talk about a whirlwind! Despite my reluctance to work on the show at first, all my hard work—all the long, redundant hours in a dark studio, striving to be the best I could be—paid off. It felt really good to get the recognition. Winning the Emmy moved to the top of the list of the most monumental moments in my life.

Over the next year, I worked with Tyra on both of her shows. I still loved working with her, but it was getting harder to build up my portfolio because the work with her was taking up more and more of my time. Plus, I couldn't flex my creative muscle and didn't have any diversity in my portfolio like I used to. I had gotten good at maintaining continuity in my craft; there were even times when the show did reruns and I would have to do Tyra's hair the same way I'd done it months prior. But after a while, I started to feel restless. Doing the same hairstyles day after day became monotonous. I was ready to move on.

I loved Tyra so much, but I knew it was time to put in my resignation, and Tyra started looking for another hairstylist. Once she found one, I phased out midseason. I didn't want to be out of Tyra's camp fully, though, so I continued to work with her on *Top Model,* which was more stimulating because it allowed for more creativity.

Just as I'd made my move out of the daytime TV show world, I got the news that I was nominated for a second Emmy Award! Nobody was more surprised than me. When the Television Academy announced that I was among the winners, I was in awe. Because I'd already left the show, I shared that Emmy with the hairstylist who had taken over my role as Tyra's key hairstylist.

Not only was I the first African American hairstylist to win a Daytime Emmy Award, I was also the only hairstylist of *any* race or gender to win *two* Emmys in that category back to back! Whenever I look at my two Emmy statues—one I keep in my salon and the other at home—I think about what would have happened if I hadn't taken that plunge into TV. What if I had listened to those naysayers? By praying, believing, and looking to God for the desires of my heart, I got double for my trouble!

Tyra and I have worked together for over a decade on *The Tyra Banks Show* and *Top Model*, among tons of press, magazine shoots, and more— and we're still running. We've traveled to amazing destinations throughout Europe and Asia, staying at beautiful hotels and always having a good time! I will always be grateful to Jay Manuel, who introduced me to Tyra and gave me the opportunity to work with a fierce Black woman entrepreneur and boss chick. Tyra is one of the most inspiring women I have ever met and worked with, and she displays so much respect for her craft.

• • •

I thought my break from TV would be a long one until music artist and actress Brandy lured me back not even two years later.

After all my drama about being bored and unchallenged on TV stages, it's crazy to believe I'd be doing it again so soon, right? Well, not really. You see, Brandy was a judge on the first season of the competition show *America's Got Talent,* so I figured I could handle the start of a seasonal show (just seven episodes) that was only going to be in production for a couple of months. Besides, I needed to earn those six hundred union hours so I could keep my union insurance going.

As it turned out, working on Brandy's show was totally different than doing Tyra's daily TV talk show. I have to admit I had fun! It felt like I was watching a concert all day. It's also where I first met Kim Kardashian, who was Brandy's personal stylist at the time—we would sit backstage together every day. Before I knew it, the show was over.

Since then, I've done a lot more TV work, including starring in my own show, a docuseries on Oprah Winfrey's OWN called *Love in the City*. It was an unscripted Black girl's version of HBO's *Sex and the City*, and focused on the fast-paced lives of four best friends living in New York and facing the challenges of love, dating, surrogacy, breast cancer, divorce, and separation while balancing love and career. Yep, we had a lot of stuff going on in our lives! Even though the series drew a lot of viewers and positive reactions, it was short-lived. But I had fun doing it, and of course, I did everyone's hair, so we all looked fabulous!

From left to right, that's Chenoa, Tiffany, Bershan, and me of course, having fun during one of our photoshoots for our TV series on OWN.

PHOTO BY KEITH MAJOR

My TV resume grew to include shows like *Black-ish* and other shows. And even as I write this book, I'm pitching new projects for TV that I would also produce.

So, does working in TV still appeal to you? Right now, there are a lot of opportunities for hairstylists and makeup professionals in TV and film. The need is even greater for those who know Black hair and skin.

Unless you've been living under a rock, I'm sure you've heard that people like Gabrielle Union, Taraji P. Henson, and a handful of other prominent Black talents are using their clout to push for diversity on union styling teams in TV and film. And in this era of Black Lives Matter, I'm already starting to see changes.

Breaking into TV and Film

If you're looking for ways to get experience so you can break into doing hair and makeup on TV and film productions, there are several ways to build your on-set credits, even if you don't live in a major city like Los Angeles, New York, or Atlanta:

- Style hair on independent and student films
- Style hair for local talent on newscasts
- Be an assistant on a larger project
- Network with others in the TV and film industry who may offer referrals
- Build your online Instagram page (portfolio)

If you're already working in LA or New York, networking is still your best bet to break into the TV and film worlds.

As a reminder, while I was winning Emmys and doing hair for Tyra Banks, I was still working in the salon and doing some freelance work with my other celebrity clients. So doing TV and film doesn't necessarily mean you have to give up your bread and butter behind the chair. If TV and film is what you want to do full-time, then cool! Either way you go, you'll find that it can be rewarding as well as fun.

One stream of income that, after a certain point, doesn't require as much of your daily time is launching your own product line.

RESOURCES

Want to join the Makeup Artists and Hair Stylists Union? Visit local706.org, then select "About" and "How to Join" for information on membership qualifications and how to apply.

My Emmys Acceptance Speech:

CHAPTER 14

Product Lines: From Selling to Launching Your Own

I WON'T put a product out
that I don't 100% *believe in.*
—Bobbi Brown, founder of Bobbi Brown Cosmetics

Doing hair or makeup or providing esthetician services may be your bread and butter, but selling products or, better yet, launching a product line is the icing on the cake if you want a profitable stream of income that leads to mass wealth. Look at Madam C.J. Walker, who became a millionaire with her hair-strengthening product line targeting Black consumers. Huda Kattan's lashes—the first product in her cosmetics line—are what helped the makeup artist and blogger create a billion-dollar beauty brand. There's also my idol and muse John Paul DeJoria, who used a $700 loan to help develop John Paul Mitchell Systems. He sold haircare products door-to-door by the day and slept in his car at night before growing his company's brand to a valuation that now hovers around $3 billion. Yes, *billion*!

For as long as I've been in this business, I've aspired to be the Paul Mitchell of textured haircare.

I'll never forget October 9, 2008. I was busy pumping and busting cuts and color from my stations at the Warren Tricomi Salon in Los Angeles when one of the other hairstylists spotted John Paul DeJoria walking into the Net-a-Porter boutique across the street from the salon.

Oh, my God! I thought. *I cannot let this moment pass; it'll never happen again! I have to go over there and say something.*

Working with celebrities, I don't usually get unhinged when I meet legends, but he's such a visionary businessman in the hair industry, I couldn't contain my excitement. I convinced myself to walk over as fast as I could to introduce myself to the self-made billionaire. I was thrilled to be face-to-face with him. I told him who I was, how I'd like to be a millionaire just like him one day, and how I wanted my company to be just like his. He was super friendly. He smiled at me as if he'd heard it all before from other hairstylists. But for me? I was serious!

It was a huge moment for me. After I left, I even ran back to the store to give him my business card!

A few years after that chance meeting with John Paul DeJoria, I bumped into him again at the NBC Upfronts, where the network was to announce plans for their new season of shows. When he walked into the room, I was like, *Wow, this can't be a coincidence.* I took it as a sign that it was finally time for me to launch my MuzeHair product line.

BIRTHING A PRODUCT LINE

The early knowledge I gained about developing a product line came from Kaz Amor, the owner of Warren Tricomi in Los Angeles, who I worked alongside for thirteen years. Kaz was a business owner but also knew a lot about product sales, marketing, customer service, and the global hair business, and his relationships were endless. I picked his brain almost every week about various products and how to use and sell them.

"What makes that hair have so much body?"

"What are the best products for volume?"

"Beyond hairspray, what other products give the best texture?"

Kaz patiently answered all my questions, and he also taught me about product sales and how they account for 40 percent of sales in the salon business. Forty percent!

Most Black salons don't sell products—no hairspray, no curl cream, no conditioners, no nothing! It's rare that clients can go to one and expect to buy the products used on them—not even travel-sized products for vacation. Any salon that isn't selling the products it uses on its customers is missing out on profits and client demands.

The more I learned about how much products contributed to making haircare a multi-billion-dollar global industry, the more it fueled my passion for building my own haircare brand and product line. I wanted to become the first African American woman to change how the textured haircare market is represented. I wanted to bring a premium haircare line and solutions to women of varying ethnicities and hair textures globally.

The first product I decided to roll out was a hairspray because it would be an easy start to test the market. Kaz was a big help in getting my hairspray into the marketplace, even introducing me to his friend Andrew Dale, who had developed a brand called Unite Hair. Andrew's professional brand, which offers shampoos, conditioners, and styling products, is highly successful today and sought after by top salons and high-profile clients. Kaz and Andrew's insights about product development and branding were invaluable. I invested $15,000 to do a private label hairspray at their suggestion rather than starting at ground zero.

I picked out a product from the lab based on what I liked and how I wanted it to perform. I knew I wanted something with a light, flexible, brushable hold so the hair wouldn't feel stiff and crunchy and could easily curl the next day. I was looking for something like Sebastian Hairspray—an old reliable favorite.

Once I found exactly what I wanted, I added my name to the label. That was that! I called it MuzeHair Last Look Hairspray because when women get their hair done, they might want to freshen it up, set their curls, and take that one last look before they conquer the day. I touted the holding spray as a product formulated to add a lightweight yet firm hold, minus the sticky buildup. It sets any style while protecting hair from humidity and maintaining plenty of movement! "Inspiration in a bottle!" became my tagline.

I spent a lot of time developing the product design, including all the renderings. I knew I wanted the packaging to look clean with white and turquoise blue accents, making whoever used it feel beautiful and special. So I used a color scheme inspired by what Tiffany & Co. uses because when a woman gets a box from Tiffany's, she feels super special. The bags, boxes, and all the other packaging had the same blue color. For my $15,000 investment, I got 2,500 tall and travel-sized pieces. The packaging was all turnkey, including labels. I got boxes and five hundred samples for a little extra money—some of these samples I sold, but most I gave away as a promotion.

Right away, I started using my Last Look Hairspray on all of my clients. I got major press in 2012 when I used the product on Jennifer Hudson to create a faux mohawk for her *American Idol* performance and Kerry Washington's mega shiny chic and simple chignon updo for the Emmy Awards.

MARKETING THE PRODUCT

Since I didn't have a large budget to promote my Last Look Hairspray, I relied on my years of experience doing editorial shoots and photography to handle the initial marketing myself.

Then I produced a photo shoot with models, going way more high-end than I should have for a first product. But I was used to working with the best, and the best gotta be paid! Not all of my models were pros, but I did a small casting on social media and found the prettiest women I could on a budget.

I insisted that all my models be diverse-looking enough to appeal to multiple markets. She couldn't be too dark or too light. She had to be a medium brown, which catered to my clients who had curly, kinky, textured, wavy hair. My first model was the seventeen-year-old daughter of a makeup artist I knew. Evidently, my eye for picking talent was spot on even back then because this newcomer went on to become an in-demand Victoria's Secret model.

I created a lot of print ads and even put myself in some of them as the pitchman, figuring that if self-branding was good enough for billionaire entrepreneurs like John Paul DeJoria and Oribe Canales, it was good enough for me!

My print ads were effective initially, but then around 2011, social media blew up and changed the marketing game. I went from just putting up pictures and ads to posting video shorts that promoted my product.

There were lots of hiccups along the way, and I didn't make a lot of money initially, but I have absolutely no regrets about launching my Last Look Hairspray. Having the line boosted my MuzeHair presence and added prestige to my brand. Plus, the advantages of designing the product *I* wanted the *way* I wanted for my clients definitely outweighed the headaches.

• • •

OK, now it's your turn. If you've ever wanted to create a product line—whether it's a hairspray, edge cream, aromatherapy face cream, oils, whatever—follow my Wright Steps to launch one that will give you a competitive edge.

THE FIRST *Wright* STEPS TO LAUNCH A PRODUCT LINE

- **Hone your vision.** I knew I wanted to launch a hairspray, and I knew the attributes I wanted it to have. You will have to think about how you want the product to react and perform.
- **Research the Marketplace.** After you decide what product you want to launch, check out the competition and the demand. You may not want to develop a specific product if the market is saturated with them and your clients are already satisfied with an effective brand. However, if your mind is set on coming out with that product, figure out what you can offer to make it more attractive. Perhaps it's a lot cheaper. Maybe it dries quicker. Maybe it's firmer. Figure it out before you commit.
- **Find a hair product supplier.** This is a turnkey process where one company oversees all aspects of a project's production from beginning to end. This approach can be affordable and less time-consuming than starting from scratch. The manufacturer

does all the leg work—creating the formula, testing, manufacturing, private labeling, shipping, packaging—and they'll do it to your specifications so you can customize your product and get it out to the market fast.

- **Create a budget.** The days of launching a product line for a $700 investment like John Paul DeJoria famously did are over. I invested $15,000 for my line of hairspray in 2011. Be prepared to invest anywhere from $2,500 to as much as $20,000 to get started, including the costs of your business license, packaging, insurance, advertising and promotion, and distribution.
- **Find a name.** Come up with a catchy or clever name that suits your product and is easy to remember. Just like when you named your business (see chapter four), do a domain search. Here's a common one on the Google platform: https://starter story.com/tools/google-domains. Register your product name and grab all the social media handles.
- **Decide on your design.** I knew I wanted the packaging for my Last Look Hairspray to have a luxury appearance inspired by Tiffany & Co. Sketch out your ideas to share with a graphic designer or directly with a supplier. Make your designs stand out from the competition.
- **Get the necessary licenses and insurances.** When you have a product line, you'll most definitely need a seller's permit, operating agreement, and likely a nondisclosure agreement to protect your "secrets" from your competition before you have time to get to market.
- **Identify your customer base.** Keep in mind that the customer who will buy your product may not necessarily be one of your loyal book clients. Identify who is most likely to need your product.
- **Set your pricing.** Just like when you set prices for your salon services, don't overprice or undersell your products. Check out what other stores are charging and why some charge more than others. Consider the costs to make the product competitive, the

cost of packaging including labeling and shipping the product, the cost of labor, the costs of photo shoots to market and promote the line, any shipping fees, and how much revenue you want to make before setting your price. Typically, you'll want to mark up three times what you've paid for an item or service.

- **Market your products.** Create a detailed plan covering how you will introduce your products to the marketplace and how you intend to promote your brand (refer back to chapter five and chapter ten for guidance on creating a niche marketing plan). Be sure to have a well-designed thought-out marketing budget and stick to it.

Let's say you're not ready or interested in launching a product line. Selling products in your salon is still a great way to create added income to your base revenues. Here are a few sales strategies to help you with that:

Wright **TIPS FOR SELLING PRODUCTS IN THE SALON**

- **Display products at the entrance.** Have products displayed in a prominent place where customers see them the moment they enter and there is an opportunity to buy and ask questions about them. The display should look professional and appealing. And please, keep them dusted! Nobody wants to purchase products that have cobwebs or look like they've been sitting on a shelf for years.
- **Display products in work areas.** Whether your client is at the shampoo bowl or your station, try only to use or show the products you are selling in the salon.

- **Pitch products during service.** Talk up the product you want to sell while you're using it on the client. Explain the benefits, then turn them to the mirror to show how you're using the product so they can use it at home.
- **Pitch products during checkout.** When your client makes a beeline to the door, you should walk with them toward wherever you have your products displayed. Show them what you've used and recommend what they can buy to use at home.

Remember, whether you're selling products from your own brand or products that you trust enough to sell in your salon, *all product sales* are profitable streams of income a beauty professional should not be without.

I was aggressive with marketing and selling my Last Look Hairspray for a couple of years until I switched focus to pursue what has become my real money-maker: *wigs*!

RESOURCES

Getting a Seller's Permit:

Seller's permits are issued by state. You can usually find the form by typing "obtaining a seller's permit [YOUR STATE]," then follow the instructions for filing. Depending on where you live, it can take at least five business days to receive the permit and the resale certificate by mail.

Check Out This Video:

This QR code links to the sixty-second commercial I created for my Last Look Hairspray that got a lot of attention after I blasted it all over Twitter and Facebook.

CHAPTER 15

Weaves to Wigs to Wealth—Taking Your Product Line to the Next Level

Don't find CUSTOMERS for your product.

Find *products* for your customers.

—Seth Godin, author and entrepreneur

My exclusive collection of MuzeHair wigs and extensions are by far one of my largest streams of income; it's been a moneymaker for my brand. Believe it or not, my vision for creating the line didn't come about because I am such a brilliant entrepreneurial visionary—even though I believe I am! But in this instance, my brand's success initially came mainly from me doing so many doggone weaves.

Back in 2014, weaves accounted for 25 percent of my income. Weaves had been popular for years, but when the Kardashians started wearing them, it's like they became a mass market. I believe they helped break down many of the biases that existed around weaves. So, finally, your boyfriend could accept it. Your close girlfriends who you tried to keep your weave a secret from could accept it. No more scrutiny!

At one time, I was doing an average of three weaves a day, and even though I pride myself on being a multitasker, in the time it took to put in a weave, take it down, color, and cut, I could've done at least three other clients. So, weaves were definitely affecting my bottom line.

Of course, weaves are still popular, but the trend for wearing them took a major shift once artists like Beyoncé came out and made it OK to admit to wearing *wigs and extensions*. J-Lo, Kim Kardashian and family, and Tyra soon followed, so the demand for lace front wigs crept up. These were nothing like those old-school granny wigs they used to buy from the beauty supply store. They were more evolved. I'm talking about wigs that became stylish hair accessories for stage or TV. They were so freakin' convenient and versatile that I even started wearing one—well, actually, several!

PHOTOS BY CHERYL FOX (TOP LEFT, TOP RIGHT, BOTTOM LEFT) AND TYREN REDD (BOTTOM RIGHT)

With my hectic schedule, the wigs gave me more freedom to experiment with color and style without compromising my natural hair's integrity. I would go from being a redhead with a mohawk one day to wearing a blonde bob the next—no need to wait for hair to grow. Before I knew it, wearing wigs became an effective marketing tactic that helped me sell them. Instant beauty! My clients would see me in my different wigs almost every day and say, "Oh my God, Kiyah! I love your hair!" It took a minute, but I finally got them around to saying, "I want one, too!"

I never had an official brick-and-mortar store for my wig sales. I used a local vendor at first. When my customers wanted a wig, I was like, "All right, let me order it!" I'd ask the next client, "You want one, too? Let me order it." I'd be ordering two, three, or four at a time. It worked! Before I knew it, my clients requested me to order wigs faster than I could get them.

At the time, my supplier was an entrepreneur sistah named Shira Jacobs, who owned Espy Hair Boutique in Beverly Hills. For years, she had been supplying me with most of the hair I used for my weaves. She also had the most beautiful high-quality wigs. Shira sourced her products from all over the world, including India, China, and sometimes the Philippines.

I bought as many as three or four wigs a month from Shira for my clients and me. And even though I was getting a 15 percent commission off of every sale and my celebrity clients were willing to pay her rates, I felt that her $1,500 to $2,500 price tags were a bit impractical for the everyday woman.

"Can't you find a wig that's cheaper?" I asked her.

"No," she said, "because it comes with too many complaints. Better quality means fewer complaints!"

Shira was a bit of a skeptic for sure, but she had found her rhythm, stuck with it, and was less concerned about sales than about selling low-end wigs.

"Sourcing lesser quality hair may look good out of the pack," she said, "but you won't know how well it performs until it's on somebody's head. I don't want to take that risk."

I understood her point because hair is an emotional purchase. Women have to see a wig, feel it, and be comfortable with it before they buy one. It has to be perfect. I was concerned about the quality, too, but I also knew there had to be a more tangible way to bring the cost closer to weave pricing.

I tried to talk Shira into maybe going into business together, but she wasn't budging. Meanwhile, my customers' requests for her wigs increased to as many as five or six a month. I hated that I always had to wait to get her inventory before I could promise them to my clients.

Just as I started looking at using other suppliers, the light bulb went on for me: *I need my own wig line!*

It worked out that by the time I was ready to pull the trigger on my wig line, Shira was moving toward getting out of the hair business. It was becoming too much of a hassle, and she wanted to devote more time to her family. So, I was off to the races! I got my prices down, my color down, and I launched my MuzeHair Collection of wigs, extensions, and bundles.

The whole process of creating a wig line proved to be a lot of work that stretched over a year and a half.

First, I researched various manufacturers and suppliers—many of which were based in Asia—trying to learn about what was driving the cost for buying these wigs and how I could get these vendors to understand our customers' needs. I wondered if they could make the wigs so our customers could keep the hairline natural or if they could make the wigs denser so we could sell more tangle-free quality hair.

I met with many of the vendors face-to-face to be sure I found one with the right vibe and integrity. Once I found my vendor, I had to order the hair, wait for it to come, then wear-test the wig to see how the hair would respond. It was risky, but hey, I had to figure out how to supply the demand with a quality product.

The first few rounds of wigs were too full of tangled, shedding hair, which was too hard to color, so I rejected them and refused to launch my line until I could find the right hair and vendor. Once everything aligned, I started my collection small with six different textures, which was hard to do. My strategy was that if a customer bought a kinky-haired, long, flowy wig in dark brown but decided to wear it in a short blonde bob, no problem! I would upsell the cut and color and customize their wig for the exact look they desired.

I liken this type of upselling to buying ice cream at Pinkberry. They may sell only three flavors, but they remix them five times, and you can add toppings to get even more variety. With my wig line, the "toppings" are the color, cut, style, and extra bundles for some thickness.

When I first launched my MuzeHair Collection, I priced the wigs from $700 to $1,300, which was a steal compared to Shira's wigs. Still, some people complained about the price.

I'd say, "Yeah, you can get a wig somewhere else for less, but I guarantee you they won't have the same quality, color, cut, and signature style of a Kiyah Wright Wig! Plus, I stand behind the quality of every one of my wigs."

In three years, I only had maybe three complaints. One time I had a client who complained that her wig tangled. I said, "Let me wear it." I washed it, sanitized it, cleaned it up, and then put it on to see how it performed. If it was going to tangle, it would've done so within two or three wears. I know it was a bit extreme, but I didn't mind taking the extra effort to make sure my customer was happy.

I've now tightened up the business even more by tracking down the best manufacturers and distributors of kinky, curly, and, yes, textured straight hair that serves my clients and my standards, and it's been well worth the effort.

THE BUSINESS OF SELLING YOUR PRODUCT

I had no idea what my "net profit" was supposed to be in the early stages of selling my wigs. Everything for me had always been trial and error. I do the work, then figure it out—which is not to say that's the right way to do business, but it was how I handled things, and I hadn't had a lot of error. But when it came down to calculating how much I was actually making on each wig after expenses, I had to learn to pay close attention to five key things:

1. What it cost to buy the wig from the vendor
2. The cost for the vendor to ship the wig to me
3. The cost of my high-end packaging, including labels in the wigs
4. The percentage of labor costs
5. The cost of photo shoots to market and promote the line

Even after considering all the amortized costs to package and promote my wig line, I profited a minimum of 100 percent on each wig sold. When I would upsell the cut, color, and extras, my profit margin jumped as high as 150 percent. If I calculated maintenance services, which may include shampooing, conditioning, and rebraiding the customer's hair, plus doing whatever else was necessary to maintain the look of their wig every two to three weeks, my profit margins jumped as high as 300 percent. Since then, especially considering COVID, the price increases and cost of manufacture have gotten even crazier.

Finding the Niche Audience for Your Product

Thankfully, business was profitable from the jump. But before I took my MuzeHair Wig Collection full blast, I seized the opportunity to expand my niche market.

Once so many of my celebrity clients like Ciara and Tyra—who were iconic for rocking natural-looking wigs in so many styles—started wearing my wigs, I would tell my everyday clients, "If you like the look I gave to Ciara, I can get that same look for you." Of course, who wouldn't want to look like Ciara?

Clients started buying wigs from me left and right—two, three, sometimes even four wigs at a time so they could change up their looks. That significant boost in sales led me to refocus the line and launch my celebrity wig collection to give the everyday woman that total Hollywood celebrity look—out-of-the-box instant beauty!

BRANDING AND PROMOTING YOUR PRODUCT OR BRAND

Early in my career, I was identified as a celebrity hairstylist, but branding my celebrity wig collection was at a whole other level. Sure, there were other celebrity wig lines out there, but I had A-list celebrities actually wearing my wigs, and I had the Hollywood accolades to give me the credit I needed.

My first marketing priority for the celebrity wig collection was to put together a mission statement (you can refer back to chapter ten for a refresh on creating a niche marketing mission statement) and come up with the best keywords for branding. My team and I brainstormed a lot before coming up with "Be the star that you are with red-carpet-ready hair!"

I spent a ton of money on print ads and videos to promote the line, then blasted them all over social media.

The messaging worked! When my posts went up, my wig sales went up. The key was to *post, post, post,* and business boomed! After three months, I took my marketing even further: more ads, more posts, more promos. By the end of the first year of dedicated marketing efforts, my wig line grossed six figures!

BE THE STAR THAT YOU ARE WITH RED-CARPET-READY HAIR!

A-List COLLECTION

LIMITED EDITION CELEBRITY-INSPIRED WIGS, DESIGNED BY *EMMY AWARD-WINNING* HAIRSTYLIST, KIYAH WRIGHT.

PURCHASE NOW

PHOTOGRAPHY BY TYREN REDD

Someone once told me, "You should always spend time on the thing that makes you the most money." That got me thinking. When I launched my wig line, I was in the salon 30 percent of the time, on the road 50 percent, and prepping and selling wigs only 20 percent, yet wigs were my most profitable stream of income. So I decided to put more focus on my wig line!

After making six figures selling wigs the first year, I set my goals to kill it again in year two, and I did: I was up 37 percent! By then, I had gotten my groove down. I had vendors who were reliable. My quality control was more solid. My schedule for orders was getting more consistent. I had a good rhythm going.

But by my third year, the market had changed. Young girls were now into wearing lace fronts every day and buying multiple wigs for multiple looks, which significantly increased demand and, in turn, the number of other wig companies out there. To survive the competition, I needed to pay attention to the market's needs and trends. I needed to find a niche within a niche.

FINDING A NICHE WITHIN A NICHE

It was 2018, and the hot thing in haircare was pastels! Since I was known for my color, it made perfect sense to introduce a "Pretty in Pastels" collection of wigs.

BLACK & WHITE IS BORING...
LET YOUR HAIR LIVE IN COLOR!

PRETTY IN

Pastels

COLLECTION

Wigs in limited edition shades & hues
that past any test with flying colors.

GET COLORFUL

PHOTOGRAPHY BY TYREN REDD

I introduced my new collection just in time for spring. It featured gorgeous shades of lavender, mint greens, and soft shades of pink. I was feeling excited about this new, more targeted venture for my wigs.

One thing was for sure: a new niche meant I needed a new niche marketing strategy and materials to promote a new product.

To appeal to that younger demographic obsessing over lace front wigs even further, I expanded my budget, got younger models, and targeted my messaging to that specific audience. With the cost of shooting, models, on-site assistants, meals for everybody, editing, photo retouches, and the venue for a day, early on, I was spending damn near $8,500 for the main shoot. But they were worth every dime. I paid the models either a flat fee or bartered, offering my wigs and services as currency.

The models were carefully selected, not just because of their looks, but because they were already fans of my work, my wig line, and more importantly, because they had big social followings. This "double up on marketing" strategy is critical because not only does it allow you to market your products and services, but it allows your models to sell, too.

PHOTOGRAPHY BY TYREN REDD

Here are my top tips for creating a niche-within-a-niche marketing strategy:

Wright TIPS FOR CREATING A NICHE-WITHIN-A NICHE MARKETING STRATEGY

- **Narrow your overall mission statement.** Unlike with creating a mission statement for your overall brand, home in on the specific demographic/customers you want to target, the product you want them to buy, and how you plan to reach them.
- **Use keywords in your messaging** that specifically target the clients you want to buy your products.
- **Utilize multi-platform marketing.** Invest in print ads, YouTube videos, social media—wherever your customers spend the most time.
- **POST. POST. POST.** Along with your consistent social media posts, hire models with big social media followings and have them spread the word about your product. Likewise, have any other team members promote the product.

• • •

Staying on top of the trends and my market needs helped me be taken seriously as an expert in the field and generate customer trust, which resulted in more sales, making MuzeHair Wigs one of my most profitable side-stream incomes.

Even if you never plan to go into the business of selling wigs, what I hope you'll take away from this chapter is how to find a niche within a niche to brand your product, services, or even yourself.

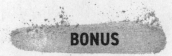

Check Out This Video That
Promotes My Pastel Wig Line:

Principle 5

Grow Your Platform to
Grow *Your Profits*

Marketing, Part 3: Platforms and Strategies to Boost Your Brand

Your *brand* is what other people SAY
about you when you're *not in the room*.
—Jeff Bezos, entrepreneur and founder of Amazon

Two marketing buzz words get tossed around a lot by entrepreneurs: brand and platform. They are notoriously overused, interchanged, and so often misunderstood.

When someone says, "My brand is blah, blah, blah," I ask them, "What does that mean to you?" Most of the time, they don't fully know. It just sounds good.

So, here's the deal: Your **brand** is your expertise and achievements as a beauty professional. Your **platform** is all the available resources you have to promote your brand. Your **brand strategy** is your plan for how to deliver the message of your brand over various platforms.

When people hear MuzeHair, they automatically think "Kiyah Wright," which is great because I own that brand. It encompasses my work as a celebrity hairstylist, my wig line, product line, ambassadorship, expertise in the beauty industry, online retail store, and affiliate programs. It's my **business brand**.

Kiyah Wright is my **personal brand** that reflects my achievements as an authority in the beauty industry. It's who I am. It's what I do!

One of the best tools available in our marketing toolbox to promote our brand is a **press kit**. These modern-day digital or print calling cards are perfect for letting media, agents, sponsors, buyers, funders, clients, and new customers know everything you want them to know about you and your brand.

The best part of having a press kit is that *you* control the narrative. Here are the elements that go into one and how to organize them.

CREATING YOUR PRESS KIT

When you create a press kit, you sell yourself and your brand, so do it up *right!* Make it look as professional as possible. Hire a designer if necessary. Make sure the overall look of your kit and your brand's marketing materials is consistent and complements any products or other branding you use, if possible. It's a work in progress, just like your brand, so it will require updating as you grow.

What goes into press kits can vary, but there are seven elements I've found that work best for beauty professionals:

- One-Page Bio
- Career Highlights
- Press and Features
- Social Reach
- Your Niche
- Your Brand
- Contact Info

One-Page Bio

This is a one-page capsule of who you are and what you've accomplished. It's where you let the reader see you and know how to find you. Resist cluttering this area with any other info.

Kiyah Wright is a TWO-Time, Emmy Award winning celebrity hairstylist whose genius has not only set the precedent for image making, but has redefined the appearance of sexy, successful and confident women around the world. As a highly sought after beauty and style trendsetter and recipient of a Hollywood Beauty Award and Golden Scissor Award, Kiyah draws much of her inspiration from her deep love of fashion when creating her signature hair designs and transforming the image of her clients. Kiyah's diverse clientele reflects her impeccable ability to reveal and effectively translate a woman's beauty, inside and out.

As a celebrity ambassador for Head & Shoulders and Clairol Professional, she continues to inspire with cutting edge developments. She has established her mark in the industry and has several groundbreaking achievements.

Her list of distinguished clients includes stars such as Halle Berry, Tyra Banks, Laverne Cox, Lala, Ciara, Jennifer Hudson, Taraji P. Henson, Kerry Washington, Halsey, Iggy Azalea, Mel B, Gabrielle Union and more.

Over the years, Kiyah's innovations have been featured on hit television shows like Pose, Power, Black-ish, The Late Late Show with James Corden, Celebrity Apprentice, Jimmy Kimmel, America's Next Top Model and America's Got Talent. In addition, Kiyah's creations have been prominently displayed in publications like Vanity Fair, GQ, Elle, InStyle, Essence, and Vogue. Alongside her remarkable work schedule, Kiyah still manages to remain loyal to her client base in Los Angeles at her Beverly Hills salon.

Kiyah has also launched her **Muze | Hair by Kiyah Wright** hair care collection which aims to address the unique needs of the ethnic and texture hair markets and bring awareness and knowledge to the proper care of "textured hair," whether it is curls or kinks.

Her **Muze | Hair by Kiyah Wright Collection** consists of Celebrity Wigs, Hair Extensions, Hot Tools and Hair Maintenance Products, all exclusively available online. (www.muzehair.com)

This bio should be quick, easy to read, pleasant to look at, and skimmable.

Career Highlights

You've worked hard. You have bragging rights to your achievements. Use this section to promote them, but limit your text. Instead of a lot of words, use a lot of photos. After all, we're in a creative industry. I know you must be taking pictures of your work. If not, get started because you'll need them in this era of digital marketing and social media.

I used lots of photos in my press kit to show my career highlights that spread over five pages. Since I'm a celebrity hairstylist, I included a page featuring all my celebrity clients' images, a page of my magazine covers, logos of the TV shows I've been a part of, and awards ceremonies I've worked on. I took bragging rights to a whole other level.

2x Daytime Emmy Award Winner
"Tyra Banks Show"

Hollywood Beauty Award
Sterforn Demmings
Hairstyling Award

EXCLUSIVE TO OWN: Oprah Winfrey Network has created a new original docu-series, **Love in the City**, about the fast-paced lives of four fabulous friends living in New York City.

Press and Features

If you've gotten press coverage in print, online, or on TV, it goes here. Include thumbnails to give a visual. This section doesn't have to include everything you've done, just the highlights.

Social Reach

In the age of social media, you must be able to show your engagement and following online. If your presence is lackluster, no worries; just make sure your work speaks for itself and is diverse. Later in this chapter, I'll offer tips on how to grow your platform to boost your profits. But for this area of your press kit, demonstrate that you have social media reach, including how many followers you have and which platforms are most prominent.

Highlight Your Niche

Devote a section of your press kit to your specialty, your niche. I'm a celebrity hairstylist but also an imagemaker, so I use this section to highlight my on-camera makeover series. A second page highlights my work as a brand ambassador for Clairol.

Contact Info

The final page of your press kit should provide your contact info, including your website. It's also not a bad idea to reiterate your social media reach.

. . .

With your press kit complete, you now have a great marketing tool to present to media ahead of interviews, submit for consideration as an expert guest or keynote speaker, submit to publishers, or refer to as a roadmap when speaking about your brand to potential customers.

I guarantee you'll be happy to have the kit as you begin to take advantage of the marketing platforms available to you.

MARKETING PLATFORMS

There are many marketing platforms you can use to promote your brand. You don't need to utilize all of them, but you do need to home in on the ones that will most effectively reach and speak to your target audience. I mostly use social media, online videos and tutorials, podcasts, TV, Clubhouse chats, classes and workshops that I teach, blogs, my work in magazines, and yeah, even this book. I cover all my bases.

Gone are the days when beauty influencers like makeup expert Michelle Phan can create an empire by relying on just one platform—although, I'll always be in awe of how she first blasted her brand on the scene through You-Tube, which propelled her to be able to launch EM Cosmetics, which is now a $500 million company. But in today's multi-platform universe, you need to consistently be on multiple platforms if you want to get noticed and amass crazy wealth. It's no different than having multiple streams of income. Here are five traditional and digital platforms I consistently utilize to build my brand:

- Online Videos and Tutorials
- Personal Appearances (hair shows, seminars, webinars, virtual tours)
- Interviews (radio, online, podcasts, chats)
- Blogs and Newsletters
- Social Media

Online Videos and Tutorials

When COVID-19 hit, I'll bet I cranked out more than fifty how-to videos so my clients and any other DIYers out there could learn how to maintain their looks while staying sheltered at home. I focused on everything from "How to Cut Layers and Bangs" to "Installing Wigs," "Styling Braids," and "Virtual Consultations on New Styles."

Doing these tutorial videos was nothing new to me. I had been producing and posting them long before everyone else jumped on the bandwagon. The idea for my first video came to me after years of doing endless amounts of weaves—sometimes three a day. My assistant, who I was mentoring, said to me, "You're so good at doing this and showing me what to do; you should teach weave classes." I was like, "Wow, I never thought about it." It made sense; weaves were a popular, classic option for most women, so the potential audience was significant.

Taking advantage of the trend, I got permission to use some Aveda locations to host a series of Weave and Extensions 101 classes I created for hairstylists called "Perfect Your Weave to Increase Your Income." I recorded videos of my classes to promote for the next classes. These pre-COVID classes offered veteran stylists a hands-on opportunity to learn 101-level styling from an expert and take their skills to the next level while increasing their profits, and they were the basis of a series of online videos I created.

For an $850 investment, my students got an instructional weave kit consisting of two packs of 14" virgin Indian hair (1B equivalent, six ounces total), a needle and thread, razors, a net, catered breakfast and lunch, and my hands-on twelve-hour intensive one-on-one boot camp where I taught them how to create flat, flawless weave extensions. I included a lot of technical training on the weaves themselves—like creating a strong foundation, braiding patterns, and different ways to install a weave—and I also talked about customer service, consultation, marketing, and how to upsell a weave with cut and color. For the first half hour, I gave my students a chance to ask me all kinds of questions. Each stylist had to bring a model. Most of the time, we helped them find one, which was easy to do because there was always someone living in the area who appreciated the incentives: a free weave and hair.

I held these boot camps all over the country with anywhere from fifteen to thirty students per class. Thirty students, in reality, meant sixty people when you counted the models. It was a lot of work for me because I had to make sure everyone got one-on-one attention and make sure everyone's weave was detailed, precise, and secure.

These classes translated well to online videos. Post-COVID, I have a whole YouTube channel devoted to my hair and beauty tutorials because online videos are increasingly one of the most effective platforms for me to reach clients, showcase my niche, market myself as an expert, and fulfill my mission, which is to help women look and feel beautiful. In an era when feature-length movies are being made with cell phones, it's too easy to take advantage of this low-cost marketing strategy and make videos that promote your skills and brand.

Maybe your videos are DIYs or possibly Q&As related to your niche. Whatever your topic, grab your high-def smartphone or camera and start filming.

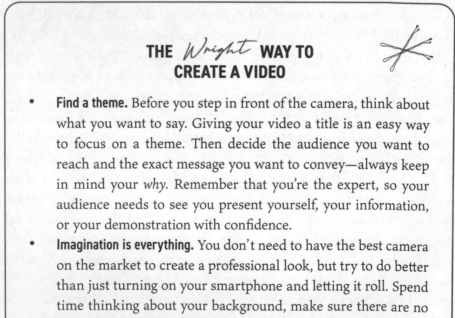

THE *Wright* WAY TO CREATE A VIDEO

- **Find a theme.** Before you step in front of the camera, think about what you want to say. Giving your video a title is an easy way to focus on a theme. Then decide the audience you want to reach and the exact message you want to convey—always keep in mind your *why*. Remember that you're the expert, so your audience needs to see you present yourself, your information, or your demonstration with confidence.
- **Imagination is everything.** You don't need to have the best camera on the market to create a professional look, but try to do better than just turning on your smartphone and letting it roll. Spend time thinking about your background, make sure there are no distractions in the frame (including sound), and use plenty of light. You can add your own sound later. Also make sure to

dress for the part. Dress the way you do when you want to be taken seriously. If you use your phone to record, turn it horizontally (the long way) in landscape mode, so it's in the proper aspect ratio for editing and playing on large screens. And make sure you're filming in HD or 4K, if possible.

- **Content is king.** It's good to be cute and personal as if you're in someone's home, but make sure to offer enough information and details to make your video hold up to its title and theme.

- **Keep it short but engaging.** When people watch videos online, they want to get in and out with the information they need. Make the message clear. Currently, the sweet spot is short (thirty seconds to one minute) and so straightforward that even a fifth grader could understand it. If the video drags on too long, edit it. Go into the recording session with talking points to keep it engaging, so you're focused on the message and won't stray. Rehearse before you start recording if you're uncomfortable being on camera. Remember, *you are the expert*!

- **Include a call to action.** End each video with a shout-out or graphic that leads the viewer back to your website or salon.

- **Optimize for YouTube posting.** Later in this chapter, we cover adding the best title, tags, and keywords to your posts—that goes for videos as well. Take it one step further and add descriptions about your video so they are easy to find and show up in search engines. The video's thumbnail should be something pleasing to look at, like a title graphic or another image that identifies what the video is about. Save all your videos and categorize them in one directory or, better yet, create your own channel. It's something you can monetize; after building one thousand followers and four hundred total channel views, you can get paid. And try to keep each video under three minutes because if we have short attention spans, you can expect that people who watch do, too.

Personal Appearances

Personal appearances are another valuable way to market your brand. Before everything got sidelined because of COVID-19, I was looking forward to speaking on panels and workshops at the Essence Festival, the National Association of Black Journalists Conference, and a bunch of other mainstream and Black beauty expos and events that I'd been invited to attend. It didn't matter if I was paid or not; these were marketing opportunities, and I wanted the exposure. Personal appearances are excellent platforms for us to network, showcase our talents, sell products and services to hundreds of potential customers and distributors, and get the attention of media professionals who can talk us up online, in print, on podcasts, and on every other kind of platform.

• • •

Participating in hair shows is another huge platform for us hairstylists. When I lived in DC in the nineties, hair shows were the hairstylist's holy grail for personal appearances. Back then, they were more like after parties—almost club-like—with a stage show in the middle of the floor that featured people sporting the hottest hairstyles. The template to stage the shows was pretty simple: the sexiest girls, excellent choreography, interesting theme, killer hairstyles, and good music. After being to so many of those hair shows, I got inspired enough to know I wanted in on one.

Barely twenty-two years old and just a few years into doing hair professionally, I started putting together full-out productions. I held auditions, choreographed weekly dance rehearsals, picked the music, bought all the outfits, and did damn near everything else to get ready for those shows. I was also really creative with the set design and lighting. I remember producing one show with an African tribal theme. I did about a half-dozen of them in total, and thank God, they were all pretty successful—with maybe a few exceptions.

Fast forward to today, hair shows are more like expos or conventions. There's Beautycon, International Beauty Expo, and TrendVision in Las Vegas that offer workshops, classes, competitions, and big mainstage performances. There are also festivals like Essence. What's great about all of them is that they attract tens of thousands of attendees who are your peers, potential customers, distributors, potential sponsors, and of course, the media.

If you can get yourself booked as a guest speaker or instructor at a Beauty Expo, go for it! You're sure to reach a broad demographic and are likely to make good money through product sales.

MY *Wright* TIPS FOR MAKING THE ROUNDS AT PUBLIC AND INDUSTRY BEAUTY EVENTS

- **Know your messaging and your value.** Be able to explain to organizers in one sentence why you need to be there as a speaker or host. Articulate the value you bring to their attendees. And be sure to show them your press kit!
- **Be prepared.** Whether you're at an event as an expert to demonstrate, teach a class, or lead a workshop, have a plan for your presence. Know your message. Know your audience. Prepare PowerPoint presentations and make sure the venue will be equipped to present them. Calculate your expenses because you'll probably have to come out of pocket to be there.
- **Ask for incentives.** Since you won't likely be paid for your participation, ask the organizers if you can have a complimentary table or booth to sell your product or just meet and greet people one-on-one.

Many of these events temporarily or permanently went virtual since COVID hit, but much of this advice still applies!

Interviews

I'll bet I've done hundreds of interviews on radio, online, podcasts, and in print. I never get tired of them because I get a chance to showcase my expertise every time I speak, which usually translates into reaching new customers.

If there's a podcast you like, a magazine you read religiously, or a beauty segment online or on TV that you love to watch, it's OK to contact the creators and let them know you'd like to share your expertise and insights on their platform. If you have the right chops, most organizers will welcome your offer. Be prepared to provide the following:

- **Bio or press kit.** Review your bio and press kit. Make sure they are up to date and highlight key issues that are relevant to your appearance. Also, provide a photo of yourself in advance of your arrival that can be used to promote your appearance online or on flyers. Don't leave it to the organizers to find a snap of you on the internet. Give them one of your choosing so you control your image.
- **Indicate the topics you'd like to cover.** Even if it means providing questions for the host to ask you, be sure to focus on the issues that are in your wheelhouse. And it's OK to let the interviewer know there are questions you don't want to cover. For instance, since many of my clients are celebrities, I clarify that I will not share private or personal information about them, so don't bother asking.
- **Provide contact information** for the host to share with listeners or readers who want to follow you online, on your website, or visit you at your salon.

Blogs and Newsletters

I love blogs because, unlike writing media articles for outside publications, I can share my message without fear of being edited. My blogs cover topics that offer everyday women solutions on everything from wig maintenance to managing their hair at home. If my catchy titles, like "Black Hair Don't Tell No Lies," don't draw their attention, my images do.

My team posts the blogs on my Muzehair.com website, where I include hashtag links to my social media accounts and relevant keywords so my blogs can pop up on all kinds of searches. You can also create a blog separate from your website by assigning it a domain name and address.

If you're hesitant about blogging because you're not sure what to write, check out these prompts to help get your juices flowing:

- What questions do your customers ask you the most?
- What topics can you speak about with confidence and little preparation?
- What topics related to our industry do you have a strong opinion about? Remember, writing a blog is not like posting on social media. Blogs generally offer useful information and resources, whereas a social media post might not be as lengthy, detailed, or informational.
- Use catchy titles.
- Write clear, easy-to-read content.
- Keep the writing catchy, informative, and brief.
- Offer help, not just ideas.
- Incorporate an eye-catching image.

The same advice applies to writing a newsletter, which is similar to a blog post but feeds out directly to your email subscribers. For either medium, if you run out of ideas, you can always invite a guest blogger to contribute on occasion.

Harness the Selling Power of Social Media

Like many people, when it first started, I used social media just for fun and to show off. I posted pictures of what was going on in my life with no real business focus. It was mainly fun stuff like, "Hey, look at me. Look at what I'm doing."

I was also never consistent with my posting because I was on the road a lot. When I did get around to posting a few times a month in my earlier days, we had to respect celebrity clients' privacy, so we never showed backstage images or footage. That was the unspoken rule until the mid-2000s. I had no idea what phrases like "Subscribe now" meant.

I didn't understand that real money could be made using social media until people started coming into the salon and asking for products I'd posted about online. They'd seen me all over Instagram using my Last Look Hairspray and saw videos of me using it on my celebrity clients.

The more I paid attention to the whole social media phenomenon and realized how it had an immediate effect on my sales, I doubled down on the number of posts I made in a single week.

By the time I launched my wig line in 2017, I had become more familiar with the market. I was hooked on using *all* of the social media platforms. It took a lot of hard work, but the benefits were huge!

If you put in the effort and planning behind your social media strategy, you're bound to see the rewards, too.

Steps for Creating a Social Media Brand Strategy

1. **Define your why.** What are your goals? Why is your audience here? Why do they care? What are your expectations for using social media for your brand? Is it to attract more customers? Sell more products? Brand yourself as an expert? Be very clear about what you want to accomplish, then give yourself a realistic timeline for achieving your goals. Maybe you want results to be ongoing. Perhaps you want to build up interest for your salon opening or anniversary celebration that's six months away. Identifying goals and setting expectations will help you stay on track with whatever goals you create and the platforms you use. Start with small steps. Collecting emails seems simple, but emails are your potential customers.

2. **Know your audience.** Before you know how to reach your audience, you need to define them. Are they upscale baby boomers, middle-class millennials, blue-collar housewives, influencers, actors, models, or savvy but starving students? Like we covered in chapter ten, make sure you know everything about the *ideal* customer you want to reach. Remember how, when I first started my wig line, I targeted upscale women who wanted that glam celebrity look, quality, and easy maintenance? When I discovered that the trend for lace front wigs was becoming popular with millennials, I refocused my brand, which meant my pricing had to change, and I had to speak to a new demographic.

3. **Choose your platform wisely.** There are over a dozen social media platforms in existence and counting. You have to know what they are before you can know which ones will work best for you. Here's a rundown of the most popular platforms at the time of this writing:

THE *Wright* MEDIA PLATFORMS FOR BEAUTY PROS

- **Instagram** is a powerful visual platform owned by Facebook. It is mainly used to share images and videos. This platform has proven to be my most profitable sales tool. It accounts for 30 percent of my wig sales, 15 percent of my salon sales, and currently, 2 percent of my minimal product line. If you want to be an influencer, you absolutely need to be here. You can expand your reach with hashtags, going live, and uploading lots of videos. I even use it to post inspirational quotes to inspire my followers.

- **Facebook.** Even though it's still the largest social media platform in the US, the site created for people to stay connected with family and friends is becoming less popular with young people. However, currently, more and more businesses are placing ads on Facebook. As a marketing tool, it's a good platform for you to make official announcements and promote discounts and offers. To reach that younger crowd, include hashtags, keywords, and other targeted messaging to redirect these potential clients to your other social media platforms. Once your page reaches twenty-five likes, you can claim your vanity URL, which looks like Facebook.com/YourBusinessName. This makes it easier for you to promote your Facebook page on your marketing material.

- **YouTube.** Now it's all about video, and YouTube is famously the second most popular search engine in the world. Your videos can be long-form or short, and you can even have your own channel where you organize your videos into themes. It's a perfect platform for showcasing your products and videos, especially DIYs and tutorials.

- **Twitter.** It's not as popular in my personal world, but stats show you *must* have a presence on Twitter because your competition will undoubtedly have one. It's a great platform to reach out to new customers and generate brand awareness. Potential sponsors look to the platform to scout for influencers and ambassador candidates to represent their products. The posts, also known as tweets, are, for now, limited to 280 characters. Most beauty pros use this platform to post updates or comment on hot issues. I like to use it to post reminders like, "Hey, I'm back in the salon!" As often as I can, I incorporate images to make my posts more engaging.

- **LinkedIn** is a business relationship–building platform that connects professionals, so be sure to create a business page on this platform. Think of it like a dating site where you can create a profile that lets you showcase who you are, your interests, expertise, milestones, etc. A big no-no here, though, is hard selling. In other words, don't post that you're looking for work or post an advertorial about your services. The advantage of using LinkedIn for what we do is to grow our email and marketing lists. You might also attract the interest of media types that are interested in using your services.

- **Pinterest** is used mainly by women and millennials, which is excellent for beauty pros. It's a platform that uses pictures instead of words to share anything from ideas to products. I like it for showing before and after looks or trendy hairstyles, even for presentations. It's also a perfect place to create your vision boards and collect your favorite items all in one location (see chapter one).

- **Snapchat** is a lot like Instagram in that it is used mainly for sharing between friends. Fashion stylists, designers, and younger generations also like Snapchat because it's suitable for tutorials. But be aware that the videos on this platform expire every twenty-four hours.

- **TikTok.** There's a lot of talk about how long this platform will be around, but as of this writing, it's primarily been used to post trendsetting, fun, and quirky short videos. The younger generation goes wild for this.

- **Quora** is an amazing platform to engage in relevant conversations and display your business expertise. Many people ask questions and queries on Quora, and by answering some of these queries, you build your reputation as a thought leader. Find new ideas to talk about, ask good questions, build your presence, and engage with your audience.

- **Clubhouse** is another conversation starter. It's a social networking audio chatroom that's a lot like a podcast and hosts anywhere from two to five thousand people per chat at the time of this writing. I took advantage of the platform to promote my brand by teaming with brand strategists to have talks about beauty, money, branding, and relationships. Any chance you get to have an entire platform dedicated to promoting your niche and brand, take it.

When you use multiple platforms as part of your overall social media strategy, be sure to select only the ones that make sense for you to achieve your selling goals. For instance, if your goal is to attract followers with DIY videos, Pinterest is not the platform for you, so cross it off your list unless you want to use it to post stunning before and after photos. Otherwise, you'll have a better chance of finding a broader audience on YouTube, Instagram, or even Facebook Live.

A big part of the early marketing strategies I used for my wig line involved Facebook to appeal to my mature, upscale customers. But once that wig-wearing trend shifted to a younger audience, I changed my focus to the platform they visited the most: Instagram. Once I hooked them on IG, I used links that directed them to where they could actually purchase my wigs on Instagram or Facebook.

Again, being on just one social media platform is not enough. So, here's what you should do to maximize your social media strategy:

- Commit to a consistent presence on at least two or three platforms
- Create a business page on each
- Create a social media brand strategy for each page you create. For instance, my social pages for Kiyah Wright and MuzeHair employ two different strategies.

Once you get it all set up, you'll need to figure out what's working. That's where online analytics come into play with business accounts.

Track and Measure Your Impact

Most social media platforms give you access to online analytics if you have a business account. These will help you gauge if your message is on point and if you're successfully attracting your target audience. Most social media platforms can show you who your visitors are and how many user clicks convert into sales. I still prefer Instagram over all the other platforms to track and measure sales for my wig line because their analytics allow me to not only highlight and sell my products, but also check out additional factors that affect my sales, like:

- How well the wigs are selling
- The number of people that visit my site with details about their age, gender, and where they live
- When to post
- Which hashtags are used most often
- Which photos received the most views
- Are people swiping more often than looking at still images?
- Do people prefer video or pictures?
- How and when do they shop?

The key here is to closely review your preferred platform's analytics to measure how close you've come to reaching your goals. The results may help you decide if you need to use different hashtags or keywords, post later in the day, or offer more discounts like your competitors.

> **KEY TIP:** When you're posting content, remember to place your keywords in the first paragraph of a post, in the subtitles, and of course, throughout your text so you appear at the top of online searches.

Be the Expert, Focus Your Content

Don't just post about your services or products. Share a little about who you are and why followers should trust your reviews and expert advice. If you're selling products, let your followers know why they should buy yours over the competition. Whether your focus is "I'm an expert at this" or "My product is the best," make sure the message you want to get out is relevant, clear, and one that the niche market you defined wants and needs to hear. Offer product and service reviews. Create videos. Comment on other posts or articles you find that are interesting and worth sharing. Post pictures or testimonials. Mix it up, but in terms of the content, *focus, focus, focus.*

When I wanted to focus on increasing my wig sales, I posted a series of do-it-yourself videos that covered everything from "How to Create a Natural Hairline with a Lace Front Wig Application" to "How to Cut the Lace, Wash the Wig, and Avoid Wear & Tear." I even created one on "How to Determine Your Perfect Wig Size." By focusing my content on wigs, traffic increased, and my sales grew exponentially—so much so that I had to add employees to help prepare, color, and sell the wigs to keep up with the demand.

And when you comment or respond to comments, remember they may last a whole lot longer than you intended, so watch what you write. Think about the long-term goal and remember that pictures and videos are forever. On your business page, heed the following advice:

- Consider before posting controversial content.
- Consider what you would hate for your mom, kids, or pastor to see.
- Consider before posting profanity, nudity, poor grammar, or colorful language.

When to Post

Believe it or not, there's a rhythm to posting, depending on who you're trying to reach. When I became the celebrity brand ambassador for P&G Brands, Head & Shoulders Royal Oils, and Pantene Gold Series Collection, I had to consider *when* to post and *why*. Do I post in the morning when people first pick up their phones? Is it better to post when they're getting their kids ready for school or getting themselves ready for work? Should I post during their commute to work and again at lunchtime? It took a lot of thought to post at strategic times. Now, almost all social media platforms have analytics that help you decipher the best times to post.

Come up with a schedule for posting that suits your goals of reaching your audience. People get annoyed if you post too much, especially if the subject matter isn't relevant to them. Be sure to consider diversity in your work as well. If you feature photos of people in your ads, look for a wide array of body, skin, and hair types. Reserve posts for the good stuff, like images that are well lit and show off your best work! And there's no need to post every day manually; you can schedule your posts for weeks in advance. Facebook provides a built-in tool to schedule posts. For prescheduling on other platforms, you can use free tools like Planoly, Buffer, TweetDeck, Calendly, CoSchedule, and Sprout Social, and I am sure more to come. This will ensure your social accounts feel alive and active without you putting in a lot of effort.

Check Out the Competition

Lastly, always keep one eye on your competition and how many views and likes they get. Their shortcomings present opportunities for you to fill a void or step up your game.

Effectively harnessing social media's power will not only generate customers and boost your sales, but it just may help you get noticed by corporations looking for brand ambassadors. I have had a lot of success this way. I'm living proof of how becoming a brand ambassador can bring you closer to your success and wealth goals and put you and your brand on a whole other level.

KEY TAKEAWAYS

A **press kit** is a perfect tool to sell yourself and your brand. Try platforms like Canva.com or even Fiverr.com to help you with the design. Use your press kit to:

* Tell people who you are
* Present your career highlights
* Highlight press coverage
* Show social reach
* Define your niche
* Showcase your brand
* Provide contact info

Marketing Platforms

When appropriately used, marketing platforms can grow your brand, reach consumers, and grow profits. Here's a summary of a few of the most effective strategies:

* Online Videos & Tutorials
  - Find a theme
  - Make content useful
  - Keep short but engaging (thirty seconds, one minute, five minutes)
  - Include a call to action
  - Optimize for YouTube posting
* Personal Appearances (hair shows, seminars, webinars)
  - Know your message and value
  - Be prepared
  - Ask for incentives
* Interviews (radio, online, podcasts, chats)
  - Provide a bio or press kit
  - Indicate the topics you'd like to cover
  - Provide contact info, including a professional photo of yourself

✳ Blogs and Newsletters
 - Focus on questions you're asked the most
 - Use catchy titles
 - Write clear, easy-to-read content
 - Keep your writing brief
 - Offer help, not just ideas
 - Incorporate eye-catching images

✳ Social Media Brand Strategies
 - Define your objective
 - What is your *why*?
 - Know your audience
 - Choose your platform wisely
 - Track and measure your impact
 - Be the expert, focus your content
 - Know when to post
 - Check out the competition

Check Out One of My Online Tutorials:

Remembering Your Why Even When Times Are Hard:

CHAPTER 17

Attracting Sponsors, Securing Sponsorships

I DON'T believe in endorsing a product
that you don't *want* to endorse.

—Taylor Swift

ompanies are always on the lookout for influencers they can collaborate with to help promote their brands. You can see these "brand ambassadors" all over Instagram endorsing everything from shampoo and hair growth treatments to magnetic lashes and Botox creams. A lot of times, all they do is say, "Hey, I love this product; you should, too!" or "Watch me use this product; it's great!" Some make five figures doing just that.

So, how do you land an ambassadorship?

Brand ambassador programs. Some companies offer brand ambassadorship opportunities to anyone who can meet their guidelines of posting. These opportunities usually include terms with specific objectives, including a certain number of posts, reels, or stories for PR usage. These are generally paid positions where you may be given free products and a monthly or weekly fee for your brand support. Or you may receive a check for the duration of the contract, which is typically anywhere from three to twelve months.

Open contests. Now and then, a company will host a contest to recruit special influencers. In early 2020 before the COVID-19 pandemic hit, Sally Beauty, the world's largest retailer of salon-quality hair color, hair-care, nails, and salon and beauty supplies, put out a nationwide call for influencers to become official "Sally Crew" ambassadors. Five winners would receive paid contracts of up to $150,000 each and professional business coaching, spokesperson opportunities with the brand, and access to exclusive products and brand events.

Employment and recruitment agencies advertise opportunities for beauty ambassadorships all the time that generally offer to pay per post for up to one year, which is how I ended up with P&G for so many years. Larger deals can start around $40,000 and go up to $100,000.

Social media. Another good way to get a beauty sponsor's attention is to hashtag a company to death. Force them to pay attention to you and whatever you're highlighting in your brand that complements their brand. Let them see that you have something to offer them.

So, yes, there are a few ways to nab a sponsorship if you have the passion, drive, and personality to influence thousands of followers. But here's the deal: if you're serious about building your brand, becoming an influencer, making *really good money* in the process, or you're focusing on getting an ambassadorship with a major brand, you need to stay up on keeping your brand very focused and the video and picture content for your page very consistent. Brands pay attention and can pay anywhere from hundreds to thousands depending on your following.

As far back as 2007, I knew I wanted to be a global brand ambassador for a major beauty company. I didn't want to make just a little money; I wanted it to become another significant stream of income.

Here's my journal entry from May 29, 2007:

I would love to be in bed with or have an association with a company like L'Oréal. I have a passion for a new big venture and becoming their spokesperson for ethnic haircare. I'm a millionaire in the heart, mind, and spirit.

It couldn't have been more than two months after memorializing my goal that I got a call from my agent. She had closed a deal for me to be a brand ambassador for one of the largest beauty, household, and skin care brands in the world: Procter & Gamble. P&G is the parent company of Clairol—the first, and still leading, hair coloring company in the US.

At first, when I got the news, I didn't believe it. "Now, let me get this right," I said to my agent. "The largest beauty brand in the country wants *me*?!" "Yes!" she responded, "they want *you*!"

Here's how I made it happen.

HOW I LANDED MY GLOBAL BRAND AMBASSADORSHIP

P&G had been searching for a new voice that was not only ethnic but also *ethical* to represent and spread positive messages about their Clairol Professional Color brand. Corporations usually look for clean images to be associated with their brands. That's why I keep stressing the importance of how you portray yourself online; in most cases, these corporations go on image. They go on looks. They go on who can speak to their consumers. They want their ambassadors to be **relatable**, **knowledgeable**, **confident**, **helpful**, and, most of all, **articulate**. On top of all of that, Clairol Professional could see by the nature of my social media posts that:

1. I was a serious professional.
2. Coloring was my niche.
3. I was an ethical influencer.
4. I was interesting.

In their words, "Kiyah is a charismatic visionary and trendsetter who established her mark in the industry and continues to inspire with cutting-edge developments and groundbreaking achievements." It was a huge honor to know that I mattered to a company whose name is synonymous with beautiful color and healthy-looking hair for millions of people.

By early 2008, it was officially announced that I was their ambassador and Clairol's Professional Celebrity Brand Colorist. Clairol explained that their expectations of me were to "be a supportive brand advocate, paying particular attention to the hair color needs of women and introducing new techniques, tips, and trends about their latest hair color products."

It wasn't a stretch at all for me to talk up Clairol's products because I had been using them since back in the day when their slogan was "Does she or doesn't she?" Remember that? They used to end their commercials by saying, "Only her hairdresser knows for sure." Obviously, they were referring to whether a woman colored her hair or not. It's still an iconic ad campaign to this day.

Back then, Clairol was the only company to have a do-it-yourself, at-home hair color kit that could lighten, tint, condition, and shampoo hair in one box. This was household color. I really did believe it was the best product out there for coloring because it was gentler on our hair, and it came in all the colors in the book.

It was so amazing to me that the company I had known since I was a kid and when I was just getting started in the hair industry was about to pay me a lot of money—$15,000 for that first year—to be their social media influencer, writing around ten posts over the course of the year promoting their iThrive line of maintenance products and professional color for all hair textures and tones. Wowzah!

Rather than just writing something up and, voilà, it's online, my posts needed to be approved by corporate before I could publish them. From my very first post, Clairol was beyond happy with my messages and the number of views I was getting. By year two of my partnership with the company, my agent had increased my compensation from $15,000 to $30,000!

The terms of the contract expanded that second year beyond online posts. Clairol launched an integrated campaign that ran across multiple platforms. Before I knew it, I was featured in national magazine ads, on TV, online, and in brochures at Sally Beauty.

My experience during that whole second year was a whirlwind. Besides doing editorial work for my product line, I had never focused on any other ad campaign. And for the first time, I was the one being photographed and in the spotlight. I have to admit that I loved every minute of it. Who wouldn't?

My partnership with P&G was going great—until it wasn't!

As Clairol Professional color expanded, they added more products to their line. Clairol introduced their anti-humidity hairspray, and they felt it was in direct competition with my Last Look Hairspray. So, they put a noncompete clause in my contract that prevented me from selling, promoting, or even displaying my product for the next three to four years of my contract's duration.

Damn! Really?

It was a huge blow—not that I was making a ton of money selling my Last Look Hairspray, but I was making plans to go all-in promoting my product. Instead, I got stuck with thousands of cans of the spray sitting in a storage unit for a while.

It was tough to swallow at first because I didn't want to give up on the product line I had nurtured. But once I considered how much P&G kept sweetening the pot to make up for me losing potential sales, I started to look at the brighter side. Over the term of the contract when I was promoting Clairol products, I was concurrently raising my profile, which helped my business as a celebrity hairstylist and my credibility as an expert. That's also when I began my on-camera transition to TV!

Just a few years into my contract, Clairol asked me to be a red carpet host on a live TV segment at the Billboard Music Awards with Jeannie Mai Jenkins from *The Real*. On one level, I was thrilled, but I was also nervous as hell about the idea. So, I started paying closer attention to ads on TV to see how the talent carried a show. It helped that I got media training early on. I thought back to when I was on the sidelines at various awards shows and premieres with my celebrity clients who were always getting direction from their producers and publicists:

"OK, make sure you say this."

"We need to get that list of questions first."

"Let's make sure we tie all this back to the brand."

Even though I had a fearless personality, I was always a little uncomfortable speaking in front of people, especially with a more intimate audience setting like hair shows or presentations. I knew I needed media training—some I got from P&G, and some I got on my own.

Media Training

I signed up for a weekend media training boot camp with Marki Costello in Los Angeles at the "Become a Host Academy." She taught me how to speak on camera and have confidence in myself. It was intimidating at first because my speaking style can be kind of random, so she worked on giving me structure with strategies and techniques, like making sure I brought the interviews back to the product and sharing relevant stories in my life that could be related to whoever I was interviewing or whatever I was talking about.

My on-camera debut at the Billboard Music Awards took place in Las Vegas. Clairol had bought a slot on the red carpet for the awards preshow. My main job was to interview the "Globe Girls" who presented the awards on stage.

My cohost, Jeannie Mai Jenkins, was a pro at being on camera, so she gave me some tips like, "Be yourself. Take a deep breath. You can do this." The whole bit. I was like, "Oh my God! Just guide me, Jeannie. Just guide me." That whole red carpet thing made me so nervous. Once we got going, I actually had a good time being on camera. In between the interviews and pitching Clairol's products, Jeannie and I would move to some video clips that were shot in my salon earlier in the week. The whole live segment happened in just seven minutes. It was over before I knew it.

My sponsor was so thrilled with my presentation, they wanted to renew my contract for a third year.

After several years into my contract, Clairol decided to lift my noncompete clause and allow me to go back to promoting my Last Look Hairspray product line. *Hallelujah!*

Four years into my contract, I got a bit more favor after asking Clairol, "Can you consider a budget for me to have more media support?" Given my innovative and marketing mindset, I decided to produce an online video series for them. They agreed to give me an extra $10,000 to cover the costs of shooting, producing, and editing a high-end six-part series of four- and five-minute hair coloring tutorials that I posted online.

Nearly a decade in, I'm still having a good run with P&G. When COVID hit, I was sure they'd end my contract. Like a lot of corporations, marketing is the first area they cut. And what were they doing with their ambassadors? But to my surprise, they not only gave me a sweet renewal deal, but they had me doing some really fun things, like virtual consultations with beauty blogger families. We did about six episodes on YouTube. This was a great pivot for me during a time when no one could really leave the house.

Brand Friendliness

I'm convinced that I was born to be a brand ambassador, but I can honestly say this income stream is not for everybody. Why? Because not everybody is brand-friendly!

Brand friendliness encompasses a lot of traits that sometimes mean being very shallow. I'm not trying to encourage superficial behavior, but sometimes you have to dress the part and look the part. Think about it: how can you expect to sell beauty and ask for a specific rate if you don't have beauty regimens in your own life or with your clientele? You're not convincing if you don't. Your clients notice, and so do corporate brands.

That's why **image** is at the top of my list if you want to become an ambassador for a major brand. Sponsors look at both you, the person, and the version of yourself you present online.

MY *Wright* TIPS FOR GETTING AN AMBASSADORSHIP DEAL

- **Brand Image.** Look the part and act the part twenty-four seven. Do your homework about the company you want to represent and make sure you have the same values they espouse. Family-friendly? Wholesome? Trendy? Hardcore (although I doubt you'll find many companies looking for this one)? It's OK to have some personality in your posts, but keep in mind that companies are looking for influencers who reflect their brand. Companies don't just look at your experience and expertise; they look at *you*.

- **Build followers.** Brands expect you to have mass appeal and bring your followers with you—not thousands, but tens of thousands—enough for you to call yourself an influencer. If you're not there yet, work on boosting your numbers. Write blogs and accept speaking engagements. As you build your brand, you'll grow your platform. Remember to *post, post, post*. So much about social media has changed, but the model for gaining an audience is still the same.
- **Sell yourself and your niche.** Show potential sponsors and all of your followers that you're an expert or at least qualified to offer advice that they can believe in.
- **Have online cred.** Your followers don't have to agree with everything you say, but they should respect your opinions about the products you endorse.
- **Post, blog, and write reviews.** You don't have to wait for a brand to pay you to talk up their product. Take the initiative to blog, post, and give honest reviews about it. The more comments and views you get, the more attention you'll get from the company behind the brand.
- **Believe in the product.** I feel it's always best to *only* get behind a brand you believe in. Brands want ambassadors who really believe in their products. When you use the products, your job is to use visuals to show how they work and how well they perform, which isn't going to work if you don't believe in what you're promoting.
- **Show passion.** Just using a product is not enough. You have to show passion for the products you want to represent. Share with your followers how long you have been using it. Why do

(*continued*)

you use it? Why would you recommend it? How is it the best over the competition? Write reviews. Believe in it and share that belief as passionately as you know how.

- **Embody the brand's mission and values.** Select companies that share your core beliefs. It may be women's empowerment, beauty inside and out, or Black Lives Matter. Make sure you believe what they believe because, at some point, they'll want you to voice it in your messaging.

CHECK OUT THESE VIDEOS

All of my friends who saw me live on TV hosting a segment for Clairol on the 2015 Billboard Music Awards red carpet told me later, "Girl, you were great!" I wouldn't say I was "great," but I guess I did show out just a little bit! Here's a clip from the show. You be the judge!

Scan the QR code to watch a video I filmed as part of my partnership with Clairol and iThrive.

Principle 6

Prepare **for the Unexpected**

Preparing for and Surviving Natural Disasters and Other Crises

By failing to *prepare,*

you are preparing to FAIL.

—Benjamin Franklin

March 17, 2020, started like any other day.

I woke up early feeling good mentally and physically, with my head on right. I had my business and life goals all laid out. This year would be all about rebranding and moving the needle forward in a dramatic way! On the way to work, I thanked God for blessing me with the resources to remodel my salon. I thanked Him for insight and clarity, not just in business but also in my health and wellness. Just thinking about what laid ahead as I was driving had me so excited, but that was about to change.

Reports about the COVID-19 virus' growing and deadly impact consumed the airwaves and social media, and then Governor Newsom ordered all California beauty professionals to close our doors "immediately and indefinitely."

I was like, *What? Are they serious?!*

There were 200, 250, 300 cases a day in Los Angeles alone at that time. Mayor Eric Garcetti posted on Instagram that "Angelenos are safer at home. All non-essential businesses are ordered to cease operations that require in-person attendance by workers at a workplace." By the time I arrived at my salon, I had received an email that said I had just twenty-four hours to move whatever belongings I wanted out.

My mind started spinning. *I don't believe this. I can't really work anymore?! I don't know what I would even need for later. How will I survive? Hair is all I know! What now?!*

By nightfall, the streets of Beverly Hills were deserted! Restaurants and all of the high-end boutiques that were ordinarily bustling had closed their doors. The few people I saw walking around wore masks. The city had completely shut down for real.

Inside MuzeHair, I packed all my things, shaking my head as I loaded the last piece of equipment into my car. Too devastated to do much else, I pulled out my phone and started recording a message to all my fellow hairstylists out there.

"This shit is real!" my post read.

On Instagram, I encouraged them to stay strong and prayed up.

"I'll pray for you. Pray for me," I said before I totally lost it.

The video got more than 24,000 views that night. Scan the QR code to check it out.

Within days, the pandemic grew worse, with as many as four hundred new cases in a single day in LA. Although I had multiple income streams, my monthly salary from just salon work shrank from over $10,000 to zero dollars overnight. With the salon sitting empty, that part of my income totally slipped under my feet.  My assistants still had to be paid or let go. The rent for my apartment had to be paid, and let's not even talk about the tons of money I had just sunk into the salon remodel.

That first week, I had no idea of my next move. I had survived challenging times before, but none felt like that. I eventually retreated to my go-to: God! I asked Him, "What's my next move?" Then I prayed and meditated.

The stillness helped me focus on coming out of the storm. Within a few days, my darkest moments morphed into a season of manifestation.

I'm a fixer, so I went into fix-it mode and applied for everything I could: Employment Development Department (EDD), Paycheck Protection Program (PPP), and Small Business Administration (SBA) loans, an LISC Small Business Relief Grant, you name it. And guess what? I got 'em all!

When my colleagues asked me, "Kiyah, how did you get all that aid?" I told them, "It's because I had my business and paperwork together, *pre*-COVID!" My books were in order. My credit was good. I paid myself a salary. I'd paid my taxes. I had a business plan for growth, and I had a good relationship with my banker. So when it came time to apply for loans, grants, and every other kind of aid I could get my hands on, I moved right through the system while everybody else was still trying to get a live person on the phone.

Getting all that financial aid and support was a huge blessing. Still, the biggest takeaway here is that disruptions and disasters—whether natural, humanmade, or plain unexpected—will always threaten an entrepreneur's survival. Like taxes and dying, you should assume you will have to deal with harsh dilemmas in the future at some point. So the best thing to do now is to prepare yourself before they happen.

Three factors determine the measure of a successful entrepreneur amid a storm: how you prepare for a crisis, your action plan *during* a crisis, and how you survive your new normal.

PREPARE FOR A CRISIS BEFORE IT HAPPENS

Like I said, your ability to handle a crisis depends on the legwork you've done beforehand. Here's my best advice for preparing for the unexpected.

Review your contracts. Booth, suite, and salon renters, this is for you. Make sure you understand your rights and obligations when it comes to the contracts you signed with your "landlords." Is there a clause in there that says your rent must still be paid even in the event of a natural disaster or other crisis? Can it be waived and added to the back end of the lease agreement for a period of time that the salon is closed? Are you protected under the landlord's liability policy? Don't wait for the next disaster to strike before you look into these important details. It's during the calm when you'll want to ask questions and get clarity. If there's something in your contract you don't like, change it.

Review your insurance policies. I'm sure you already know that no one will give you flood insurance during the threat of a Category 3 hurricane or earthquake protection right after a magnitude 4.1. That's just not happening. So make sure you have all the proper interruption coverages that protect you from losing everything during a natural disaster. Don't assume that just because you have hazard insurance, you're protected from floods or earthquakes. Most of the time, you have to add a rider or get a separate policy for those high-risk coverages. Refer back to chapter four for a list of the necessary insurances you should have when you operate as a beauty professional, then review your policies with your insurance broker and ask the most critical question, "What am I *not* covered for?"

But let's not forget about the most important part: our own personal coverage for our mental and physical health. Be sure to acquire an insurance that covers you in case of illness, emergencies, or damages. I personally have State Farm for my business and Northwestern Mutual for my personal.

Tally your inventory. If you have to file a claim with your insurance company for damages due to a disaster or even theft, you'll need to have a list of all of your business equipment that was affected. So be proactive and create an inventory of everything you own or lease, from hair dryers and reclining foot spas to computers and furniture. It's a good idea to take pictures of everything and keep a record of this inventory in a location where you can easily access it even if you can't get back into the salon.

Create a backup system. Not only should you be able to quickly put your hands on your insurance policies, lease agreements, inventories, and other contracts, you should also create a digital backup system for all of your customer and vendor information. Store this information somewhere offsite or in the cloud, Dropbox, Office 365, Google One, or any secure place you can access the information at a moment's notice.

Keep emergency funds. For years, I've made sure that a large chunk of what I earned went back into the salon. But after experiencing COVID-19, I now put aside a set amount of funds for emergency reserves just in case my loans run dry or I have to purchase supplies or equipment or relocate temporarily. Try to make a habit of putting away some amount into an emergency account each month. It doesn't have to be a lot. It just needs to be something tangible and regular. If you don't think you're disciplined enough to stick to a manual savings plan, set up auto deductions into your account. If you never see it, you may never miss it.

Another way to get emergency funding is to apply for a business line of credit or a business credit card with a generous limit *before* that plumbing goes out, *before* a recession, *before* you need it. It's a whole lot easier to get a line of credit before disaster strikes than while the rest of the world is trying to apply for the same thing.

Get a handle on your credit. The best way to guarantee you'll qualify for a loan or line of credit is to have a good credit score, which is a rating based on your payment history and ability to repay your debts on time. Check your credit score often to see where it stands (and refer back to chapter eight for a refresher on all things credit). This is important for independent contractors and solo practitioners because our personal credit scores are as important as our business credit scores, so make sure they are also as high as possible.

Personal credit scores range between 300 and 850, with 711 being the average. You'll want to keep your business credit score above 650.

Set up electronic online banking and payments. I like to go into banks to make my deposits and withdrawals and look my banker in the eye. But when planning for the unexpected, I had my banker and accountant set up electronic online banking, bill pay, and salary distribution options that I can access online if the banks are closed or I can't easily get to them.

Ask the tough "what if" questions. If you work with an accountant or financial planner, now is the time to ask the tough questions like, "Financially, how long can I survive if I have to shut down?" and "How do I pay my assistants if no money is coming in?" And in the event of a disaster that puts you out of your regular place of business, ask yourself, "Where can I relocate until it's safe to return to the salon?"

No matter how much you've prepared for a crisis, you simply can't prepare for everything. Here's how to weather a crisis as it's happening.

SUMMARY OF THE *Wright* WAYS TO PREPARE BEFORE DISASTER STRIKES

- **Review your contracts.** Can your rent be waived or deferred? Are you covered under your landlord's liability policy? If the answer is no, look into these concerns before disaster strikes.
- **Review your insurance policies.** Your hazard insurance may not cover you for all disasters. Make sure you understand your coverage and determine if you need an extra rider.
- **Tally your inventory.** It's easier to file claims when you have an up-to-date inventory list with photos.
- **Create a backup system.** Don't just back up your computers—which you should automatically do anyway—back up electronic *and* paper files of all your agreements, financials, and contracts.
- **Keep emergency funds.** Start a "just in case" fund you contribute to regularly and secure a line of credit that you tap into only for emergencies.
- **Get a good handle on your credit.** Manage your credit wisely so you are preapproved for credit increases and eligible for emergency loans.
- **Set up electronic banking and payments.** Make sure you can access your money electronically at any time and have a plan for how you will pay vendors and your team if you can't get to the bank or salon.
- **Ask tough "what if" questions.** Ask your accountant or financial planner about your "Survival Plan B" if your salon has to close and there's no money coming in.

WEATHERING THE STORM DURING A CRISIS

I can't say I had the foresight to ask all the tough questions before COVID-19 hit, but I sure as hell asked about a week after we were forced to shut down.

"Where do I go to get financial aid?"

My banker sent me an application, then *boom*. Just like that, I got approved. I didn't apply for a new small business loan, I already had one. But what I got under the COVID Pandemic Assistance Plan was relief from paying my existing loan for six months, including principal, interest, and any associated fees that I owed. That was a major blessing for me during a crisis. I was thankful! And keep in mind that if you pay yourself a salary as a freelance worker, you may be entitled to apply for unemployment if disaster strikes and you cannot work.

Along with government programs, several companies and beauty brands stepped up in the early days of the COVID-19 pandemic, offering relief grants to help stylists stay afloat. I also know of some salon owners who got creative and even had success with crowdfunding.

The bottom line is that you should do what you have to do to stay afloat in times of disaster and never be afraid to seek help.

Look into Loan Options

- Consult with your accounting or other finance teams for direction on what loan programs are out there that will work for you and your circumstances. If you don't have an accountant, do your homework. Depending on the nature of your need, check out these resources:
  — **FEMA** (Federal Emergency Management Agency):
    www.fema.gov/assistance
  — **EDD** (Employment Development Department) for the state of California:
    www.edd.ca.gov
  — **SBA** (Small Business Administration):
    https://disasterloanassistance.sba.gov/ela/s/
  — **US Chamber of Commerce:**
    https://www.uschamber.com
- Act fast. Apply early. Money allocated for most aid and relief loans is not unlimited.
- Keep your finances in good order and your credit in good standing so it's a no-brainer for you to qualify for aid.

Inform Creditors

If an emergency comes up where you have to close your doors for longer than a month, make sure you call your creditors and bank right away to let them know what happened. See if they will give you a break on your payments or even help you out by raising your credit limit or line of credit or even getting you a quick hard loan.

Focus on the Customers

Some cities are hit worse than average when natural disasters or pandemics strike. Focus on your location and what is going on, which affects you *and* your customers. Listen to business news, local news, and social media to see what your clients are saying about their jobs and how the crisis may affect them.

Your customers are the lifeblood of your business. It's natural to focus on staying afloat, but once you get a plan in place, you need to shift your focus to those who kept you going before the crisis. Here's how:

- **Communicate with clients.** Send out emails and newsletters to let your clients know how and when things are looking to return to normal.
- **Consider house calls.** If another crisis hits that prevents your customers from coming into the salon, offer to go to them if that's an option.
- **Create DIY (do-it-yourself) kits.** When COVID-19 hit, I focused on DIY and product recommendations along with instructions for how to use them so my clients could supplement their stay-at-home routines. If they needed me to walk them through usage, I was just a phone call away.
- **Offer virtual consultations.** For more complicated services, I posted DIY videos for individual wig buyers who could benefit from maintaining their wigs from home. It's OK to charge for this service.
- **Be creative.** You can offer live-chat services on your website to answer questions in real time from your customers, or you can schedule Facebook Live tutorials that also allow customers to ask questions in real time.

Think About Your Team

Thankfully, the resources I received from the government when COVID-19 hit allowed me to keep my team on board during the crisis. But if you have to furlough your employees or vendors, make sure you communicate with them regularly so they understand what's happening with the business, when and if they can come back to work, and what you expect the new normal might look like. This way, they can plan accordingly. Also, don't let your checkups and check-ins with your teams be only about business. Crises and natural disasters are challenging for everyone. So make sure they're safe, their loved ones are safe, and they are managing what could be emotionally and financially challenging.

Prioritize Cash Flow

Just because you have cash doesn't mean you have to spend it. In times of unexpected interruptions, you'll need every resource you have to get through it, which may mean redirecting some of your funds. Ask yourself, "Do I really need to order that case of champagne for my clients when the salon will be closed for two months for repairs?" Examine your expenses to see what you can get away with for less or, better yet, skip a month or two. Consider negotiating with your vendors to see if they'll defer payment and add expenses to the back end of the agreement.

Be Efficient During Downtime

If you find that you have time on your hands due to an unexpected dilemma, be productive while trying to make the most of a bad situation. As I said before, I used my downtime during COVID-19 to record DIY videos from my home, write this book, and plan for the future. Here are a few other tasks to take on that may be hard to find time to do when you're working:

- Level up your website
- Refresh your contact lists
- Brainstorm new marketing strategies
- Update your bio
- Take an online class or make time for another way to improve your technical expertise

One silver lining to every crisis is that they don't last forever, and sometimes we even come out of it better on the other side!

After the economic crisis in 2008 hit and more than 2.6 million people lost their jobs, the hair industry grew by 8 percent. I once read that hair salons continued to thrive during the Great Depression in the early- to mid-1930s, with women spending millions on haircare services.[10]

SUMMARY OF *Wright* TIPS FOR WEATHERING A STORM

- **Get emergency funding.** In addition to consulting with your banker, look into government aid through FEMA (https://www.fema.gov/assistance) and disaster funding assistance through the Small Business Administration (https://disaster loanassistance.sba.gov/ela/s/) and the US Chamber of Commerce (https://www.uschamber.com), among others.
- **Inform creditors.** Alert your creditors immediately about your situation to make payments. Request credit limit increases or deferred payments if necessary.
- **Provide frequent updates.** Keep your clients and team in the know about when it's safe to resume operations.
- **Consider house calls.** If it's safe and makes sense, go to your clients' locations until you're ready to resume services in the salon.
- **Create DIY kits.** Prepare DIY kits that your customers can use to get by until services resume.
- **Virtual consultations.** Create and post how-to videos for more complicated services that customers can do themselves but may need directions for.
- **Prioritize cash flow.** Cut out any perks or services that were line items in your budget but may not be practical or cost-efficient during a storm.
- **Make good use of downtime.** Use the downtime to organize, update your skills, plan ahead, and level up your website.

Of course, there are no guarantees that your business will spring back to what it was after you get out of a crisis, so don't overexpect. But give serious thought to when it *is* safe to go back to work. Will you be prepared?

SURVIVING AFTER A CRISIS WHEN IT'S NOT BUSINESS AS USUAL

Update Your Policies

Just like the airlines do after a nationwide crisis, it's an excellent practice to rethink policies like cancellation fees. You never want your clients to come to you sick, for instance, and some of them may not be able to guarantee that they'll be available at the time of their scheduled appointment. So, depending on the crisis, set up some new guidelines that let your customers know that they can cancel without penalty.

Update Your Services

You may not be able to get back to business 100 percent those first weeks after a crisis. In fact, after COVID reopenings, we were limited to 25 percent capacity all throughout 2021, so I am adjusting as well. Look at the circumstances and decide what makes sense in terms of the services you offer and when you offer them. Maybe you need to reduce your hours on some days for a short period, or perhaps it no longer makes sense to do weaves during the week because they take up too much time and prevent you from booking more basic services with more clients. If that's the case, try doing weaves on a Sunday and Monday when you're otherwise typically closed.

Be creative in your thinking and make changes as necessary, even if it's only for a short time.

Offer Discounts, Not Raised Prices

Offer discounts on services to reward your loyal customers who rode out the storm with you and are eager to get back. The deals will also likely attract new customers and increase your sales to make up for time lost. Of course, doing hair, nails, brows, facials, and other beauty services is a business, and you have to make ends meet, but do your best to avoid raising your prices. The disaster you got through may be even more challenging for your clients to overcome, so try to keep rates steady as long as you can to help them out.

Develop New Normal Safety Measures

In addition to following all the protocols set by your state's cosmetology board for opening safely, consider contactless and cashless payment offerings, online scheduling, cleaning between services, and drive-by services for customers to pick up products and for wig maintenance.

Take Advantage of Lower Costs to Advertise

A lot of independent and small businesses are hurting after a natural disaster, recession, or epidemic. Often, that results in a trend of lowered rates for advertising on local TV, radio, or online. This may be the break you need to get the word out about your brand at a discount.

SUMMARY OF THE *Wright* WAY TO PREPARE AFTER TRAGEDY STRIKES

- **Update your policies.** In times of disaster, your clients may need support, too. Consider relaxing your cancellation and payment policies.
- **Update your services.** As you ramp back up from a structural setback, natural or manmade disaster, or epidemic, consider offering limited services on limited days if that's what it takes to get back on track.
- **Offer discounts, not raised prices.** You may have lost money while the salon was closed, but your clients may have also taken a hit. Rather than raise prices, offer incentives to build goodwill and bring clients back.
- **Develop "new normal" safety measures.** Always check protocols for operation with your state cosmetology board before resuming business after a disaster.
- **Look for advertising savings.** When tragedy strikes, media rates tend to be more affordable. Take advantage of advertising your services, products, or brand.

We've all experienced some type of unexpected crisis that has affected us personally, professionally, and financially. I've lived through many, and I've survived them all.

Still, a lot of salons close because they have no survival plan. So, like Sean Puffy Combs famously said, "You gotta *stay* ready, so you don't have to *get* ready!" And in this case, that means preparing yourself for the unexpected.

While you're thinking about what to do ahead of the next big one, give even greater thought to growing your financial portfolio (see chapter nineteen) and preparing for retirement (see chapter twenty).

It's never too early to prepare for your future!

USEFUL RESOURCES

* **USA Unemployment Benefits:** https://www.usa.gov/unemployment
* **FEMA** (Federal Emergency Management Agency): www.fema.gov/assistance
* **SBA** (Small Business Administration): www.sba.gov/services/disasterassistance or https://www.sba.gov/funding-programs/loans
* **U.S. Chamber of Commerce:** https://www.uschamber.com
* **SBDC** (Small Business Development Centers): https://americassbdc.org
* **EDD** (Employment Development Department) for the state of California: www.edd.ca.gov

Principle 7

Prepare Your Future, *Today*

CHAPTER 19

Growth and Start-up Funding

An entrepreneur without *funding*
is a musician without an INSTRUMENT.

—Robert A. Rice, Jr., author

I firmly believe that every five or so years, we hairstylists, makeup artists, estheticians, beauty professionals, and salon owners need to not only redefine our creative niches and reinvent ourselves, but also upgrade our environments.

I'm constantly redecorating my home, making personal adjustments in my life, or refreshing my niche. I consider it an investment in myself and my craft. After having redecorated my salon before, during, and immediately after the COVID-19 pandemic, I welcomed my clients back with a new look and attitude, feeling refreshed!

We all need a little pick-me-up every now and then. However, when it comes to remodeling or upgrading your salon, many investors will tell you, "Do not use your own money!"

You've likely heard the horror stories swirling around about people who use their own money to start, purchase, upgrade, or expand their businesses, then wish they hadn't. They spend, spend, spend, and get everything they want the way they want it, but then end up with so much debt that it messes up their credit scores and purchasing power. Well, that was me once! All my cash was going back into my MuzeHair business—everything! This was when a colleague suggested that I apply for my first business loan.

GETTING A TRADITIONAL BUSINESS LOAN

At first, I was hesitant about getting a business loan. MuzeHair had been up and running for quite a while, and I was good at keeping my bills paid up, but, *oh my God!* My debt was sky-high. I didn't think I could even qualify for SBA (Small Business Administration) assistance. But when my wig vendor Shira decided she wanted to get out of the business, I knew I needed big money to transition my business.

I scrambled.

How can I get this money?

On a leap of faith, I applied for a hard money business loan.

Hard Money Business Loans

Hard money loans come from lenders who are individuals or companies, not banks. These loans make it easier for entrepreneurs to get unsecured capital, regardless of how bad our credit is. And what's great is that you can usually get the money in just a few days after applying.

I first applied in 2017 when there were a lot of companies out there offering hard money loans. I chose LendingTree, and—*bam*—just like that, I got the $45,000 I asked for to launch my MuzeHair extensions and wig business. I couldn't believe how easy it was to apply and then get the money in just a few days.

But by not having done my due diligence to figure out exactly how much money I needed to borrow, I blew through that $45,000 so fast, I could barely blink. That meant I had to go back and ask for another $15,000. Believe it or not, I got that too in just a few days! The extra money was enough to get me over the hump—it gave me the jump start I needed and totally paid off when I ultimately made major profits.

The hard money loan was precisely what I needed at that time and is always an excellent option for anyone who needs money fast but may not have the best credit rating.

I do have one caution, though. These types of loans utilize predatory lending practices with exorbitant interest rates—some greater than 30 percent—and quick repayment schedules, so if you get one, make sure you have the confidence that you can quickly pay it back. Thankfully, I was able to pay mine off in six months.

By the time I was ready to expand my MuzeHair Wigs line and remodel and rebrand my salon space, my profit and loss statements looked good and my credit was also in good standing. That put me in a better position to apply for a traditional small business loan that offered lower interest rates and a more reasonable payback schedule.

Small Business Loans

The SBA offers a variety of loans that are popular with salon owners:

- **SBA 7(a) Loans** can be used to buy new equipment, purchase supplies, and even pay employee salaries. You can get one to buy a salon or refinance existing debt. But it can never be used for personal expenses.
- **SBA Express Loans** can be approved much more quickly and are capped at $350,000.
- **SBA Microloans** are capped at $50,000 and don't usually have strict credit requirements that may keep you from getting other kinds of SBA loans.

The consulting team I hired before I even thought about applying for my SBA loan handled everything for my brand, including my website, marketing strategy advice, and social media. Plus, they helped me update my existing business plan with what I needed to apply for the loan. One of the two owners of the consultancy team even acted as CEO of my business for an hourly rate. With their help, I got my first traditional small business loan for $150,000, with the promise of getting more within a year.

I applied for an SBA 7(a) loan in 2018, got the money in 2019, but then things got tight, and the bank stopped lending. But not before I landed another loan for $110,000 in the nick of time! And here's the good news: when COVID-19 happened, because my loan fell under the SBA 7(a) category, my loan payments were forgiven for six months during the pandemic.

There used to be a time when you had to have a comprehensive business plan to be considered for a business loan. Today, if you're already up and running with your business, most lenders care more about your finances. If this is the case for you, you should still prepare what I call a "**mini-business plan**," a single document where you should include answers to the following:

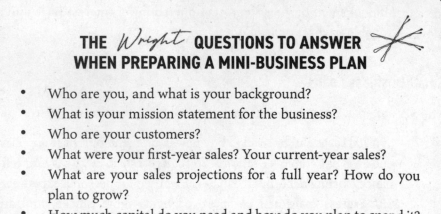

THE *Wright* QUESTIONS TO ANSWER
WHEN PREPARING A MINI-BUSINESS PLAN

- Who are you, and what is your background?
- What is your mission statement for the business?
- Who are your customers?
- What were your first-year sales? Your current-year sales?
- What are your sales projections for a full year? How do you plan to grow?
- How much capital do you need and how do you plan to spend it?

If you're just starting, have little credit experience, have never had a loan, and need a substantial amount of money from a bank, you'll need to create a **full-blown business plan**. In this instance, I recommend getting expert advice, particularly with the required financial information.

Although what's required for full-blown business plans can differ based on the lender and other variables, there are certain things you can expect to be asked to provide.

Creating a Full-Blown Business Plan

The requirements for a full-blown business plan for traditional bank loans are fairly comprehensive and can vary based on several variables.

THE *Wright* COMPONENTS OF A FULL-BLOWN BUSINESS PLAN

- **Background and team.** Include your location, website, the services you provide, and all the people involved with the business, including their qualifications and experience.
- **Mission statement.** What is your service or product? Who are you selling to? How do your services benefit your customers? What makes your service unique? What are your objectives—short term, medium term, and long term?
- **The market.** Who is your target market? Where is your target market based? Why do they want your services or product?
- **Competitor info.** Who is your competition? How do the services, products, and price points you offer differ from your competition?
- **Marketing plan.** Include an outline of your marketing and advertising ideas and strategies.
- **Current funding.** What capital do you currently have available? Who are your suppliers, and what are their terms?
- **Financials.** For new businesses, what are your start-up costs, running costs, and projected income for a full year? For existing companies, provide a monthly cash flow, bank statements for the last three months, annual financial statements, and any outstanding debts.
- **Press kit (optional).** You can also include a digital presentation that promotes you and your business, including clients, credits, photos of your work, and industry affiliations.

The Small Business Administration offers a free business plan template online at: https://www.sba.gov/tools/business-plan/1.

ADDITIONAL FINANCE ROUTES FOR START-UPS

If you're just getting started and *don't* have financial statements or a track record for being in business, there are other options to get start-up funds:

- Crowdfunding
- Seed money from friends or family
- Private investors

Continue reading for my best tips on securing each of these kinds of funding.

Crowdfunding

I recently read about a woman from Cleveland Heights, Ohio, who wanted to create her dream salon but didn't have the money. So, she asked a handful of her loyal customers to make a $500 to $1,200 investment in her dream. In return, they would get services equal to their investment, plus a little something more, to make it all worthwhile. It took her no time to raise the $20,000 she needed, which she paired with a supplemental loan from the SBA, then voilà! She opened her dream salon. I love her thinking! It's crowdfunding without blasting your business over social media.

If you decide to look into more traditional crowdfunding methods like Kickstarter or Indiegogo, make sure the agency you use does the following:

- Specializes in crowdfunding full-time
- Will partner with you
- Manages your expectations and is transparent about their role

Seed Money from Friends or Family

A lot of entrepreneurs get their start-up money from family or friends. Hey, if you got it like that, great! Most "angels" back *you* more so than your business because they believe in you and may not necessarily expect a return. But don't take their generosity for granted by asking for more than you need.

And don't even think about spending your business loan on personal stuff. Think hard about how much is enough. Be totally transparent up front. Make sure everybody understands the expectations about the money, and get absolutely everything in writing.

Private Investors

Private investors who lend expecting to get some kind of return on their investment also tend to want to invest in you, the entrepreneur, more than your business. So, you'll have to tout your experience and work ethic and convince them that you can run and succeed in your business if given the resources. Once assured that you are worth the investment, they'll want to know things like, "What customers do you already have, and how do you plan to attract more? Who are your target customers? Where are you operating now in your home? Where do you want to operate eventually?"

• • •

You'll find many examples of how to write a business plan online. I recommend that you review them, as well as what I've provided here, as guides. And importantly, trust your judgment and be as transparent as possible.

While this chapter's primary focus is on how to start, grow, or sustain your business, it's never too early to start thinking about retirement!

RESOURCES

The Small Business Administration offers a free online business template at https://www.sba.gov/tools/business -plan/1.

To inquire about SBA 7(a), Express, and Microloans, visit https://www.sba.gov/funding-programs/loans.

Press Kit

Including a press kit with your business plan is by no means a requirement, but it can't hurt! Scan the QR code to have a look at my most recent press kit.

CHAPTER 20

Planning for Retirement

*Asking for **financial advice** from a financial planner*
*is like asking a barber if you **NEED A HAIRCUT**.*
—Warren Buffett, billionaire business tycoon and investor

My mother worked hard all her life but died at age thirty-eight with no savings, retirement, or insurance. Our family barely had enough money to bury her. What's crazy, though, is that she had hit the lottery and won $4,000 a week before she passed.

I'll never forget that day. It was the Friday before Christmas back in 1989. After picking up her winnings, she took my brother Chance and me Christmas shopping. We must've gone to a dozen stores where we scored big with all kinds of gifts like toys and Sergio Valente and Guess jeans, which were a big deal back then.

On the ride home, my mom was unusually quiet. At one point, she turned to me and said, "I just want you to know that if anything happens, be sure you take care of your brother."

Huh? I thought. *Where is this coming from?*

Then she said, "And remember always to hold your head up high." She had totally lost me with that one. I was fourteen freakin' years old. We continued the drive home in silence but not before I noticed for the first time that she had an orange plastic hospital band around her arm. But again, I knew not to ask.

A day or so later, I was in the basement of our home that we shared with my grandmother and aunts when I heard a commotion upstairs. I ran up as fast as I could to see what was going on. As I reached the end of the hall that led to the living room, I heard my mom scream, then a big thump.

Seconds later, I was standing over my mother's limp body stretched lifeless against the mantel on the cold floor, watching her chest expanding and contracting. Her eyes never opened.

"Call 911!" my grandmother yelled.

My aunt called out my mom's name, but she wouldn't respond. Instead, she gave one massive heave, then let out a slow exhale. I stood there, numb. Before I knew it, we were all at Holy Cross Hospital. My mother was lying in bed on a respirator with tubes coming out of her. A doctor explained that she had had a brain aneurysm. He couldn't tell us right then what might have caused it.

I flashed back to when I was riding in the car and noticed that bright-colored orange band around my mom's arm.

Maybe she had been in the hospital before and we didn't know it.

Did she know something like this would happen?

Is that why she was talking so crazy in the car?

The next day, before going to the hospital, one of my aunts said to me, "Tell your momma you love her 'cause you never know."

Never know what? What the hell are you talking about?

I had no understanding of the concept that I might never see my mother again, but she transitioned from this earth on December 28, two years shy of her fortieth birthday.

Everybody knew my mom wanted to be cremated. She used to say so many times, "I don't want no worms crawling all over me in the ground!" And yet, for lack of funds, they buried her in a DC cemetery. No tombstone. No memorial.

In retrospect, I can understand why my mom didn't have life insurance. Back then, a lot of Black folks didn't; they were barely saving. What little they did save was hidden away in their houses instead of in banks. They didn't trust banks and wanted to be able to get to their money when they needed it.

My grandmother, who died shortly after my mom, faced a similar situation. After working hard for twenty years at the same job, she had no life insurance, benefits, or retirement fund. I guess you could say the apple didn't fall far from the tree.

Despite what happened with my mother and grandmother, it took me until I got into my mid- to late thirties before I started seriously thinking about life insurance and retirement.

The first thing I did was find Ms. J., an excellent certified financial planner who helped me focus on my goals and objectives and create a roadmap to get there. Until I met her, I never realized how little I knew about life insurance, investing, IRAs, savings accounts—all of that. Thank God I have a good handle on it now. So let me help you by first breaking down the basics.

LIFE INSURANCE 101

When you buy a policy, you are the **insured**. Every month or year, you make a payment on the policy, which is called a **premium**. The amount of the premium is based on the coverage you decide you want. When you die, the policy pays out a lump sum of money called the **death benefit** to whoever you designate to be your **beneficiary**. It's that simple!

Some life insurance policies have a face value and a cash value; these are two different numbers. The **face value** is the dollar amount your beneficiaries will receive after you die. The **cash value** is the amount you would receive if you surrendered the policy early because you needed the cash.

Not all policies are created equal. There are three different kinds, each with their own advantages and disadvantages:

- Term Life Insurance
- Whole Life Insurance
- Universal Life Insurance

Term Life Insurance

Many people think that when someone dies, their debts die with them and their loved ones are not responsible for those debts. *Wrong!* Even if you're single and have no children but you have more than $10K in credit card debt, some creditors (depending on probate laws where you live) can sue your estate to recoup those funds from your next of kin or whoever is handling your affairs.

A term life insurance plan doesn't benefit you while you're alive, but it can wipe out your debts, cover your burial, and even replace income that's missing from your household, like monies you may have wanted to go toward an education fund for your kids. When you get a term life insurance plan, you pay premiums every month or year for a term of usually ten, twenty, or even thirty years. Your death benefit typically never changes during that term. Once the term ends, you can continue paying on the insurance, but the rates are guaranteed to skyrocket! After you die, the benefits are paid in one lump sum to your beneficiaries.

Think of term life insurance like renting a house where you pay rent for as long as you live there. With term life insurance, you pay a premium for the term of the policy.

Whole Life Insurance

While term life insurance is like *renting* a house, whole life insurance is like *buying* a house that you don't own until you've made all your mortgage payments. Still, you can borrow against it to take out an equity line of credit on your insurance policy if you decide to make upgrades or just need some extra cash.

Whole life insurance is more long term than short term. It gives you coverage for a lifetime that pays out when you die. The best benefit, though, is that your cash value accumulates with every payment on an annual basis, oftentimes depending on when you established the policy.

Here are a few tips when looking for the right policy:

- Ensure the company is owned by their policyholders, not by a shareholder—in other words, a "mutual company." That way, the company's profits come back to you, the insured, and that's what helps the policies grow so strongly. You get guaranteed growth plus dividends, if they're issued.

- Look for companies that have a high death benefit payout rate. How do you know? Do your research for the companies that have the highest financial strength from the credit agencies. This will help build your confidence in knowing that the company will keep their end of the contract and pay your beneficiaries as intended.

• • •

Premium payments for whole life insurance policies are higher than with term life insurance plans and are usually fixed at one price. The tax advantages of this are outlined by the IRS. Visit IRS.gov and type in "IRC Code 7701 and 7702."

Universal Life Insurance

Universal life insurance policies also give you coverage for your lifetime, but you can increase or lower your payments as needed. These policies are more attractive for people who can live off their wealth rather than their income because the second you stop funding the policy, the cost of insurance that's baked inside goes up because you're not putting in enough money. And every year you get older, the cost of the insurance goes up. So if you start taking money out early, you may find that you have no more cash value by the time you reach sixty or seventy. Worse yet, you may be in jeopardy of losing your policy altogether.

Doubling Up on Insurance Coverage

You can totally do a "blend" and have both whole and term life insurance, which covers all of your bases for the long and short term. If you're not sure if one policy is enough, Ms. J. advises that some coverage is better than no coverage at all. But be sure what you have is adequate to protect your family. For instance, if you're a single mom with three kids and you can only afford one policy, then you should probably get the term life insurance to protect your entire family. After that, you can decide how much more you may want and how much you're willing to pay per month or year for the insurance.

Life Insurance Payments

The price for all life insurance policies depends on your age and health. I liken the payment options to those offered by car insurance companies who let you pay monthly but give you a discount if you pay for a full term.

Whichever way you choose to make your payments, *do not pay from your business account*. Otherwise, you'll lose the tax benefits that the IRS will otherwise give you for having these policies. So make sure you pay your premiums from your personal bank accounts. If you pay yourself a salary, include enough to cover your premiums so you get the deductions.

I like that you never have to pay income tax on life insurance—not when you're dead and not when you're alive. It's the IRS' way of thanking you for contributing to a better society.

SUMMARY OF THE *Wright* LIFE INSURANCE OPTIONS FOR BEAUTY PROS

- **Term Life Insurance.** Think of term life insurance like renting a house where you pay rent for as long as you live there. With term life insurance, you pay a premium for the term of the policy—every month or year for the term. Once the term ends in ten, twenty, or even thirty years, your payments also end. If your policy "matures" because you died, it can wipe out your debts, cover your burial, and replace the lost income from your household.

- **Whole Life Insurance.** Think of whole life insurance like *buying* a house that you don't own until you've made all your mortgage payments. Like an equity line of credit in your home, you can borrow against it if you decide to make upgrades or just need some extra cash. Plus you get coverage for a lifetime that pays out when you die.

- **Universal Life Insurance.** Universal life insurance policies also give you coverage for your lifetime, but you can increase or lower your payments as needed.

If you're unsure which plan works best for you, seek advice from an insurance broker or financial planner. And while you're at it, it's a good idea to start looking into your retirement options like 401(k)s and other investments.

Oh yeah, one other great advantage of life insurance is that it's a deductible business expense when it is a paid expense/benefit for an employee (not the owner) and the business/owner is not a policy beneficiary.

401(K)S AND OTHER INVESTMENTS

It doesn't matter if you think you'll work forever because, at some point, you owe it to yourself to take a break. Hopefully, you've got some multiple streams of income that will work for you long after you step away from behind the chair. Or maybe you have a product line that lets you make money while you sleep. Even though I like to think I got it like that, Ms. J. insisted that I still needed to make financial plans for my retirement. Of course, there's always the stock market to consider, but it can be risky because it offers no guarantees—it's up one day and down another.

Depending on how you structured your business—as an LLC, C Corp, or S Corp—you have several options available to you, including an **SEP-IRA**, **Solo 401(k)**, and a **SIMPLE IRA**.

Solo 401(k), SEP-IRA, and SIMPLE IRAs

Many people think 401(k)s are only for people who work for corporations that offer them as perks to their employees and sometimes even match their contributions. This is not entirely accurate. For most of us beauty pros who work independently—running our own business—we can still get the benefits of a traditional 401(k) through what's called a **Solo 401(k)** (for sole proprietors only, not employees) or an **SEP-IRA** (Simplified Employee Pension), which, like a 401(k) that employers offer, allows us to put in as much as $58,000 per year, according to 2021 tax rules. Another option is a **SIMPLE IRA** plan (Savings Incentive Match Plan for Employees) that, as of 2021, allows a maximum annual contribution of $13,500.

These retirement accounts are pretax, meaning the tax will need to be paid when you hit age fifty-nine-and-a-half and now have access to that money. So, like with a traditional 401(k), you can defer up to $58,000

($19,500 for employees only) a year depending on your income without being penalized by the IRS.

As business owners, we have the enormous advantage of contributing an additional $38,500 compared to what the average employee can contribute.

If you do happen to work as an employee where the owner offers a 401(k), take it. It's a great way to save for your future, especially if they also contribute. Here's how it works: You decide how much you want to contribute to your 401(k) every month. Your employer can match your contribution up to an employer-designated percentage of your annual income. So, let's say you make $100K a year, and you commit to putting in $500 month ($6,000 a year). If your employer agrees to match your contribution to the max of 4 percent (which equals $4,000), you will have saved $10,000 toward retirement that year with taxes deferred, unless you touch it before you turn sixty (or fifty-nine-and-a-half, to be exact).

A RECAP OF THE *Wright* PENSION PLAN OPTIONS FOR BEAUTY PROS

Each of these retirement plans gives us beauty professionals many of the benefits of traditional 401(k)s.

- **SOLO 401(k)** is designed for any sole proprietors—no employees. As of 2021, we're allowed to put in as much as $58,000 per year.
- **SEP-IRA (Simplified Employee Pension).** This plan also allows us to put in as much as $58,000 per year, but it is not limited to sole proprietors. Your employees can also contribute.
- **SIMPLE IRA (Savings Incentive Match Plan for Employees).** This plan is for employers who have fewer than one hundred employees, including self-employed, sole proprietors. As of 2021, this plan allows a maximum annual contribution of $13,500.

If you're a salon owner and want to offer 401(k), SEP-IRA, or even SIMPLE IRA options to your employees, you should ask your financial advisor (more on this below) to walk you through the steps to get a plan set up.

Once you commit to taking the plunge with a 401(k), do your best to avoid taking a 401(k) loan before age 55. If you must, then understand that the IRS will penalize you 10 percent in addition to the income tax you'll pay on the loan. Pay it back as soon as you can. But start as quickly as possible, so by the time you're ready to retire, you have a pretty good nest egg.

In addition to a dedicated retirement plan, it's also important to have a dedicated savings account.

SAVINGS PLANS

Of course, having a savings account is one of the easiest ways to start planning for your retirement, as well as the not-so-distant future. They're pretty easy to open, but if you've never had one, here are some tips to start you on the right track:

- Check out Google or Bankrate.com to search for banks and other financial institutions that offer savings accounts. Most big banks give you a 0.01 percent interest rate, which is not great. Those rates are tied to the Federal Reserve, so whenever Fed interest rates drop, so do the bank rates. Look for high-yield saving accounts.
- Make regular deposits based on a percentage of your income that feels most comfortable for you. Maybe it's 10 percent of your earnings. Whatever the number, stick to it.
- Take the control out of your hands. Have the money go into your savings account automatically through direct deposit. If you give yourself a paycheck every week, every two weeks, or every month, have that 10 percent come out automatically, then *boom*. You're done.

You don't need a financial planner or advisor to open a savings account, but if you want more bang for your buck and you're serious about planning for your retirement, I highly recommend you look into getting one.

FINANCIAL PLANNERS & ADVISORS

A financial planner will help you create a plan to meet your long-term financial goals. A financial advisor is a broader term for someone who helps manage your money, including investments and other accounts.

These professionals will clearly explain options that will allow you to make the best-informed decisions about your money and future. Here's what to look for when you're seeking a financial planner or advisor to join your team:

- **References/Credit Rating.** Check out all of the references for that company, including how they are rated from a credit standpoint. I would never sign anything with a company that does not have a AAA rating. That's key! If they don't have a good credit rating, they are not managing their money well. If they can't manage *their* money well, they can't manage *your* money well, which means they may not be around ten or fifteen years from now. So then what happens to your investment account? You'll be relying on SIPC insurance.
- **Certifications.** Although a financial planner or advisor doesn't need to be certified, it can be the icing on the cake. Certified financial planners (CFPs) are held to the highest code of ethics in the financial planning industry. To find one in your area, visit www.cfp.net.
- **Fees.** Certified financial planners are compensated by fee-based arrangements, which can average $5,000 for a twelve-month engagement. So this may not be the best way to go if you're just starting in the industry. Another option would be a financial planner or advisor who charges based on solutions rather than a flat fee.

ESTATE PLANNING

I totally get that no one likes to talk about death or retirement when building or growing a business, but I urge you to use my mom and grandmother as cautionary tales. Plan now so all of your hard work today will take care of you and your family for the rest of your lives—and beyond.

My last piece of advice comes from having experienced how my mom died without enough money to give her a proper burial and meet her intentions. **Meet with an estate planner.** Don't leave people guessing about what to do and how to do it after you're gone. Do the right thing and leave instructions behind for how you'd like your estate handled after your death, especially if you're single and don't have children.

Lastly, if you own property, I highly recommend having a living trust. Unlike a will, a living trust passes property outside of probate court. There are no court or attorney fees after the trust is established. Your property can be passed immediately and directly to your named beneficiaries without the additional expenses and time required by a probate court. Currently, even cryptocurrency is another form of investment to be considered, but be careful to keep your eye on it and learn all you can.

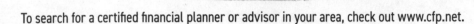

RESOURCES

To search for a certified financial planner or advisor in your area, check out www.cfp.net.

To search for **accredited estate planners in your area**, check out:

* **National Association of Estate Planners & Council:** naepc.org
* **American Academy of Estate Planning Attorneys:** visit aaepa.com and browse through the member directory

For more information about **retirement plans for small businesses,** including SEP, SIMPLE, and qualified plans, check out:

* IRS Retirement Plans for Small Business Guide
  https://www.irs.gov/pub/irs-pdf/p560.pdf

CHAPTER 21

A Positive Mindset Breeds Opportunity

Every problem is a *gift*;
without **PROBLEMS**, we would not *grow*.

—Anthony Robbins, self-help motivational speaker

If you've gotten this far, I trust that you care about your brand as a hair-stylist or other beauty professional. You care about your business, future, and responsibility as an entrepreneur. I've done my best to equip you with the information and encouragement you need to *pay attention to your money*! Now it's your turn to make it all happen.

My last piece of advice is to stay optimistic! Never give up on your dreams. Set goals for yourself, and until you reach that pinnacle of success you're striving for, continue to believe that you *will* make it. Start each day on a positive note and remember to take the time to celebrate your successes and *again*, pay attention to your finances.

The goal is to stay ahead of entrepreneurial burnout by taking care of yourself physically, mentally, and emotionally. Pray, meditate, read affirmations—whatever it takes to find peace and keep your sanity. And for God's sake—you cannot be on your feet forever!

There will come a point when the constant hustle starts to get to you, or you may get bored with the way things in your professional life are going. Remember that you're not alone. Trust me—other beauty professionals have likely experienced the same feelings. If you set yourself up along the journey in all the practical ways you can—finding your niche and market and sticking to it, staying active during slow seasons, and always thinking about your future—you can afford to make the shift you need to make in order to keep growing and maintaining a positive outlook.

Don't forget: the beauty industry can be extremely lucrative, but you can spend money as fast as you make it. This industry is growing fast, and in order to succeed you have to keep your eyes on what's relevant and in some cases, what's trendsetting.

I've been able to achieve success in the beauty industry by following the advice I've laid out in this book. I've maintained my edge by becoming a brand authority, staying relevant and keeping my portfolio diverse, and always staying focused in an industry that is constantly changing. I have watched this industry change three times over during the course of my career. Above all, I know I wouldn't have achieved so much without having the right mindset.

Scan the QR code for some of my final thoughts about my journey and how I hope it can help you.

I hope this book has inspired you to work toward the career of your dreams, and given you the tools to actually get there. I see great things in your future, and now you've got everything you need to reach for the stars. You've got a network of fellow beauty pros, including myself, cheering you on. Now get to work!

ACKNOWLEDGMENTS

I want to thank God for all my life circumstances that led me to what I thought looked and felt like hardships, but ultimately turned into lessons. I thank Shirley Neal for being patient, organized, and for writing out my story so well first, then translating each story into a lesson I could share with you. This took time and Shirley nailed it.

To my agents and advocates, Regina Brooks and Ameerah Holliday.

I also want to thank Kaz Amor for being such a good mentor along the way. I moved to LA and really wanted to take my career up a level and the way you were there for me, trusting me in your salon at all types of hours, and where I was able to bring my clientele which at the time was fully all brown women, helped me do that, and elevate my personal brand. Thank you for welcoming me to the Warren Tricomi brand in LA for thirteen years and making it comfortable for all of us . . . what an experience.

I thank James for really being there for me as my friend and investing in MuzeHair very early on, trusting that I knew what I was doing, as I was learning along the way. A true friend you have been for sure.

I am so grateful to Dr. Stacia Pierce for being loyal and supporting me as an artist and for always driving me to believe in myself and my brand, to GO BIGGER and really BELIEVE, and to keep diversifying my money.

Thanks to Meriden Weems for being the best assistant, for moving up to operating the brand daily, really maintaining and staying with me along this journey, and being a believer as well.

I also have to thank my sister who is always consistent with being loving, a great listener, and most of all, patient. She has been really special along my personal journey—thanks a bunch! Thanks for remembering the best moments of MY LIFE as well as your own—LOL.

I also want to thank Jasmine Ali, who started MuzeHair with me from conception, for being a good friend and hanging in there while we learned together—thank you for such patience and love. friend.

Thanks to the team here at BenBella Books, including Glenn Yeffeth, Adrienne Lang, Sarah Avinger, Alicia Kania, Jessika Rieck, Rachel Phares, and Lindsey Sageser, as well as Lyric Dodson. Rachel, you have been so patient and great to work with this whole way; I really appreciate you for your "getting it done" spirit and keeping me on point. I love it!

APPENDIX: ADDITIONAL RESOURCES

TAX FORMS

Form 1040-ES
Estimated Tax for Individuals

Form 1099-NEC
Non-Employee Compensation

Form 940
Employer's Annual Federal Unemployment
(FUTA) Tax Return

Form 941
Employer's Quarterly Federal Tax Return

Form W-2
Wage and Tax Statement

Form W-4
Employee's Withholding Certificate

Form W-9
Request for Taxpayer Identification Number and
Certification

Form 4070
Employee's Report of Tips to Employer

Form 1099-K
Payment Card and Third-Party Network
Transactions

Form 6765
Credit for Increasing Research Activities

OTHER RESOURCES

EIN
Application for Employer Identification Number

SBDC (Small Business Development Centers)

PCR (Pacific Coast Regional)
Small Business Development Center (local office
for California residents)
jduncan@pcrsbdc.org

EDD (Employment Development Department)
for the state of California

SBA (Small Business Administration)
Small business resources including loans and other assistance, business plan templates, and more.

Consumer Financial Protection Bureau
U.S. government agency designed to help protect and educate consumers and supervise banks and other financial institutions.

Upwork
Resources for tax services, business developers, project managers, and more.

LegalZoom
Website that offers legal documents and solutions for small businesses.

Hankin Patent Law

If you're looking for a trademark attorney, this is a great resource.

Northwestern Mutual

Company that offers consultation on financial services, from wealth management and business consultation to retirement and estate planning. I also use them for my personal insurance.

State Farm

There are a ton of reputable insurance companies out there, but I use State Farm for my business.

QuickBooks

Accounting software well suited for small and medium-sized businesses.

GoDaddy

Resource for registering a website domain name.

Wix

Resource for creating a website.

WordPress

Resource for creating a website.

Squarespace

Resource for creating and hosting a website.

Mailchimp

Marketing resource for managing email lists and sending email newsletters.

Shopify

Resource for setting up an online store.

Fiverr
Resource for finding and hiring freelancers (web designers, social media help, video/animation professionals, setting up your online store, and more).

Canva
Design resource to help edit or create your own ads, blogs, flyers, social media posts, presentations, business cards, and more.

Local 706
The official labor union for make-up artists and hairstylists working in film, TV, stage, and digital media.

Check out some of these top agencies for representation:
Celestine Agency, Forward Agency, Cloutier Agency, Wall Group Agency, Creative Artists Agency, Ken Barboza, Opus Agency, Exclusive Artists Agency

INSPIRATION

Watch this video to learn more about how I stay motivated, my vision for this book, and what I hope you've gained from it.

Check out this video for my thoughts on the Boss Woman mindset.

Take a look at some fun behind-the-scenes footage from my photo shoot for this book!

NOTES

1. Stylewatch. 2008. "Oprah's Obama Inauguration Dress Plan: It's All About the 'Vision Boards.'" *PEOPLE.com.* November 04. people.com/style/oprahs-obama -inauguration-dress-plan-its-all-about-the-vision-boards/.
2. Shinn, Florence Scovel. 1989. *The Wisdom of Florence Scovel Shinn: Four Complete Books.* Simon & Schuster.
3. Empact. 2016. "Bill Gates, Warren Buffett, and Oprah Winfrey All Use the 5-HOUR Rule." *Inc.com.* July 22. www.inc.com/empact/bill-gates-warren-buffett-and-oprah -all-use-the-5-hour-rule.html.
4. Sorvino, Chloe. 2017. "Why the $445 Billion Beauty Industry Is a Gold Mine for SELF-MADE Women." *Forbes.com.* May 24. https://www.forbes.com/sites/chloe sorvino/2017/05/18/self-made-women-wealth-beauty-gold-mine/?sh=6450cf282a3a.
5. Abraham, Joe. 2011. *Entrepreneurial DNA: The Breakthrough Discovery That Aligns Your Business to Your Unique Strengths.* McGraw-Hill.
6. SBDCNet. 2020. "Beauty Salon Business." *SBDCnet.* June 23. https://www.sbdcnet .org/small-business-research-reports/beauty-salon/.
7. Ibid.
8. Henderson, Gary. n.d. "How Much Time Does the Average Person Spend on Social Media?" *digitalmarketing.org.* www.digitalmarketing.org/blog/how-much-time-does -the-average-person-spend-on-social-media.
9. W3Techs. n.d. "Usage Statistics and Market Share of WordPress." *W3Techs.com.* https://w3techs.com/technologies/details/cm-wordpress.
10. Sherrow, Victoria. 2021. *Encyclopedia of Hair: A Cultural History.* Greenwood Press.

INDEX

A

accountants, 78, 86–88, 90, 101, 105
advertising, 62, 68–69, 75–76, 103,
    119–120, 181–182, 246
affirmations, use of, 13, 16–17, 19, 271
American Idol (TV show), 180
America's Next Top Model (TV show), 167,
    169, 173–174
Amor, Kaz, 42, 133, 178–179
appointments, 43, 84, 150, 245
apps, 84, 106–108
Ash, Mary Kay, 21
assistants, 26, 28, 74, 77–88, 101, 105
Associated Hair Professionals, 48
automobiles, tax deductions, 101–102

B

Babyface, 133
backup systems, 238, 240
Bad Boys II (movie), 156–157, 165
Bad Boys Records, 81, 90, 120, 132–133,
    154, 166
Baker, Anita, 2, 131, 172
bank accounts, 53–54, 59, 103, 121–124,
    237, 239, 267
Banks, Tyra, 11, 130, 158–159, 165–170,
    172–174, 176, 188, 192
Bassett, Angela, 10–11, 165
Bay, Michael, 157
beauty industry, 21, 27–28, 68, 89–90, 272
Behar, Joy, 170
Berry, Halle, 131
Beyoncé, 188
Bezos, Jeff, 199
Biggie Smalls, 154
Billboard Music Awards, 228–229, 232

Bing, 65, 69, 75
Black Lives Matter, 175, 232
Black-ish (TV show), 175
Blige, Mary J., 154–157
blogs, 69, 120, 206, 212–213, 222, 231
bookkeepers, 78, 86–88, 90
booth rental, 28–34, 36, 42, 44, 49, 91, 95, 237
brand, 51–53, 62, 179–182, 184–185, 187,
    192–193, 199–208, 214–218, 221–222.
    See also niche
brand ambassadors, 134, 139, 147–148,
    200, 204–205, 216, 220, 223–232
Brandy, 174
Branson, Richard, 85
Broadnax, Theresa, 170, 172
Brown, Bobbi, 177
Bruckheimer, Jerry, 157
budgets, 43, 62, 70, 75, 87, 118, 158,
    180–181, 183–184, 244
Buffett, Warren, 18, 259
bundling services, 149–150, 152
burnout, 271–272
business basics for start-ups
    banking. *See* bank accounts
    checklist, 59
    compensation, 58. *See also* income
    EIN (Employer Identification Number),
        48, 53, 59–60, 92–93, 110, 121
    elements of, 47–48
    equipment, 55, 105, 123
    insurance. *See* insurance
    licenses. *See* licenses
    name of business, 51–53, 63
    permits. *See* permits
    pricing, 56–58
    resources, 59–60

business disruption, 241–247. *See also*
    COVID-19; crisis, preparing for
business mindset, 22
business models, 26–44, 141
business name, 51–53, 63
business plans, 36, 254–257

C

Canales, Oribe, 181
cancellation policies, 245–246
Carol's Daughter, 21
cash flow, 116–120, 243–244
celebrity clients, 83, 154–157, 161, 164. *See*
    also individual celebrities
cell phones, 101
Certificate of Occupancy, 49
charitable contributions, 105
Ciara, 11, 159, 192
Clairol Professional, 134, 159, 204–205,
    225–226, 228–229, 232. *See also*
    Procter & Gamble (P&G)
clients
    cancellation policies, 245–246
    celebrities, 83, 154–157, 164
    customer relationships, 62, 69–76
    customer service, 72–74, 76
    discounts, 245–246
    engaging with during business
        disruption, 242, 244
    and long absences, 120
    loyalty, 72–73, 120, 142, 165
    niche market, 138–139, 142. *See also* niche
    as problem-solver for, 141
    retention, 72–76
    stealing of by assistants, 81
    testimonials, 65
Clubhouse, 217
collaboration with other beauty
    professionals, 141, 159, 162
Combs, Sean ("Diddy," "Puffy"), 21,
    132–133, 154–156, 159, 169, 247
commission business model, 26–30,
    33–34, 162
communication skills, 23, 73, 225
competitors, 18, 37, 39, 56, 68, 135,
    137–143, 182–183, 218–220, 255
complaints, 73, 76, 189, 191
confidence, 11–12, 22, 30, 81, 225
Confucius, 25
content management system (CMS), 64
contests, 70–72, 76, 224
Costello, Marki, 229
COVID-19, 34, 44, 54, 207, 211, 230,
    235–237, 241, 245, 254. *See also*
    business disruption

Cox, Laverne, 159
Craigslist, 82
credit bureaus, 121–122
credit cards, 54, 59, 107, 121–124
credit score, 121–122, 239, 241, 253
creditors, 242, 244, 262
crisis, preparing for, 236–240, 247
crowdfunding, 241, 256
cryptocurrency, 269
Cuban, Mark, 18, 129
customer service, 72–74, 76

D

Dale, Andrew, 179
DBA (doing business as), 51–52, 59
debt, 122–123. *See also* loans
DeGeneres, Ellen, 13
DeJoria, John Paul, 21, 177–178, 181
Dior, David, 27, 131
disability insurance, 49–50, 59
Disney, Walt, 14
DIY (do-it-yourself) kits and videos,
    242–244. *See also* online videos and
    tutorials
DNA, entrepreneurial, 22–24
domain name, 63, 75, 183, 212
domain searches, 52, 59, 63, 183
Dr. Dre, 154
Dr. Phil (TV show), 171
dreams, importance of, 4, 11–18, 271
dues, 103, 168, 170

E

Ebony (magazine), 159
editorial work, 158–163
EIN (Employer Identification Number),
    48, 53, 59–60, 92–93, 110, 121
electronic records, backup system for,
    238
Elle (magazine), 159
EM Cosmetics, 206
email accounts, 64
email marketing, 66–68, 70–71, 75, 120,
    206, 212, 214
emergency fund, 238–240
Emmy Award for Outstanding
    Achievement in Hairstyling, 2,
    139–140, 170–174, 176, 202
employees, 33–34, 50, 78, 81, 83, 86,
    106–107, 239–240, 242–244, 253. *See*
    also assistants
Employer Identification Number (EIN),
    48, 53, 59–60, 92–93, 110, 121
employer's liability insurance (workers'
    comp), 33, 50

Employment Development Department (EDD), 237, 241, 247
entrepreneurship, 21–24, 26, 28, 36–41
equipment, 55, 105, 123
Espy Hair Boutique, 189
Ess, Kristin, 133
Essence (magazine), 2, 154, 159
estate planning, 268–269
estheticians, 34, 40, 148, 177, 251
Evans, Faith, 10, 132–133, 154–155, 1157
expenses, 31, 38–39, 52, 57, 101–105, 117–119, 168
expert, status as, 129, 141, 206, 208–209, 211–212, 214, 219, 222, 231. *See also* niche

F

FABLife (TV show), 130
Facebook, 82, 215, 217, 220, 242
family leave, 33
FEMA (Federal Emergency Management Agency), 241, 244, 247
Fenty Beauty, 21
fictitious business name (DBA/doing business as), 51–52, 59
financial planning, 267–269. *See also* money management; retirement plans
financial statements, 86–87, 255–256
Fishburne, Laurence, 10
flexibility, 28, 35, 47, 154
focus, 14, 16, 24, 80, 156, 170, 219, 242, 272
401(k), 265–267
Franklin, Benjamin, 89, 235
fraud and identity theft, 123–125
freelance work, 10, 90–91, 108, 110, 148, 153–163, 166, 176, 241
friends and family, seed money from, 256–257
Full Frontal Fashion (TV show), 171
furniture, salon, 43, 55, 105, 238

G

Garcetti, Eric, 236
Gates, Bill, 61
gifts, 74, 101, 103, 105
goals, 12–18, 214, 271. *See also* dreams, importance of
Godin, Seth, 137
Google, 65, 68, 75, 107, 238, 267
GQ (magazine), 167

H

hair shows, 210–211
hard inquiries (credit checks), 122
hard money business loans, 252–253

Harvey, Steve, 13
hashtags, 66, 215, 218, 224
Hasselbeck, Elisabeth, 170
Head & Shoulders, 159, 220
health insurance, 49, 103, 167, 238
Heitman, Stacy, 133
Henson, Taraji P., 159, 175
Hill, Lauryn, 157
home-based salon, 36–38, 44
hosting services, 63–64, 75
Hudson, Jennifer, 11, 130, 158–159, 180

I

illness, absence due to, 120
image, 28, 79–80, 116, 132–133, 225, 230
income
    brand ambassadorships, 224, 226. *See also* brand ambassadors
    cash flow planning, 118–119
    compensation methods, 58–59
    diversification. *See* multiple streams of income
    freelance work. *See* freelance work
    taxes. *See* taxation
    tips, 29, 33, 58, 81, 89–90, 106–107
    unemployment benefits, 33, 241
independent contractors, 32–34, 91–94, 101, 110
influencers, 206, 216, 223–224, 231. *See also* brand ambassadors; social media
Instagram, 68, 70, 75, 82, 160, 176, 213, 215, 217–218
InStyle (magazine), 159
insurance, 12, 33, 49–51, 59, 103, 124, 167, 183, 238, 260–265
interest rates, 253
Internal Revenue Service (IRS)
    EIN (Employer Identification Number), 48, 53, 59–60, 92–93, 110, 121
    estimated tax payments, 93–94, 111
    Form 940 (Employer's Annual Federal Unemployment (FUTA) Tax Return, 95–97, 112
    Form 941 (Employer's Quarterly Federal Tax Return), 95, 98–100, 112
    Form 1040-ES (Estimated Tax), 94, 111
    Form 1099-K (Payment Card and Third-Party Network Transactions), 107–108, 111
    Form 1099-MISC, 95
    Form 1099-NEC (Nonemployee Compensation), 92, 95, 111
    Form 4070 (Employee's Report of Tips to Employer), 106, 112

Internal Revenue Service (*continued*)
  Form 6765 (Credit for Increasing
      Research Activities), 109–110
  Form W-2 (Wage and Tax Statement),
      91–92, 113
  Form W-4, 113
  Form W-9 (Request for Taxpayer
      Identification Number and
      Certification), 92–93, 110
  Retirement Plans for Small Business
      Guide, 269
  Tax Guide for Small Business, 113
  Tax Tips for the Cosmetology and
      Barber Industry, 113
interviews, 141, 206, 211–212, 221, 229
inventory, 43, 55, 238, 240
iThrive, 226, 232

J
Jacobs, Shira, 189–190, 252
Jenkins, Jeannie Mai, 228–229
J-Lo, 188
job applications, 26
Jobs, Steve, 77
Jodeci, 133
John Paul Mitchell Systems, 177
Jones, Star, 170
Jordan, Barbara, 147

K
Kardashian, Kim, 174, 188
Kattan, Huda, 177
keywords, 66, 75, 195, 209, 218–219
Khan, Chaka, 11

L
LaBelle, Patti, 11
Last Look Hairspray, 70, 178–183, 185,
      213, 228–229
Lawrence, Martin, 156
leases, 31–32, 39, 55, 63–64, 102, 237–238
licenses, 26, 38–39, 48–49, 59–60, 87, 103,
      117, 183. *See also* permits
life insurance, 260–265
lighting, 41, 160–162, 169–170
Lil' Kim, 154
line of credit, 239, 242
LinkedIn, 216
LISC Small Business Relief Grant, 237
loans, 54–55, 103, 121–122, 237, 239–242,
      244, 252–255, 267. *See also* Small
      Business Administration (SBA)
local codes, 38, 49
location of salon, 36–39, 142
Long, Nia, 131, 159

Love in the City (TV series), 74, 174–175
Lover, Ed, 154
loyalty
  assistants, 80–81, 88
  clients, 72–73, 120, 142, 165
  rewards, 62, 74, 76, 245

M
Mack, Craig, 154
Madonna, 2, 172
magazines, 69, 103, 212. *See also* specific
      magazines
makeup artists, 10, 34, 157–159, 161–163,
      165, 167, 170, 175–177, 251
manifestation, 2, 13–15, 17–19, 173, 237
Manuel, Jay, 165, 174
marketing
  advertising. *See* advertising
  brand. *See* brand
  budget, 62, 75, 180–181, 183–184
  contests, 70–72, 76
  customer relationships, 62, 69–76
  email, 62, 66–68, 75
  free trials for products, 70
  marketing plan, 61–62, 75, 255
  multi-platform, 195
  niche, 137–143
  platforms. *See* marketing platforms
  press kit, 200–206, 221
  print ads, 181–182
  product lines, 180–181, 184
  promotional, 69–72, 76
  rule of three (price anchoring), 149, 152
  self-branding, 181
  social media. *See* social media
  special offers, 69–70
  target market, 36, 62, 69, 75, 137–141,
      183, 192, 194–195, 206, 214, 255
  website, 61–66, 75
  word-of-mouth, 70
marketing platforms
  blogs and newsletters, 206, 212–213,
      222
  defined, 199
  interviews, 206, 211–212, 221
  online videos and tutorials, 206–209,
      221–222. *See also* online videos
      and tutorials
  personal appearances, 206, 210–211,
      221
  social media, 206, 213–220, 222
Martinez, Angela, 154
Mary Kay, 21
Mase, 155
maternity leave, 120

McGrath, Pat, 21
McQueen, Alexander, 42
meals and entertainment, 104
mentorships, 26–28, 30, 44, 85–86
mission statement, 138, 143, 192, 254–255
mobile business models, 28, 34–36
mobile devices, 65, 67–68
mobile payment apps, 107–108
money management, 115–125, 147, 239, 241, 253, 272
multiple streams of income
    freelance work. See freelance work
    importance of, 147
    options for, 148
    product lines, creating and selling. See product lines, creating and selling
    products, salon sales of, 40, 184–185
    sponsorships and brand ambassadors, 148
    teaching and speaking engagements, 148
    TV and film work. See TV and film work
    upselling, 148–152
multitasking, 23, 78–80
MuzeHair, 51, 178–179, 182, 187, 200, 212, 252
MuzeHair Wig Collection, 187, 191–194, 196, 253
MuzeWorld, LLC, 52, 108

N
nail salons, 38–40, 149
name of business, 51–53, 63
natural disasters. See business disruption; crisis, preparing for
Neutrogena, 159
newsletters, 120, 206, 213, 222, 242
Newsom, Gavin, 235
niche
    developing, 130–134, 138–140
    ebook, 142
    marketing strategies, 140–143, 195–196
    niche market vision statement, 137–140, 143, 195
    passion and talent, 129–130, 134–135
    target market, 137–141, 192, 194–195
noncompete clauses, 228–229
nondisclosure agreement (NDA), 83, 183
Northwestern Mutual, 50, 238, 279

O
Obama, Barack, 13, 18
Olay, 159
online booking, 43, 84

online videos and tutorials, 65, 103, 141, 182, 192, 195, 206–209, 213, 215–217, 219, 221, 229, 232, 242–244
The Oprah Winfrey Show (TV show), 171

P
Pantene, 159, 220
partnering. See collaboration with other beauty professionals
passion, 22, 85, 129–130, 134–135, 231–232
Pat McGrath Labs, 21
Paul Mitchell, 21, 178. See also John Paul Mitchell Systems
Paycheck Protection Program (PPP), 237
payment apps, 106–107
Pebbles, 133
permits, 48–49, 59, 183, 185. See also licenses
personal appearances, 206, 210–211, 221
personal assistants, 78, 82–84
Phan, Michelle, 206
photo shoots, 90, 153–154, 158–159, 161, 163, 166, 169, 181, 184, 191. See also freelance work
photography, knowledge of, 161, 169
Pierce, Stacia, 14, 16
Pinterest, 216–217
planning, 25–28. See also business models; retirement plans
podcasts, 141, 206, 210–212, 221
portfolio, 158, 160–162, 164, 176
positive mindset, importance of, 22, 24–25, 271–272
prayer, 2, 13, 17–19, 167, 174, 236, 271
press kit, 200–206, 211–212, 221, 255, 258
Priano, Timothy, 160
Price, Lisa, 21
The Price is Right (TV show), 171
pricing considerations, 56–58, 183–184
print media, 69, 75, 181–182
private investors, 256–257
Procter & Gamble (P&G), 134, 139, 148, 205, 220, 224–225, 228–230. See also Clairol Professional
product lines, creating and selling, 148, 177–185
products, salon sales of, 40, 184–185
products liability/professional treatment insurance, 50
professional development, 103
professionalism, 28, 63, 120, 142
profit and loss statements, 86–87
promotional marketing, 69–72

promotional tours. *See* freelance work
public liability insurance, 50
punctuality, 23, 74, 76, 156

Q
Quora, 217

R
read, write, and reflect, 13, 18–19
The Real (TV show), 228
receipts, 54, 101, 104, 107–108
reception area, 40, 105
receptionists, 43, 53, 78, 84–86
references, 87, 268
referrals, 74, 87, 162
repairs and maintenance, 31, 101–102
research and development (R&D),
    108–110, 182
retail display, 40, 184–185
retail sales permit, 48–49, 59, 183, 185
retirement plans, 103, 265–267, 269
Rice, Robert A., Jr., 251
Rihanna, 21
Robbins, Anthony, 271
Roberts, Damone ("The Eyebrow King"),
    141
rule of three (price anchoring), 149, 152

S
Safari, 65
safety measures, 41, 44, 246
sales tax, 49, 57
Sally Beauty, 159, 224, 226
Salon Republic, 43
salon suite business model, 28, 34, 41–44,
    141
salons
    atmosphere, 37–39, 41, 43, 72, 76, 79,
        142, 251
    business models. *See* business models
    location of, 36–39, 142
    nail. *See* nail salons
    salon suites. *See* salon suite business
        model
    starting. *See* starting a salon
Salt-N-Pepa, 27, 131
savings accounts, 267
search engine optimization (SEO), 65–66,
    75, 209
seasonal promotions, 69–70, 119–120
Sebastian Hairspray, 179
secure sockets layer (SSL) certificate, 64
security systems, 41
seed money, 256–257
self-branding, 181

self-discipline, 24
self-employed business owners, 87, 91–95,
    110–111, 124, 266
SEO (search engine optimization), 65–66,
    75, 209
SEP-IRA (Simplified Employee Pension),
    265–267
setbacks, coping with, 23. *See also* business
    disruption
shampoo area, 40, 43, 184
Shinn, Florence Scovel, 16
Silva, Rea Ann, 10
SIMPLE IRA (Savings Incentive Match
    Plan for Employees), 265–267
slow seasons, planning for, 116, 119–120,
    147, 272
Small Business Administration (SBA),
    49, 237, 241, 244, 247, 252–254,
    256–258
Small Business Development Center
    (SBDC), 247
Smith, Will, 156–157
Snapchat, 216
social media
    analytics, 72, 218, 220
    assistants, ads for, 82
    and brand ambassadors, 220, 224–226,
        231
    brand strategy, 214, 218
    business versus personal accounts,
        160
    clients, staying connected with, 120
    comments, 219
    competition, checking on, 220
    content, 219
    contests, posting about, 71–72
    hashtags, 66, 215, 218, 224
    influencers, 206, 216, 223–224, 231
    keywords, 218–219
    managing, 23–24
    as marketing tool, 61, 182, 195, 206,
        213–220
    photos, use of, 202
    platforms, 195, 215–218. *See also*
        specific social media platforms
    posting, 219–220
    power of, 213–214
    press kit, 204, 206
    product marketing, 182–183, 192–194
    reach, 204, 206
    time spent on by users, 63
    wig sales, 193–194
    work images, separate from personal
        accounts, 160
Solo 401(k), 265–266

solo practice as salon owner, 26, 28, 36–41, 44
speaking engagements, 210–213
special offers, 68–71, 76
specialties, 29, 129. *See also* niche
specialty events, 141
sponsorships. *See* brand ambassadors
Sports Illustrated (magazine), 167
Sprout Social, 220
SSL certificate, 64, 75
starting a salon
    business basics. *See* business basics for start-ups
    business loans, 252–255
    commercial space (brick-and-mortar salon), 38–41, 44
    crowdfunding, 256
    friends and family financing, 256–257
    home-based, 37–38, 44
    private investors, 257
    Small Business Administration (SBA) loans, 253–256
State Farm, 50, 238, 279
state regulations and laws, 48–49, 52, 57. *See also* licenses; permits
success, steps for achieving, 11–19, 25
success journals, 13, 15–16, 19
success mindset, 24–25
supplies, 34, 38, 43, 91, 101, 156
Swift, Taylor, 223

T
target market. *See* marketing
tax identification numbers, 48, 53, 59–60, 92–93, 110, 121
taxation
    accountant, need for, 86–87
    booth renters, 95
    credits, 108–110
    deductions, 101–106
    depreciation, 102, 105
    documentation, 104
    employees, 91–92
    employers, 95–100
    estimated tax payments, 93–94
    federal unemployment tax (FUTA), 96–97
    life insurance, 264–265
    mobile payment apps, 108
    nonemployee compensation, 95
    overview, 110–113
    penalties, 90, 94
    research and development credits, 108–109
    resources, 113–114

sales tax, 49, 57
Section 179 deduction, 105
self-employed business owners, 92–94
separate business entities, 53
state income taxes, 106
tax credits, 55
tax forms. *See* Internal Revenue Service (IRS)
of tips, 89–90, 106–107
TikTok, 216–217
time management, 74
tips, 29, 33, 58, 81, 89–90, 106–107
Total, 154
trademarks, 9, 53
treatment rooms, 41
TV and film work, 148, 159, 166–176
Twain, Mark, 47
Twitter, 215–216
The Tyra Banks Show (TV show), 2, 82, 167–174

U
underpricing, 56–57
unemployment benefits, 33, 241, 247
uniforms, 103
Union, Gabrielle, 130, 157–159, 175–176
unions, 159, 167–168, 170, 175
Unite Hair, 179
upselling, 56, 148–152, 184–185
Uptown Records, 154
US Chamber of Commerce, 241, 244, 247
utilities, 102

V
Vanity Fair (magazine), 2, 159
Vibe (magazine), 154
Victoria's Secret (catalog), 167
videos
    creating, 208–209
    DIY (do-it-yourself) kits and videos, 242–244
    marketing platforms, 206–209, 221–222
    photo and video shoot freelance work, 10, 90, 153–154, 158–159, 161, 163, 166
Vieira, Meredith, 170
The View (TV show), 170–171
virtual consultations, 242, 244
vision, 18, 23, 82, 182
vision boards, 13–19, 216
Vision Plans, 36–37, 44
vision statement for niche market, 137–140, 143
Vogue (magazine), 2, 159, 167

W
Walker, Madam C.J., 177
Walters, Barbara, 170
Warren Tricomi Salon, 42, 73, 79,
    133–134, 178
Washington, Kerry, 11, 158–159, 180
websites, 63–66, 72, 75, 183, 209
Westwood, Vivienne, 42
What's Love Got to Do with It (movie),
    10–11, 165
why, 22, 24–25, 37, 62, 208, 214, 222
wigs and extensions, 187–196, 207, 252. *See
    also* niche
Williams, Serena, 11
Williams, Venus, 11
Williams, Wendy, 154
wills and trusts, 269
window displays, 41
Winfrey, Oprah, 9, 13, 18, 174
The Wisdom of Florence Scovel Shinn
    (Shinn), 16
work ethic, 23, 169, 257
work kit, 156, 163–164
workers' compensation insurance, 33, 50
work-share business model. *See* booth
    rental
workshops, speaking at, 210–211
Wright, Kiyah
    America's Got Talent (TV show), 174
    Bad Boys Records, touring with artists
        from, 81, 90, 120, 132–133, 154,
        166
    Billboard Music Awards host, 228–229,
        232
    booth rental, 30, 32, 42
    brand, 200
    as brand ambassador, 134, 139, 147–
        148, 200, 204–205, 220, 225–230
    brother (Chance), 259
    career journey, 272
    COVID-19 business disruption, dealing
        with, 235–237, 241
    early interest in beauty industry, 1–3
    editorial work, 159–160, 163
    education and training, 2–3
    Emmy Award for Outstanding
        Achievement in Hairstyling, 2,
        139–140, 170–174, 176, 202
    Imagine This salon, 26–27, 29–30, 32,
        51, 131
    Last Look Hairspray, 178–182, 185
    Love in the City (TV series), 74, 174–
        175
    Millennium salon, 10
    mother, death of, 2, 16, 259–260
    MuzeHair, 51, 178–179, 182, 187, 200,
        212, 252
    MuzeHair Wig Collection, 187,
        191–194, 196, 253
    MuzeWorld, LLC, 52, 108
    niche, 130–134, 138–140
    online videos and tutorials, 207–208
    press kit example, 200–205
    promotional tour work, 154–157
    Salon Republic, 41–43
    SBA 7(a) loan, 241, 253–254
    sister (Jalannia), 171–172
    TV and film work, 166–176
    Tyra Banks Show, work on, 2, 82,
        166–174
    Warren Tricomi Salon, 42, 73, 79,
        133–134, 178–179
The Wright Salon, 1

X
XXL (magazine), 154

Y
Yahoo, 65
YouTube, 206, 208–209, 215, 217, 230. *See
    also* videos

Z
Zendaya, 11
zoning laws, 38, 49
Zuckerberg, Mark, 18, 115

ABOUT THE AUTHOR

Kiyah Wright is a two-time Emmy Award–winning celebrity hair-stylist, beauty expert, and Image Maker. Kiyah's ultimate goal has been to give women a look that makes them feel confident and beautiful. She has been a celebrity stylist for over twenty-eight years while remaining relevant. She works with stars such as Tyra Banks, Ciara, Gabrielle Union, Halle Berry, Laverne Cox, Jennifer Hudson, Kerry Washington, and Halsey, and television shows including *The Voice*, *Black-ish*, *The Tyra Show*, *Jimmy Kimmel Live!*, *America's Next Top Model*, and *America's Got Talent*. Kiyah also manages her Beverly Hills salon and her MuzeHair product line, and has been a celebrity ambassador for Procter & Gamble for thirteen years. Kiyah prides herself in being a salon stylist throughout all the years, because connecting with the everyday woman, making them over, and teaching them about regime and maintenance is really the core of how beauty from the OUTSIDE IN happens.